PHP and script.aculo.us Web 2.0 Application Interfaces

Building powerful interactive AJAX applications with script.aculo.us and PHP

A complete how-to guide for building web sites using script.aculo.us and PHP to get your project up and running

Sridhar Rao

BIRMINGHAM - MUMBAI

PHP and script.aculo.us Web 2.0 Application Interfaces

Building powerful interactive AJAX applications with script.aculo.us and PHP

Copyright © 2009 Packt Publishing

All rights reserved. No part of this book may be reproduced, stored in a retrieval system, or transmitted in any form or by any means, without the prior written permission of the publisher, except in the case of brief quotations embedded in critical articles or reviews.

Every effort has been made in the preparation of this book to ensure the accuracy of the information presented. However, the information contained in this book is sold without warranty, either express or implied. Neither the author, Packt Publishing, nor its dealers or distributors will be held liable for any damages caused or alleged to be caused directly or indirectly by this book.

Packt Publishing has endeavored to provide trademark information about all the companies and products mentioned in this book by the appropriate use of capitals. However, Packt Publishing cannot guarantee the accuracy of this information.

First published: April 2009

Production Reference: 2280409

Published by Packt Publishing Ltd.
32 Lincoln Road
Olton
Birmingham, B27 6PA, UK.

ISBN 978-1-847194-04-6

www.packtpub.com

Cover Image by Filippo (filosarti@tiscali.it)

Credits

Author
Sridhar Rao

Reviewers
Andrew J. Peterson
Robert F. Castellow

Acquisition Editor
James Lumsden

Development Editors
Nikhil Bangera
Dilip Venkatesh

Technical Editors
Bhupali Khule
Hithesh Uchil

Copy Editor
Sneha Kulkarni

Indexer
Monica Ajmera

Production Editorial Manager
Abhijeet Deobhakta

Editorial Team Leader
Akshara Aware

Project Team Leader
Lata Basantani

Project Coordinator
Rajashree Hamine

Proofreader
Laura Booth

Production Coordinator
Aparna Bhagat

Cover Work
Aparna Bhagat

About the author

Sridhar Rao has been learning, working, and developing web applications from the time he was first introduced to the Web. The very idea of reaching out to the masses and bringing change in the behavior of the users through web applications excites him the most.

Most of his work has been in PHP, MySQL, and JavaScript. He has worked with some of the leading technology and service companies in his IT career.

Sridhar currently works for the world's leading database and enterprise company. He holds an engineering degree in Information Technology and is based in Bangalore, India.

> A book is not the work of an individual. I would like to thank my family and friends for their encouragement and support. I would like to thank the whole team of Packt who not only helped me when things were difficult, but also believed in this project. Special mention goes to James Lumsden, Nikhil Bangera, Rajashree Hamine, Bhupali Khule, Hithesh Uchil, and Navya Diwakar for their extra efforts and patience.

About the reviewers

Rob Castellow is the president of PAC Enterprises LLC, a contract and development company responsible for providing quality professional services. He has provided services in the development of several J2EE based projects for large corporations in the telecommunication and financial services sectors.

Rob graduated in 1998 with a Masters in Electrical Engineering from the Georgia Institute of Technology, and began his career developing embedded systems. Rob soon found that all the fun was in developing enterprise systems and has been working on J2EE based applications ever since.

Rob is an enthusiast of new technologies. When he is not proofreading books in PHP or script.aculo.us, he can be found developing Grails applications, attending user groups, reading books, and managing or developing several web sites.

Andrew J. Peterson lives with his wife and three daughters in San Francisco, California. He has about 20 years of experience in building and managing software systems for consumers, enterprises, and non-profits. His expertise contributes in the full life-cycle of software development, software methodologies, software architecture, software engineering, and usability.

Andrew has diverse experience in the industry. In the consumer space, he led a team in the creation of the top-selling SoundEdit 16. He served numerous roles producing enterprise software for the leading supplier of software solutions for container terminals, shipping ports and lines, and distribution centers.

He transferred this experience to web-based software. Over the past ten years, he's built a variety of web applications, including non-profit, social networking, social search, pharmaceuticals, and social e-commerce. He has built successful projects in a variety of languages, including Java, Ruby, C++, and Perl.

> I'd like to thank my daughters for sharing their energy with me.

Table of Contents

Preface	**1**
Chapter 1: About script.aculo.us	**5**
Welcome to the script.aculo.us world	5
Versions	6
The script.aculo.us fun begins	6
Effects	6
Drag and drop	7
AJAX	8
Much more fun	9
Summary	9
Chapter 2: Exploring Client-side Techniques with Prototype	**11**
About Prototype	11
The story so far: Versions	12
Compatibility	12
Prototype features—a walk-through	12
Getting started with Dollar, DOM, and more	12
AJAX components—an overview	16
Ajax.Request	17
Ajax.Updater	18
Ajax.PeriodicalUpdater	18
Ajax.Responders	19
Hands-on examples	20
Event handling	25
Description	25
Handling general events	25
Syntax	26
Handling mouse events	26
Handling keyboard events	26
Hands-on examples	27
Handling the keyboard events example	28
Handling mouse event example	29

Redefining forms with Prototype	**30**
Introduction	30
Description	30
Usage	31
Hands-on examples	32
Getting more hands-on	**36**
Hands-on example: How to use XML to read data from the server using Prototype	36
Summary	**40**
Chapter 3: Server-side Techniques with PHP and MySQL	**41**
Basic requirements	**41**
A word about PHP 5.0 or above	42
A word about MySQL 5.0	42
The WAMP server: A must-have for Windows users	42
phpMyAdmin	43
Getting the playground ready	**44**
Checking the PHP installation using the WAMP server	44
Checking the MySQL installation using the WAMP server	45
Adding Prototype library in our code	46
Adding the script.aculo.us library in our code	46
Basic classes	46
DBConfig.php	47
DBClass.php	47
Secure.php	49
Hands-on examples: Common scripts	**49**
User login management system	49
Signup.php	50
Login.php	53
Index.php	57
Logout.php	58
Adding a username availability script to the login management system	59
Creating a simple tag cloud	63
Summary	**66**
Chapter 4: Adding Effects and Multimedia to User Interface Design	**67**
Introduction to effects	**67**
Types of effects	**68**
Common parameters	69
Code usage	69
Hands-on examples	**73**
The core effects	73

Various effects	76
Combining all the effects	78
Playing sounds with script.aculo.us	**79**
Types of sounds	79
MP3 sounds	80
Code usage	80
A hands-on example	80
Summary	**82**
Chapter 5: AJAX Drag and Drop Feature using script.aculo.us	**83**
Introduction to the drag and drop feature	**86**
Explanation of the drag and drop feature	**86**
Code usage of the drag and drop feature	**88**
Hands-on example: Creating a drag and drop sample in one line of code	**91**
Hands-on example: Advanced drag and drop tutorial	**93**
Summary	**97**
Chapter 6: In-place Editing using script.aculo.us	**99**
An introduction to the in-place editing feature	**99**
Getting started with in-place editing	**101**
Code usage of the in-place editing features and options	**102**
Tips and tricks with in-place editing	**106**
Disabling the element for the in-place editing functionality	106
Entering into the edit mode	106
Submitting on Blur	107
Callbacks for onEnterEditMode and onLeaveEditMode	108
Hands-on example: In-place editing with server-side handling	**108**
Hands-on example: InPlaceCollectionEditor	**112**
Summary	**114**
Chapter 7: Creating Autocompletion using script.aculo.us	**115**
Introduction to autocompletion	**115**
Explanation of the autocompletion feature	**117**
Types of autocompletion sources	118
Remote sources	118
Local sources	118
Options for autocompletion sources	119
Options for remote sources	119
Options for local sources	120
Code usage of autocompletion using remote sources	**121**
Code usage of autocompletion using local sources	**123**
Hands-on example: Autocompletion using remote sources	**124**

Table of Contents

Hands-on example: Advanced autocompletion using remote sources for multiple fields	128
Hands-on example: Autocompletion using local sources	132
Summary	133
Chapter 8: Slider for Dynamic Applications using script.aculo.us	**135**
First steps with slider	136
Parameters for the slider definition	137
Options with the slider	137
Types of slider	138
Vertical slider	138
Horizontal slider	139
Code usage for the slider	139
Code usage for the vertical slider	140
Code usage for the horizontal slider	142
Code usage for sliders with options	143
Tips and tricks with the slider	146
Reading the current value of the slider	147
Multiple handles in the slider	147
Disabling the slider	148
Enabling the slider	149
Hands-on example: Using vertical and horizontal slider	149
Summary	154
Chapter 9: script.aculo.us in One Go	**155**
Hands-on example: Multiple script.aculo.us features mash up	155
Adding in-place editing in page	156
Adding effects to the page	157
How about adding the drag and drop feature?	157
Out of the box thinking—adding multiple features to an element	159
Hands-on example: Quick revision of all the features of script.aculo.us in one page	162
Let's start with effects	162
Some in-place editing	163
A little bit of drag and drop	164
The slider needs to be in picture too	165
How can we miss music?	167
Summary	168
Chapter 10: Todonow: A Tadalist Clone	**169**
The BIG picture	169
Features and functionality	170
Creating a database playground	170

Let's log in…	**172**
User interface comes first	**173**
View all my lists	**174**
Logic and code	174
View all my lists along with a summary of incomplete items	**176**
Logic and code	176
Creating new lists	**177**
Logic and code	177
Adding items to our lists	**179**
Adding items to the database	179
Reading the newly added item and placing it back on the page	181
Adding effects to our items	**182**
Mark items as completed	**183**
Add the item to the completed <div>	184
Delete the item from the incomplete <div>	185
Change the status of the item to completed	185
Convert completed items to incomplete status	**186**
Add the item to the incomplete <div>	187
Delete the item from the complete <div>	188
Change the status of the item to incomplete	188
Deleting lists	**190**
Let's wrap up and log out	**190**
Our Todonow is ready to go live	**191**
Summary	**191**
Chapter 11: Creating Delicious and Digg Bookmarks Manager	**193**
Application at a glance	**193**
Features and functionality	**194**
The database playground for our application	**194**
User profile home page	**196**
Submit new tutorials	**196**
Submitting a tutorial URL	197
Adding title, description, and tags to the tutorial	199
View tutorial	**202**
Deleting tutorials	**202**
Search using real-time autocompletion	**204**
Exploring the tag cloud features of 2.0 applications	**206**
Adding tags to tutorials	207
Reading all the tags in the database	208
Creating a tag cloud	208
Search using tags	209

Don't forget to log out	**210**
Ideas for life	**211**
Summary	**211**
Chapter 12: Creating a Shopping Search Engine	**213**
Application at a glance	213
Features and functionalities	214
The user management system	214
Selecting the products to buy	215
Adding effects	217
Searching products	218
Searching products using the tag cloud	221
Generating a tag cloud	222
View products for a tag name	223
Summary	224
Chapter 13: Common 43: 43 Things, 43 Places, and 43 People Clones	**225**
Getting the database ready	225
Database for places	226
Database for people	226
Database for things	226
Advanced commenting system	227
Creating a comments form	227
Posting comments	229
Edit or Delete comments	234
Modules ready to go live	234
User management system	234
Tag cloud features	235
Adding 2.0 flavour to applications	235
AJAX modules	235
Effects	236
Real-time search	237
In-place editing	237
Drag and drop	238
Putting the building blocks together	239
Features and functionalities	239
Summary	**240**
Index	**241**

Preface

Let me start by thanking the whole script.aculo.us community, which is pushing the limits of creativity through JavaScript.

This book is a humble attempt to help developers to quickly get on board and make their web applications AJAXified using Prototype and script.aculo.us. We have used PHP and MySQL as our server-side artillery to spread love among the PHP and MySQL developers and community as a whole for script.aculo.us.

Prototype library has been covered in depth and features have been explained in a way that would not only help a beginner but also amaze gurus. The script.aculo.us library has been fully explored with the help of snippets, codes, and examples.

Exclusive hands-on examples have been provided that will act as a reference guide whenever needed.

Towards the end of the book we go on to build three web applications from scratch.

"*If Prototype is giving our web applications powerful performance, script.aculo.us is making them look functionally beautiful.*"

What this book covers

Chapter 1 Kick-starts our script.aculo.us journey. We will explore the overview of the script.aculo.us library, real-world usage, and a quick example.

In *Chapter 2* we will learn about the powerful Prototype library. We will explore various features like DOM, AJAX, event handling, and helper functions.

Chapter 3 gets us started with PHP and MySQL in building our complete Login Management System, getting AJAX into the picture, and create our own Tag Cloud.

Preface

In *Chapter 4* we will learn with the help of hands-on examples, how to add multimedia and effects to web applications using script.aculo.us.

In *Chapter 5* we will learn to make simple, clean, and beautiful user interfaces using drag and drop. Drag everything and drop something.

In *Chapter 6* we will learn how to use InPlaceEditor and InPlaceCollection for editing on the fly.

Chapter 7 explores yet another 2.0 feature called autocompletion to create more robust and engaging applications.

In *Chapter 8* we will learn the hands-on examples with different types of sliders and how to integrate it into our web applications.

Chapter 9 is our reference guide for all the script.aculo.us features in one go.

In *Chapter 10* we will learn how to build our own tadalist application from scratch to live.

In *Chapter 11* we will build your own social bookmarking application from scratch to live.

In *Chapter 12* we will learn how to build a new design for a 2.0 shopping site from scratch to live.

Chapter 13 explains the build modules required to implement 43 things, 43 people, and 43 places from scratch to live.

Who this book is for

This book is for web developers who swear by simple yet agile and useful web applications. This book assumes basic knowledge of HTML, CSS, JavaScript, and PHP. A PHP beginner will surely find this book useful, and for the gurus, the book gives you a completely new way of adding interactivity to your web applications. The examples in the book use PHP, but can be adapted easily to other languages.

Conventions

In this book, you will find a number of styles of text that distinguish between different kinds of information. Here are some examples of these styles, and an explanation of their meaning.

Code words in text are shown as follows: "We are calling the function fetchArray defined in our DBClass to get the array of results and using a while loop read each row."

A block of code will be set as follows:
```
$db = new DBClass();
$newlist = new lists();
$title = $_POST['ListTitle'];
$ownerid = $_SESSION["uid"];
$query = $newlist->add_new_list($title,$ownerid);
```

New terms and **important words** are shown in bold. Words that you see on the screen, in menus or dialog boxes for example, appear in our text like this: "We click on the **Serialize The Form** link and it creates a string which is ready to be passed to the AJAX objects."

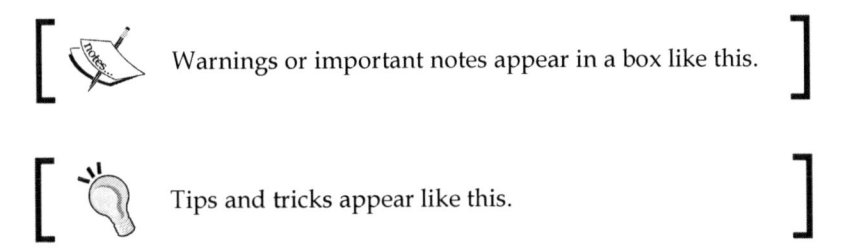

> Warnings or important notes appear in a box like this.

> Tips and tricks appear like this.

Reader feedback

Feedback from our readers is always welcome. Let us know what you think about this book—what you liked or may have disliked. Reader feedback is important for us to develop titles that you really get the most out of.

To send us general feedback, simply drop an email to feedback@packtpub.com, and mention the book title in the subject of your message.

If there is a book that you need and would like to see us publish, please send us a note in the **SUGGEST A TITLE** form on www.packtpub.com or email suggest@packtpub.com.

If there is a topic that you have expertise in and you are interested in either writing or contributing to a book, see our author guide on www.packtpub.com/authors.

Customer support

Now that you are the proud owner of a Packt book, we have a number of things to help you to get the most from your purchase.

Downloading the example code for the book

Visit http://www.packtpub.com/files/code/4046_Code.zip to directly download the example code.

The downloadable files contain instructions on how to use them.

Errata

Although we have taken every care to ensure the accuracy of our contents, mistakes do happen. If you find a mistake in one of our books—maybe a mistake in text or code—we would be grateful if you would report this to us. By doing so, you can save other readers from frustration, and help us to improve subsequent versions of this book. If you find any errata, please report them by visiting http://www.packtpub.com/support, selecting your book, clicking on the **let us know** link, and entering the details of your errata. Once your errata are verified, your submission will be accepted and the errata added to any list of existing errata. Any existing errata can be viewed by selecting your title from http://www.packtpub.com/support.

Piracy

Piracy of copyright material on the Internet is an ongoing problem across all media. At Packt, we take the protection of our copyright and licenses very seriously. If you come across any illegal copies of our works in any form on the Internet, please provide us with the location address or web site name immediately so that we can pursue a remedy.

Please contact us at copyright@packtpub.com with a link to the suspected pirated material.

We appreciate your help in protecting our authors, and our ability to bring you valuable content.

Questions

You can contact us at questions@packtpub.com if you are having a problem with any aspect of the book, and we will do our best to address it.

1
About script.aculo.us

We have been developing web applications using PHP and MySQL. But now we want to learn how to make our applications interactive in terms of usage, and build a community around them. In short, we want to build simple, yet powerful applications.

Look no further! script.aculo.us is our savior and our love, too. script.aculo.us is a JavaScript library that provides dynamic visual effects, user interface controls, and robust AJAX features. In this chapter, we will explore the script.aculo.us library with regards to versions, features, and real-world usage.

The official site of script.aculo.us describes it as *Web 2.0 JavaScript*, which it truly is. We will also see how we can delight our friends with just a few lines of code.

Welcome to the script.aculo.us world

Anyone developing a web application knows how painful it is to make cross-browser JavaScript functionality—especially when we are dealing with XMLHttpRequest aka AJAX and many more such features, as different browsers behave differently.

Thomas Fuchs wrote the initial version of script.aculo.us to solve this problem. The open-source community of script.aculo.us too added many more features that have redefined the way JavaScript is being used. From simple effects to complex **Rich Internet Applications (RIA)**, script.aculo.us does it all. script.aculo.us supports popular browsers available in the market such as Internet Explorer, Mozilla, Opera, and Safari.

script.aculo.us is an add-on to the Prototype library. If Prototype makes JavaScript simple, script.aculo.us makes JavaScript fun.

About script.aculo.us

Versions

Now that we are ready to have some *serious* fun with script.aculo.us, it's important to quickly grab the latest version. We will require the Prototype library that comes with the latest version of script.aculo.us.

 You can download the latest version of script.aculo.us from their official site at `http://script.aculo.us/`. Save the file in the web server's root directory, www, inside the specific project folder. The **Getting Started** URL explains this process in detail.

script.aculo.us 1.8 is the latest version that comes with Prototype 1.6.0.1 beta. Alternatively, if you have an older version such as 1.7 or 1.6, it should be fine. However, we highly recommend upgrading it to version 1.8, as it adds new features for multimedia support and incorporates many bug fixes which may be missing in the previous versions.

The script.aculo.us fun begins

The best way to understand and visualize what script.aculo.us can do for us is by getting our code up and running—quickly! Yes, we mean it. Let's explore some features of script.aculo.us with examples and real-world scenarios before we move on to create the next big thing on the Web.

Effects

You want to impress your application users, don't you? Effects are all about adding interactivity to your applications, which in turn gives an appealing user interface to make users fall in love with your applications.

script.aculo.us comes with an effects engine, which provides various effects such as grow, slide, highlight, and many more. When applied in applications these effects add beauty to the functionality.

And, what if I tell you that we can do this in one line of code? I know you won't believe it, so let's see it happening. Just copy and paste the following JavaScript code in your editor and you should see the magic unfold.

The HTML code, which we will use to add effects, is as follows:

```
<html>
<body>
<div id="effect-id"> </div>
</body>
</html>
```

Now let's add effects to this `<div>`:

```
new Effect.Highlight($('effect-id'));
```

You should be able to see the effects when the `<div>` is selected. A simple real-world example of what you have done now is shown next. It's a **WordPress** application using the script.aculo.us effects.

Want to try something else? Try this:

```
new Effect.Fade($('effect-id'));
```

After applying the fade effect to the `<div>`, you should see the `<div>` fading away slowly.

We will use many such effects in our applications throughout the book.

Drag and drop

Drag and drop is another feature that is quite often seen in many web applications. Imagine a simple shopping cart where you can simply drag-and-drop the items you want to buy from a list of items. Isn't it simple for users? Yes, it indeed is. And even better, it is simple for developers too.

About script.aculo.us

The complete drag and drop features of script.aculo.us will be explained in Chapter 5. For now, check out the **Backpackit** application from *37signals* at www.backpackit.com and visualize what kind of application you want to create using drag and drop.

In the following screenshot we can drag notes and lists, and re-arrange the items on the page:

AJAX

Asynchronous JavaScript and XML or **AJAX**, as it is commonly known, redefines and bridges the gap between the web and desktop applications. As a user, we send requests to the server and data is received as a response. This is then displayed to us—the user—on the same page without the whole page getting reloaded. The same applies to desktop widgets synchronizing with web applications.

script.aculo.us uses the functions and power of Prototype, such as `Request` and `Updater`, to add AJAX functionality to web applications easily. For now, all you should understand is how it will help us in our applications.

In the previous screenshot we could add a **List**, **Note**, **Divider**, and **Tag** without moving to another page. Everything is done on the same page, but the data is sent to the server using AJAX. From the user's perspective, the application is easy, fast, and simple.

As we said before, we can add a **Note**, **List**, and **Tag** without moving to another page. This feature makes use of the power of XML features through AJAX techniques, which update the server at runtime and even fetch the data from the server without loading the whole page.

Our idea of building a project is also the same. We shall go through all these features step-by-step in Chapter 2.

Much more fun

It's only the beginning of the fun. We have just touched upon an overview of the library. There are many other features such as autocomplete, sliders, in-place editing, and multimedia. All these features are fun to work with and are covered in depth in the chapters to come.

Throughout the process of learning script.aculo.us, all you need to do is visualize the possibilities of how we can make our applications more interactive and engaging.

Summary

In this chapter we saw an overview of the script.aculo.us library. Real-world scenario of WordPress and Backpackit prove that script.aculo.us has been trusted with developing and deploying simple, yet powerful user-driven applications.

In the next chapter we will explore the very powerful JavaScript library Prototype. We will learn about DOM manipulation, helper functions, and AJAX in detail. Anything and everything about Prototype will be covered – but all the while having fun. Read on!

2
Exploring Client-side Techniques with Prototype

In the previous chapter, we saw some basic features provided by the script.aculo.us library such as effects, drag and drop, and AJAX.

In this chapter we will cover the wonderful **Prototype** library. Some of the key features of Prototype that we will be covering are as follows:

- Helper functions
- AJAX components
- Forms and events handling
- Hands-on examples

About Prototype

Prototype was originally written by Sam Stephenson. It is a powerful open-source JavaScript framework, which makes it easy to develop dynamic and rich internet applications. Prototype provides both simple and advanced JavaScript extensions that assist developers, instead of making them rewrite their own code base. This includes the powerful **XMLHttpRequest (XHR)**.

Prototype natively supports the AJAX and **Document Object Model (DOM)** features. This makes it an obvious choice for developers who want to bring about rapid web application development.

A single chapter dedicated to Prototype is certainly not sufficient to cover and explain everything that Prototype can help us do. However, remember that we want to build dynamic web applications, and step-by-step we will explore features of the library that we can actually use in our applications.

As said before, Prototype makes JavaScript easy, script.aculo.us makes it fun to work with.

The story so far: Versions

The Prototype framework has seen a lot of contribution and changes from the community since Sam Stephenson released it in February 2005.

The current stable version of Prototype is version 1.6, which comes with the script.aculo.us library. Alternatively, you can grab the latest copy from `http://www.prototypejs.org/`.

Compatibility

Prototype's JavaScript framework has the compatibility to work with leading web browsers. What makes it more powerful is the fact that developers can extend it with any of their programming languages such as Ruby, PHP, and Java.

Prototype features—a walk-through

Prototype extends the DOM through extensions and also allows developers to create their own extensions and methods. Prototype provides the most powerful and the simplest way of using AJAX in any web application.

Getting started with Dollar, DOM, and more

OK, fasten your seatbelt and get ready! We are going for a long drive with Prototype.

Prototype comes with utility functions, which makes it easy to incorporate it with any server-side scripting language.

 We are using PHP as our server-side scripting language throughout the book.

A traditional way of accessing the element by ID would be like this:

```
var elementID = document.getElementById('elementID');
```

Similarly, to get the value of anything in the input field we would use this:

```
var elementValue = document.getElementById('elementID').value;
```

If we were to use a set of HTML elements—such as an input box, a `<div>`, or any other element—along with their values, it would result in typing the whole syntax repeatedly for each element. So, are there any shortcuts? In such situations, Prototype comes to our rescue.

We can achieve the same functionality with simple shortcuts, such as the following:

```
var element = $('elementID');
Var elementValue = $F('element');
```

You see how easy this is? Prototype has many more of these simple utility functions to make our code neat and simple.

The $ function extends `Element.extend()`, which is valid for all the elements and methods.

The complete cheat sheet is as follows:

Using Prototype	Description
$()	Get the element by ID
$F()	Get the value of the element passing the ID
$A()	Converts a single argument into an `Array`
$H()	Converts objects into hash objects
$R()	Used in place of writing the `objectRange` objects

These are some of the basic functions that prove to be really handy, instead of typing the same syntax repeatedly. We will be using all these and many more functions in all our applications.

Now let's create a simple example to demonstrate the power of helper functions on the web page.

First, create a simple HTML file with some elements. Call it `helper.html`.

```
<script type="text/javascript" src="prototype.js"></script>
<script type="text/javascript" src="Scripts.js"></script>
<script></script>
<link rel="stylesheet" href="style.css" >
<head>
   <title>Helper Functions!!!</title>
</head>
<body>
   <h3 class="heading">
   Trying Out With Some Helper Functions!!!
   </h3>
   <table class="FormTable">
      <tr>
      <td>Enter Your Name</td>
      <td><input type="text" name="first_name"
            id="first_name" size="35">
```

```html
            </td>
         </tr>
      </table>
<p>
   <div class="links">
      <a href="javascript:readDollar();">
         Read The Object Name Using $ function
      </a>
<p>
      <a href="javascript:readF();">
         Read Name Using $F function
      </a>
<p>
      We have used a simple example by creating an array
      <br>
      <i>var name=new Array("First Name","Last Name","Age");
      </i>
<p>
      <a href="javascript:readA();">
         Read All Inputs & Put in Array Using $A function</a>
<p>
   </div>
</body>
</html>
```

We have included the stylesheet style.css. The code that follows is inserted into the style.css file to add beauty to the code in the helper.html file. Feel free to use your CSS creativity.

```css
.FormTable {
   background: #9AAB3C;
   font-family:Verdana;
   font-size:13px;
   color:white;
   align:center;
}
.links a{
   width:300px;
   font-family:Verdana;
   font-size:14px;
   color:#13801C;
   align:center;
}
.heading {
   font-family:Verdana;
   font-size:14px;
   color:#9E5A70;
}
```

Here, it is a simple user interface using a combination of both scripts and codes. When we run it in the browser, the output that we get is similar to the following screenshot:

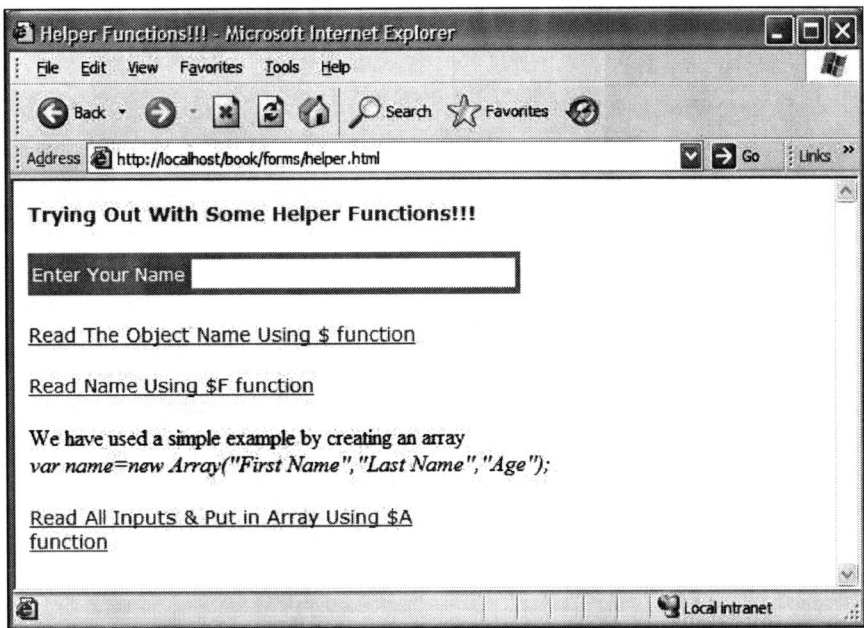

It's time to add some JavaScript to the `helper.html` file between `<script> </script>`. This is pretty simple and straightforward.

```
function readDollar() {
   alert($('first_name'));
}
function readF() {
   alert($F('first_name'));
}
function readA() {
   var name=new Array("First Name","Last Name","Age");
   alert($A(name));
}
```

Exploring Client-side Techniques with Prototype

That's the most basic example you can find and, of course, you can quickly get started. The following screenshot shows the result:

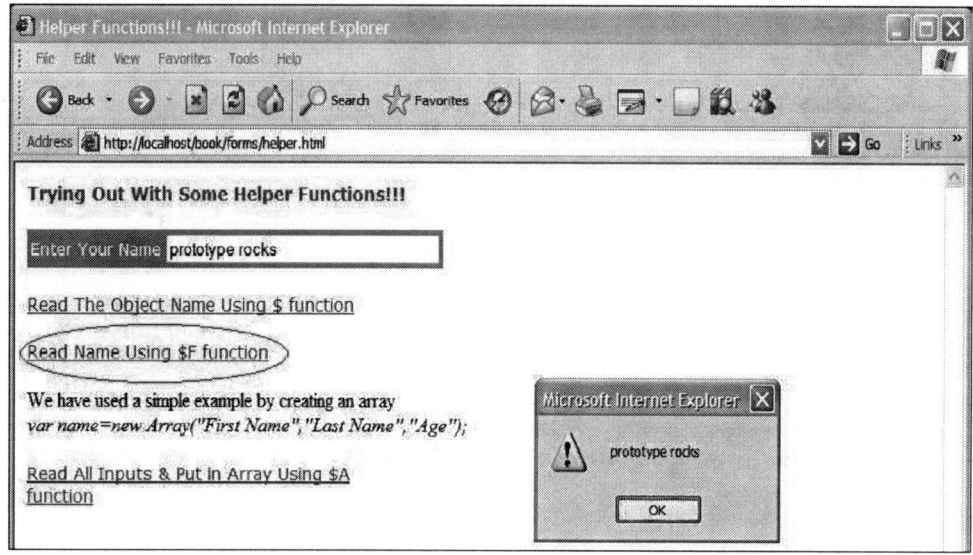

AJAX components—an overview

Ask any developer why he prefers working with Prototype and you will typically find one obvious reason—it's native and easy support for AJAX.

Asynchronous JavaScript and XML aka XHR aka AJAX has become the de facto technique for many web applications. Most of the community-centric and niche web applications are powered by AJAX these days. Prototype provides a lot of features that help us add AJAX functionality to web applications with ease. Otherwise, we would have to write the XMLHttpRequest objects. The best part is that we, as developers, don't have to worry about the cross-browser issues. Prototype takes care of them.

An AJAX object is a predefined object in the library that helps us to create objects on the fly. It comes with a lot of options for our convenience.

All AJAX functionality is contained in mainly four objects of the AJAX class. There are basically the following four types of objects:

- Ajax.Request
- Ajax.Updater
- Ajax.PeriodicalUpdater
- Ajax.Responders

Ajax.Request

`Ajax.Request` is inherited from the AJAX class of Prototype. It helps us in dynamically requesting a URL from the server, which is followed by a server response. An `Ajax.Request` object encapsulates commonly used AJAX code for setting up the XMLHttpRequest object, performing cross-browser checking for compatibility, and callback handling.

Communication with the server to establish client-side communication, based on server-side script, is easy and painless.

A simple constructor looks like this:

```
New Request = new Ajax.Request(url, options);
```

As you will notice from the syntax, in order to initiate the `Request` object we need to supply two arguments: the `url`, and the `options`.

Some of the `options` parameters are as follows:

- `Method`: It specifies whether the action is a `GET` or `POST` method
- `Parameters`: It is the input values that we will be passing to our server
- `onSuccess`: On successful completion of the request, either call a function or perform some other similar function
- `onFailure`: It is the handle used if the request fails
- `onLoading`: While requesting, show a simple image or text to notify the user about what is happening

The syntax for calling an `Ajax.Request` object with all parameters is shown in the following code:

```
var options = {
    method: "get",
    parameters: param,
    onSuccess: ShowReponse,
    onFailure: ShowError
};
var req = new Ajax.Request("url", options);
```

Alternatively, we can also define the `options` as a part of the constructor.

This would look like the following code snippet:

```
new Ajax.Request(url, {
    method: 'get',
    parameters:pars,
    onSuccess: showResponse,
    onFailure:showError
});
```

Ajax.Updater

The `Ajax.Updater` class of Prototype helps us by updating specific portions of the web page with the data that comes from the server dynamically.

The syntax looks like this:

```
new Ajax.Updater(location, url,[ options])
```

If you look at the syntax, it takes two parameters:

- `location`: It is the ID of the `<div>` or any specific part of the page that needs to be updated
- `url`: It is the URL of the server file to fetch the data

The options are the same as those of `Ajax.Request`. So, the complete constructor to be defined would be as follows:

```
var options = {
    Method: "get",
    Parameters: param,
    onSuccess: ShowReponse,
    onFailure: ShowError
};
var req = new Ajax.Updater('location', "url", options);
```

Ajax.PeriodicalUpdater

The `Ajax.PeriodicalUpdater` class of Prototype uses the `Ajax.Updater` class to refresh an element after a certain time interval. The syntax will be almost the same as the one for `Ajax.Updater`. But along with this we need to supply the frequency and delay.

A simple example that we can mention at this point of time is **Gmail**.

After a certain period of time the data gets refreshed and new data is placed inside the container, as seen in the following screenshot:

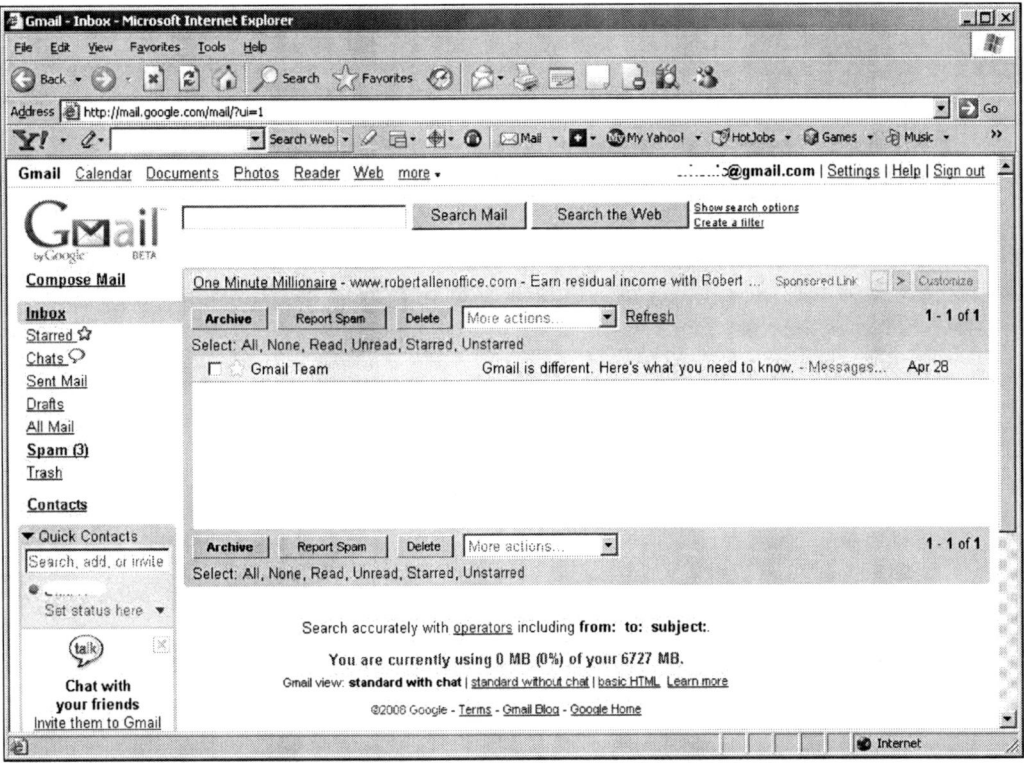

Ajax.Responders

`Responders` are global objects that monitor all AJAX activities on the page and are notified of each step in the communication process. We can always keep a track of any AJAX activity using `Responders`.

They act as *listeners* for the web page activity. We can create our own functions that will respond to any other function using `Responders`.

This generally takes place in two steps:

- Register the `responder`
- Associate the function

The simplest way of doing it is shown here:

```
Ajax.Responders.register(responder)
```

Similarly, to unregister any `responder` use the script that follows:

```
Ajax.Responders.unregister(responder)
```

Exploring Client-side Techniques with Prototype

Now, let's quickly look at a simple example of how we can use `Responders` in web applications.

```
Ajax.Responders.register({
  onCreate:callsomeFunction,
  onComplete: RemoveFunction
});
```

This means whenever an AJAX request is created, our `Responders` will automatically call the function `callsomeFunction` and once that particular request is completed, we will call `RemoveFunction`.

We have understood all the three major objects provided by Prototype for adding AJAX to our web applications. Here's a quick look at the terms that we should always keep in mind:

- `Ajax.Request`: This helps and supports the communication between the server and the client while taking care of cross-browser handling
- `Ajax.Updater` or `Ajax.PeriodcialUpdater`: This helps in updating specific parts of the web page without refreshing the whole page
- `Ajax.Responders`: This helps in responding or reacting to other functions inside the web page when triggered using AJAX calls

Hands-on examples

Enough said! Now let's see something working. Working code is not only an inspiration, but a motivation too.

Username availability script using Ajax.Request

Talking about dynamic web sites and not mentioning username scripts doesn't sound good. So, let's hack a simple `Ajax.Request` script. (And yes, once it is done, don't forget to impress your friends.)

Let's fire up our browser and see the application module.

```
<script type="text/javascript" src="prototype.js"></script>
<script type="text/javascript" src="Scripts.js"></script>
<script type="text/javascript" src="src/scriptaculous.js"></script>
<script type="text/javascript" src="src/effects.js"></script>
<link rel="stylesheet" href="style.css" >
<head>
    <title>Check Username Script</title>
</head>
<body onload="JavaScript:init();">
```

```html
    <form class="login-form">
    Username:<input type="text" name="username" id="username"
              onblur="CheckUsername();">
<p>
    <div class="yes" id="yes">
       <p>Username Available</p>
    </div>
    <div class="no" id="no">
       <p>Username NOT Available</p>
    </div>
    Password: <input type="text" name="password" id="password">
<p>
    <input type="submit" name="submit" value="Join" id="password">
    </form>
</body>
</html>
```

It creates a simple user interface layout for us.

We are also creating two `<div>`s to hold and show data whether a username is available or not. The `<div>`s are hidden in the web page using the `init()` function on load.

Let's add some spicy JavaScript to this code and make it more interactive.

```javascript
function init() {
$('no').style.display='none';
$('yes').style.display='none';
}
function CheckUsername() {
var pars = 'username='+$F('username');
var url = 'checkusername.php';
new Ajax.Request(url, {
     method: 'get',
     parameters:pars,
     onSuccess: showResult,
     onFailure:showError
  });
}
function showError() {
alert("Something Went Wrong");
}
function showResult(ServerResponse) {
var response = ServerResponse.responseText;
if(response=="available"){
```

Exploring Client-side Techniques with Prototype

```
$('no').style.display='none';
$('yes').style.display='';
}
else {
$('no').style.display='';
$('yes').style.display='none';
}
}
```

Now, let's see the application module.

We also create a simple server URL called `checkusername.php`.

```
<?php
  $usernames = array('sam', 'me', 'prototype', 'sri');
  if(in_array($_GET['username'], $usernames))
    echo 'unavailable';
  else
    echo 'available';
?>
```

That's pretty much the simplest way of checking the `username`. The important thing to note here is that we are using the `Ajax.Request` object for this example.

When you try to enter the data that is already present in the array, you will get a message as shown in the following screenshot:

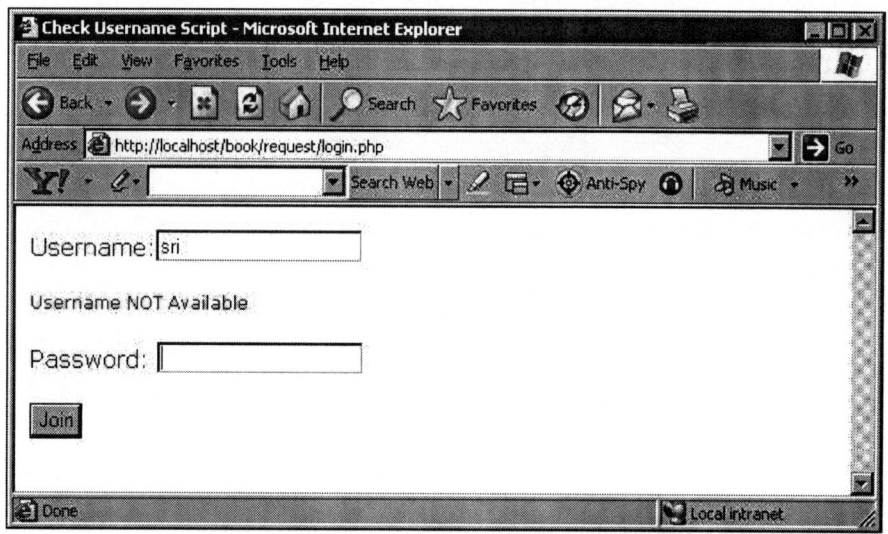

Display username availability script using Ajax.Updater

We have seen how we can implement the username-checking script using `Ajax.Request`.

Maybe it's now a good idea to implement the same using `Ajax.Updater`.

For this example, the scripts and the code would also be on the similar lines but with a little variation.

Let's explore some new ways.

```html
<script type="text/javascript" src="prototype.js"></script>
<script type="text/javascript" src="Scripts.js"></script>
<script type="text/javascript" src="src/scriptaculous.js"></script>
<script type="text/javascript" src="src/effects.js"></script>
<link rel="stylesheet" href="style.css" >
<head>
    <title>Check Username Script</title>
</head>
<body>
    <form class="login-form">
    Username:<input type="text" name="username" id="username"
            onblur="CheckUsername();">
<p>
    <div class="result" id="result" ></div>
<p>
    Password: <input type="text" name="password" id="password">
<p>
    <input type="submit" name="submit" value="Join" id="password">
    </form>
</body>
</html>
```

As you can see, we have removed the `<div>`s for each response and have introduced only a single *result* `<div>` that would generate our response from server.

The server-side script file `checkusername.php` remains the same for this example. After all, we are playing with the client-end scripts, right?

OK, so here are the modifications we need to do for the JavaScript code:

```
function CheckUsername() {
var pars = 'username='+$F('username');
var url = 'checkusername.php';
new Ajax.Updater('result','checkusername.php', {
    method: 'get',
```

Exploring Client-side Techniques with Prototype

```
      parameters:pars
});
}
function showError() {
   alert("Something Went Wrong");
}
```

We are passing the *result* `<div>` as a container that would store the result sent by the server.

Finally, it's time to see the application up and running.

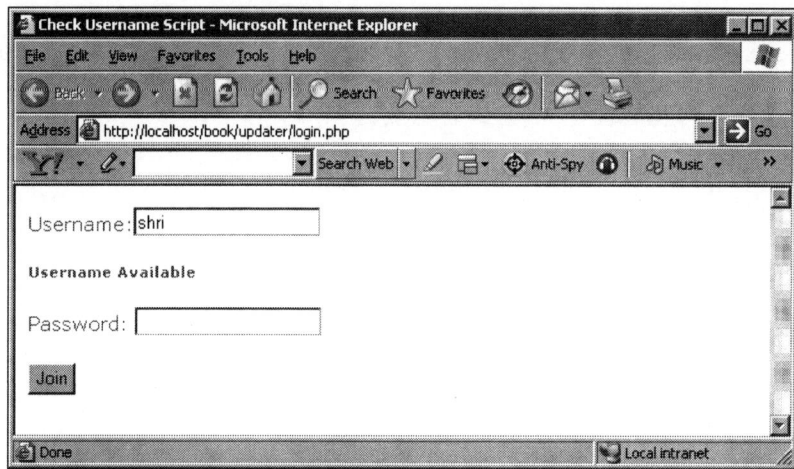

If the **Username** is already in use, the message will be displayed. Check out the following screenshot:

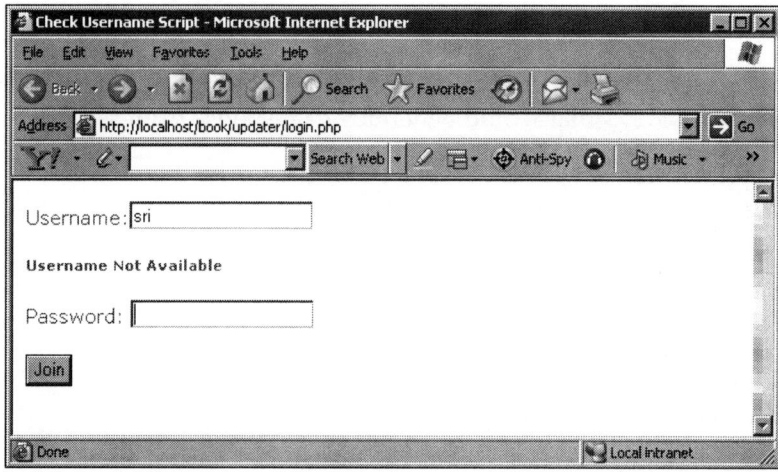

Event handling

We may find ourselves typing some of the code repetitively. That's where Prototype comes in handy for us.

Simple utility functions, a clean way of reading values, adding elements on the fly just about anything and everything can be handled by Prototype—and you thought magicians were rare.

Description

Events are a core part of web applications. Another way of saying this could be *Events talk to our users on behalf of us*. They interact, and hence are close to users.

Let's explore the power of events and of course the ease with which we can use them, using Prototype. By using events, we can handle a lot of functionality at the client end rather than making it heavily dependent on the server-side scripts.

Let's quickly dive into the methods supported by Prototype for handling Events. We have divided them into three basic categories for easy understanding.

- Handling general events
- Handling mouse events
- Handling keyboard events

Handling general events

Handling general events becomes easy using the following methods:

- `Element`: This returns the DOM element on which the event occurred.
- `Extend`: Developers are given the freedom to create and extend the `Events.Methods` class.
- `findElement`: This helps us in finding the element with a specific tag name.
- `Observe`: This method helps in registering an element for event handling. For example, if a particular link was registered, we would be able to trace how many times it was clicked on, and so on.
- `Stop`: We have control over the flow of events. We can stop the events action by calling this method.
- `StopObserving`: Like we registered an event to observe, we can also unregister it by calling the `StopObserving` method.
- `unloadedCache`: If you are using Prototype versions less than 1.6, you will not find this. But for those of you working with versions above 1.6, it's already there.

Syntax

The basic syntax for working with events would be like this:

```
Event.observe(element, name, observer);
```

We will now define the `observe` method for the event on an element when it is clicked.

```
Event.observe('ElementID', 'click', function(event)
{ alert('Element Was Clicked');});
```

Simple? OK, let's try some more examples with key press and mouse events:

```
Event.observe('ElementID', 'keypress', function(event)
{ alert('Key Was Pressed');});
Event.observe('ElementID', 'mousemove', function(event)
{ alert('clicked!');});
```

What if we were to handle the `onload` function in the window? You think it is tough? No, it is not.

```
Event.observe(window, 'onload', function(event){ alert('Loaded');});
```

Now, what if we wanted to stop some particular event? This is simple too.

```
Event.stop(event);
```

Having spoken about the events, now let's find the element on which the event occurred. Interesting? It sure is.

```
var myElement = Event.element(e);
```

Handling mouse events

Dealing with the mouse becomes painless with these methods:

- `PointerX`: It returns the horizontal position of the mouse event
- `PointerY`: It returns the vertical position of the mouse event
- `isLeftClick`: It is self-explanatory; returns with the left-click of the mouse

Handling keyboard events

Prototype has native support for the following keyboard event handlers. All these are pretty straightforward. We handle key-press events and detect which of these events were fired.

- `Event.KEY_BACKSPACE`
- `Event.KEY_TAB`

Chapter 2

- Event.KEY_RETURN
- Event.KEY_ESC
- Event.KEY_LEFT
- Event.KEY_UP
- Event.KEY_RIGHT
- Event.KEY_DOWN
- Event.KEY_DELETE
- Event.KEY_HOME
- Event.KEY_END
- Event.KEY_PAGEUP
- Event.KEY_PAGEDOWN
- Event.KEY_INSERT

So now let's look at how we can use these events in our application. A simple basic syntax will look like the code shown here:

```
$(element).observe('keyup',function);
```

A quick example can be written as follows:

```
<input type="text" id="ourElement" />
<script type="text/javascript">
$('ourElement').observe('keyup',onKeyUp);
Function onKeyUp(e) {
If(e.keyCode==Event.KEY_RIGHT)
{
   alert("Well, you pressed the RIGHT key button");
}
}
</script>
```

Now that you have got a clear picture on how we can use the keyboard events, try out the rest of the keyboard events. I will give you a simple example about the same in the next chapter.

Hands-on examples

In this section we will try out hands-on exercises related to keyboard and mouse events handling using Prototype.

[27]

Exploring Client-side Techniques with Prototype

Handling the keyboard events example

Let's see how the following piece of code, involving events handling, will look like when we fire it in a browser:

```html
<html>
<head>
   <title> determining which key was pressed</title>
   <script type="text/JavaScript" src="prototype.js"></script>
</head>
<body>
<div>
   <input type="text" id="myelement" />
</div>
   <script type="text/javascript">
   function onKeyup(e) {
      var element = Event.element(e);
      if(e.keycode == Event.ESC) {
         alert("Clicked");
      }
    }
   $('myelement').observe('keyup', onKeyup);
   </script>
</body>
</html>
```

We invoked a simple function, `onKeyup`, whenever you press a key in the input textbox. We are comparing the `keycode` of the entered input with the keyboard events. If the condition is satisfied, we display an `alert` for that.

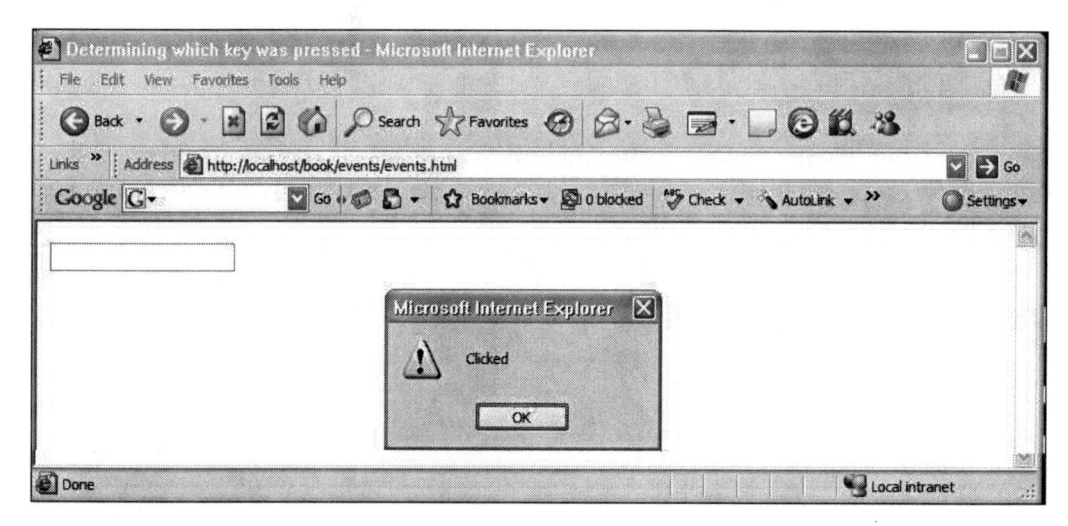

Handling mouse event example

This is a simple example, but it's important for us to understand how it works, as we will explore the drag and drop feature of script.aculo.us later. So here we go.

Let's take a pretty straightforward approach. We create a region or a simple term `<div>`, which acts as an area in which we read the coordinates when the mouse enters. When the mouse is rolled over it, we display the change of coordinates.

```html
<html>
    <head>
        <title>X and Y coordinates of the mouse</title>
        <script type="text/javascript" src="prototype.js"></script>
    </head>
    <body>
        <div id="myMouse">
            Dare You Drag The Mouse Here!!!!!
        </div>
        <script type="text/javascript">
            function onMouseMove(e)
            {
                var element = Event.element(e);
                element.update(Event.pointerX(e) + 'x'
                + Event.pointerY(e));
            }
            $('myMouse').observe('mousemove', onMouseMove);
        </script>
    </body>
</html>
```

Want to see what it looks like when we are done? Let's have a look at the screenshot that follows:

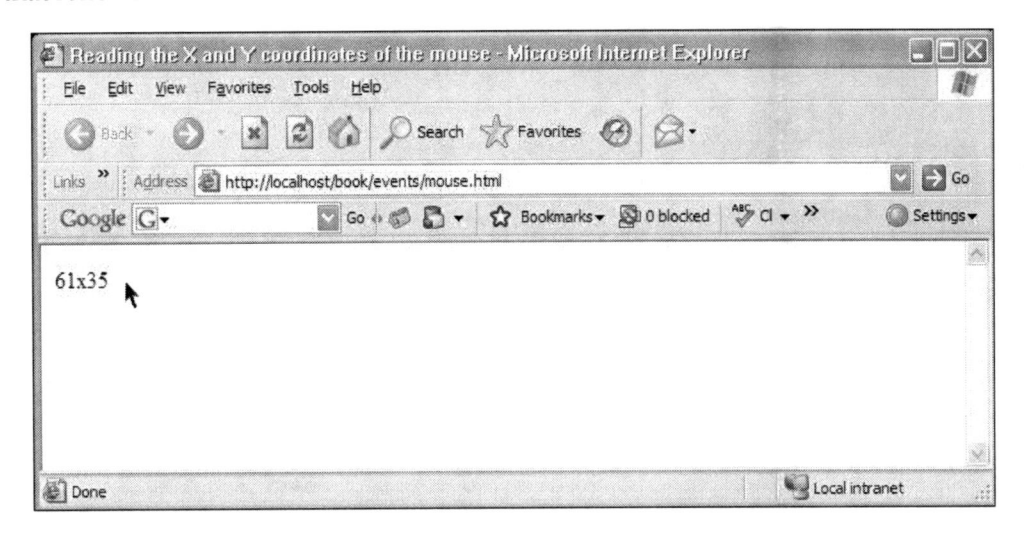

Redefining forms with Prototype

Forms are an integral part of the Web and web applications. In this section we will explore how to redefine the forms using Prototype's features. Prototype has native support for reading values, adding elements, and changing the style properties inside the forms. So let's get started and redefine our forms.

Introduction

Forms are the epicenter of any web application. For end users, they are the product. So how can we explore and make our forms beautiful? In this section we will try to make our forms interactive as well as eye-candy.

Prototype provides us with the form as a namespace that encapsulates everything related to form handling, manipulation, and serialization.

Description

The form module of Prototype comes with the following methods that handle the biggest pain that the developers face—cross-browser scripting with forms.

All these methods may not seem very powerful at first, but trust me that they take all the pain of doing the same things time and again.

We will quickly run through all these methods.

- `Disable`: Calling this method will help us disable the form. The form and the corresponding form elements will be visible, but users will not be able to edit them. Imagine a simple comment form. If a user is logged in, comments can be written; otherwise they cannot edit anything.

- `Enable`: Using this method we can dynamically make the form and its elements active. All the form elements can be made completely or partially active.

- `findFirstElement`: Using this method we can find the first non-hidden, non-disabled element in the form.

- `focusFirstElement`: This method enables the keyboard to focus on the first element of the form.

- `getElements`: Using this method we get a collection of all the elements in the form.

- `getInputs`: Calling this method will return the values from all the input elements from the form.

- `Request`: Now I am sure this would catch your attention. The request method is used to submit the form to the server using `Ajax.Request`.
- `Reset`: Using this method we can reset the form to its default values.
- `serialize`: This method is called when we need to serialize the data coming from the form, and we need to pass it as parameters to the `Ajax.Request` method.

    For example, to pass two variables to server we need to create our URL to look like this:

    `someform.php?id=1&username="proto"`

    Instead of creating the URLs ourselves, we just pass the variables in the form of inputs. Prototype's serialize function would automatically create the query string, which we can just pass to our server.

- `serializeElements`: This is the same as the `serialize` method. But here you select which elements are to be read from an array, and pass them to the `Ajax.Request` method.

Usage

Now that we have seen all the form methods that our library Prototype provides, we shall learn how to use them in our code.

Try this simple method. All you have to do is pass the ID of the form and you can find the form being disabled. OK, one more piece of advice. Don't try to disable a form before you read the values, otherwise it would result in an empty return.

```
$('formID').disable();
//again enabling the form
$('formID').enable();
```

Got it? Wasn't it fun? So why not try some more methods and get into the flow?

These methods are pretty much self-explanatory. We are trying to get the elements, values of input elements, values for a specific input element, placing the keyboard focus on to the first element of the form and reset the form to default values.

```
var myElements = Form.getElements($('formID'));
var myInputs = Form.getInputs('formID');
var firstName = Form.getInputs('formID', 'firstName');
Form.focusFirstElement('formID');
Form.reset('formID');
```

Exploring Client-side Techniques with Prototype

While we are at it, let's see a trickier one.

```
var params = $('myFormId').serialize();
```

Imagine that we have a form with five input elements. Reading the values and passing them to the server would be a real pain. But using the method `serialize`, we leave everything to Prototype to make our values ready to be sent or used as POST or GET in `Ajax.Request`.

Hands-on examples

Now that we are well-versed with the concepts of playing and making our forms intuitive, let's have some fun clubbing all the methods and features of the form together to get a clear picture of how it works in an actual web page.

Here we go:

```html
<script type="text/javascript" src="prototype.js"></script>
<script type="text/javascript" src="Scripts_old.js"></script>
<script type="text/javascript" src="src/scriptaculous.js"></script>
<script type="text/javascript" src="src/effects.js"></script>
<link rel="stylesheet" href="style.css" >
<head>
   <title>Playing With Forms</title>
</head>
<body>
   <h3 class="heading"> Playing with Forms is Fun!!!!</h3>
   <form name="addForm" class="addForm" id="addForm">
   <table class="FormTable">
   <tr>
      <td>First Name</td>
      <td><input type="text" name="first_name" id="first_name"
          size="35">
      </td>
   </tr>
   <tr>
      <td>Last Name</td>
      <td><input type="text" name="last_name" id="last_name"
          size="35">
      </td>
   </tr>
   <tr>
      <td>Gender</td>
      <td>
```

```html
            <select id="gender" name="gender">
               <option>Male</option>
               <option>Female</option>
               <option>Not Sure</option>
            </select>
            </td>
      </tr>
      <tr>
         <td></td>
         <td><input type="submit" value="Test Submit"><td>
      </tr>
      </table>
</form>
<div class="links">
   <a href="javascript:disableForm();">Disable The Form</a><p>
   <a href="javascript:enableForm();">Enable The Form</a><p>
   <a href="javascript:findFirstElement();">Find The First Element of
   Form</a><p>
   <a href="javascript:readAllElements();">Read All Elements</a><p>
   <a href="javascript:readInputElements();">Read Only Input Elements
   Value</a><p>
   <a href="javascript:serializeForm();">Serialize The Form</a><p>
   <a href="javascript:FocusOnFirstElement();">Focus On The First
   Element of Form</a><p>
   <a href="javascript:resetForm();">Reset The Form</a><p>
</div>
</body>
</html>
```

The code we just saw is in plain HTML, which would create a simple user interface for us to play with and test all our methods. When you open the file in the browser, the web page now gets a new look.

Check it out yourself.

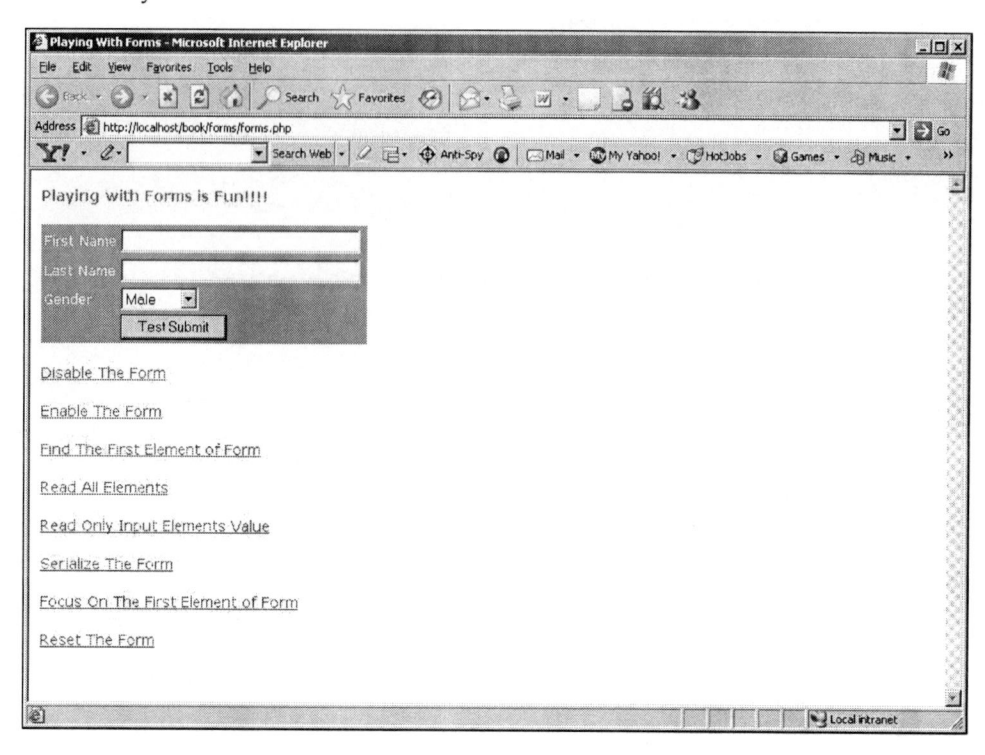

Now that we have our skeleton ready, let's add some life to it with JavaScript.

```
function disableForm(){
$("addForm").disable();
}
function enableForm(){
$("addForm").enable();
}
function findFirstElement() {
myElement = Form.findFirstElement("addForm");
alert(myElement.value);
}
function readAllElements() {
var myElements = Form.getElements('addForm');
for(i = 0; i < myElements.length; i++) {
    alert(myElements[i].value);
}
}
function readInputElements() {
var myInputs = Form.getInputs('addForm');
for(i = 0; i < myInputs.length; i++) {
    alert(myInputs[i].value);
```

```
}
}
function serializeForm() {
myForm = Form.serialize("addForm");
alert(myForm);
}
function resetForm() {
myForm = Form.reset("addForm");
}
function FocusOnFirstElement() {
Form.focusFirstElement('addForm');
}
```

I know you are eager to click on one of those links as quickly as you can. So what are you waiting for? We click on the **Serialize The Form** link and it creates a string which is ready to be passed to the AJAX objects.

It reads each of the form elements one by one and converts them into *ready-to-use* parameters.

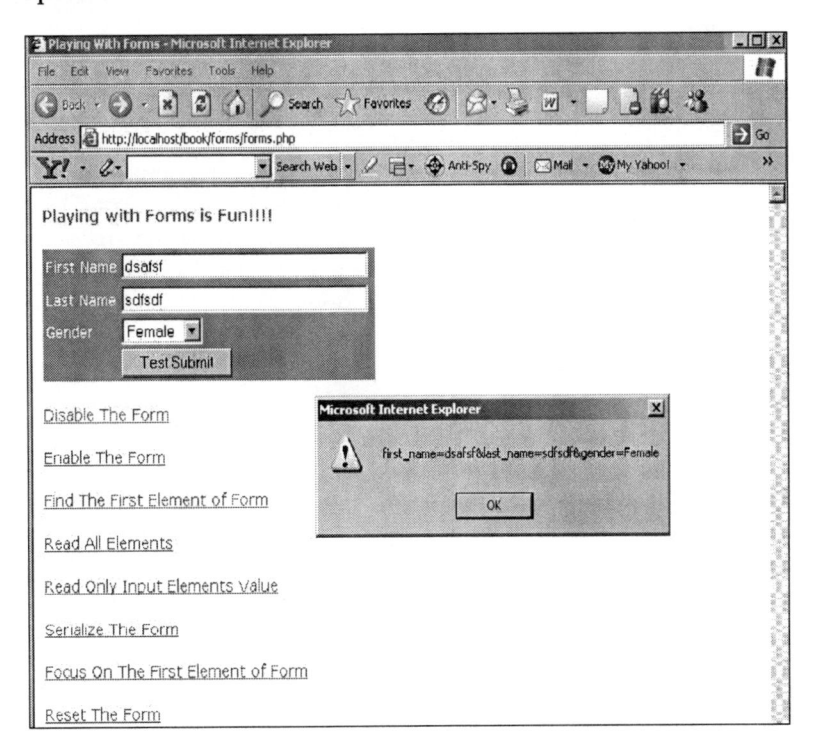

Go ahead and try clicking on some more links. You will get a clear picture as to what and how the form methods will actually work. And yes, imagination has no boundaries.

Getting more hands-on

After exploring Prototype's features, which we can implement in our applications, in this section we will learn how to interact with the server using Prototype through the AJAX calls.

Hands-on example: How to use XML to read data from the server using Prototype

By now, you are loaded with theory and have been through a simple hands-on. It's now time for us to get into a real application module.

The module we will be working with is from the fully featured project in Chapter 10, the Tadalist.

This module plays the most important role in an application. Using this module, we can add items in our page dynamically and put them back to the page without refreshing the page.

Let's quickly get the user interface part done with the following piece of code and save the file as `add.php`.

```
<script type="text/javascript" src="prototype.js"></script>
<script type="text/javascript" src="Scripts.js"></script>
<script type="text/javascript" src="src/scriptaculous.js"></script>
<script type="text/javascript" src="src/effects.js"></script>
<link rel="stylesheet" href="style.css" >
<head>
   <title>Adding New Items</title>
</head>
   <?php
   echo '<div id="ShowAddItem" class="ShowAddItem"><form id="myform"
   action="additem.php" method="post" onsubmit="return false;">';
   echo '<br>Enter a New Item to this List<br><br>';
   echo '<input type="text" name="myinput" id="myinput"
         size="25"/><br><br>';
   echo '<input type="button" value="Submit!"
         onclick="Javascript:AddItem()">';
   echo '</form></div>';
   echo '<p><br>';
   echo '<div id="ItemTree" class="ItemTree">';
?>
```

The code is pretty self-explanatory, but we will quickly run through it. We are including all the required JavaScript files such as `prototype`, `scriptaculous`, and `Scripts`. When we open the file in the browser we should able to find something similar to the next screenshot:

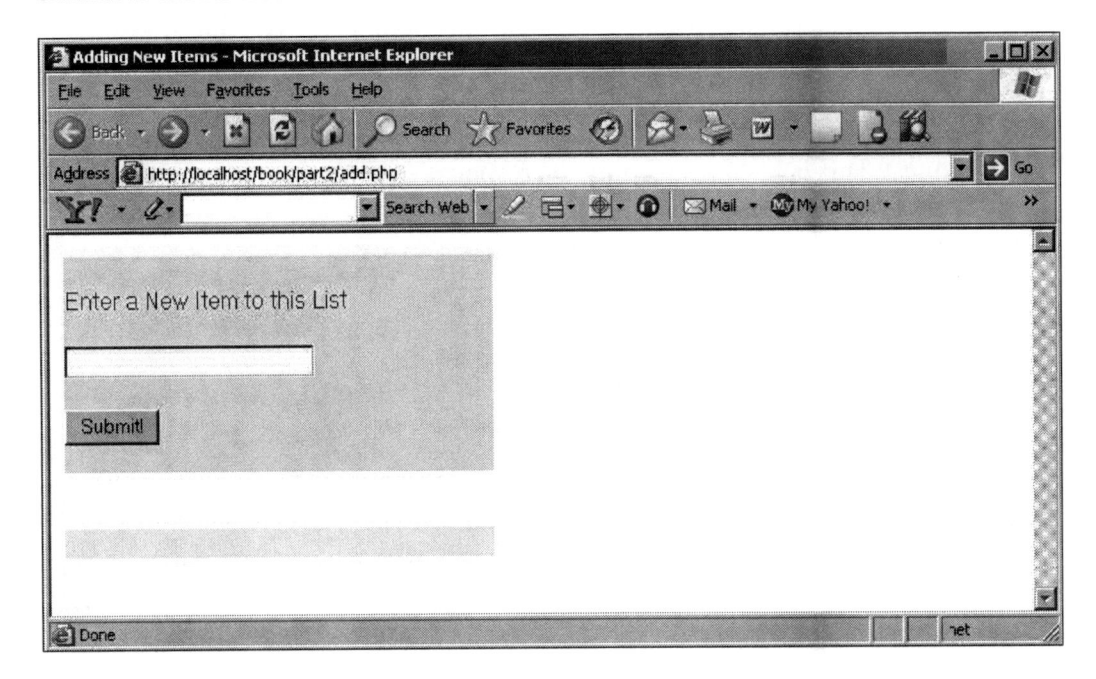

Simple isn't it? I can see you smiling.

Now it's time to add some power functionality to make our `add.php` module exciting. We have called a function `AddItem()` on the **Submit** button, so let's implement it.

```
function AddItem() {
var input = 'myinput='+$F('myinput');
var pars = input;
new Ajax.Request(
'additem.php',
    {   asynchronous:true,
        parameters:pars,
        onComplete: ShowData
    }
);
$('myform').reset();
$('myinput').activate();
return false;
}
```

Exploring Client-side Techniques with Prototype

As discussed earlier, we are making use of the utility functions such as `$F()` to read the value from the input textbox. Above all, we are making use of `Ajax.Request` and passing our parameters to the utility functions in the form of `pars`. Two interesting things to note here are:

1. `AddItem.php` is the server-side URL we are passing our parameters to. This URL would also return the response which would be handled by the `ShowData()` function.
2. We are calling the `ShowData()` function on the successful completion of the request. This helps us in reading the response from the server and displaying it back on our page.

Let's quickly get these two things ready.

Here is the code for `AddItem.php`:

```php
<?php
    mysql_connect("localhost", "root", "") or die(mysql_error());
        //connects to the mysql db or outputs an error
        mysql_select_db("test") or die(mysql_error());
        // selects the database from the choosen server or outputs an
          error
    header("Content-Type: text/xml");
        print'<?xml version="1.0" encoding="UTF-8" standalone="yes"?>';
        $the_name = $_POST['myinput'];
        $sql = "INSERT INTO items (ItemID,ItemName) VALUES
        (NULL,'$the_name')";
        $result = mysql_query($sql);
        $rowID = mysql_insert_id();
    if (!$result) {
        echo 'Could not run query: ' . mysql_error();
        exit;
    }
    else {
        $sql = "SELECT ItemName from items where ItemID=".$rowID;
        $result = mysql_query($sql);
        $row = mysql_fetch_row($result);
        $itemValue = $row[0];
        echo '<response>';
        echo '<ItemID>'.$rowID.'</ItemID>';
        echo '<ItemName>'.$itemValue.'</ItemName>';
        echo '</response>';
    }
?>
```

Scared? Don't be; it's as simple as noodles.

Before I explain further, why don't we quickly get a simple database up and running to save all our items?

Fire up your MySQL prompt and run the following SQL code to create a quick table:

```
CREATE TABLE `items` (
  `ItemID` smallint(5) NOT NULL auto_increment,
  `ItemName` varchar(20) NOT NULL,
  PRIMARY KEY  (`ItemID`)
);
```

Don't worry too much about security. At this point of time we are trying to get our basics strong. Once we have sound fundamentals we shall make our security really powerful in the later part of the book.

Let's get back to the AddItem.php script. We are making use of MySQL functions to connect to our database by passing our login credentials **Username** and **Password**. We are selecting the database through **mysql_select_db**.

Now comes the most important part of the module—handling response through XML.

```
header("Content-Type: text/xml");
print'<?xml version="1.0" encoding="UTF-8" standalone="yes"?>';
```

These lines of code will tell the server through the header that we are going to create an XML file. Further, they will also tell the server to prepare itself to handle data in the XML format.

And, finally, we have our ShowData function which is also pretty straightforward.

```
function ShowData(originalRequest) {
    var xmlDoc = originalRequest.responseXML.documentElement;
    var value = xmlDoc.getElementsByTagName("ItemName")[0].
            childNodes[0].nodeValue;
    var value1 = xmlDoc.getElementsByTagName("ItemID")[0].
            childNodes[0].nodeValue;
    divID = 'DIV'+value1;
    var div = document.createElement('div');
    div.className ='ItemRow';
    div.id = divID;
    var val = '"'+value+'"';
    var i = document.createElement('input');
    i.type='checkbox';
    i.id=value1;
    i.value=value;
    var t = document.createTextNode(value);
    div.appendChild(i);
    div.appendChild(t);
    $('ItemTree').appendChild(div);
}
```

Using this function we will read the XML file that we have created in the
`AddItem.php` file. We then create a `<div>` and add it to our `<div>`, in the
`add.php` file, to `ItemTree`. With that, we are done.

The final output should look like the screenshot that follows:

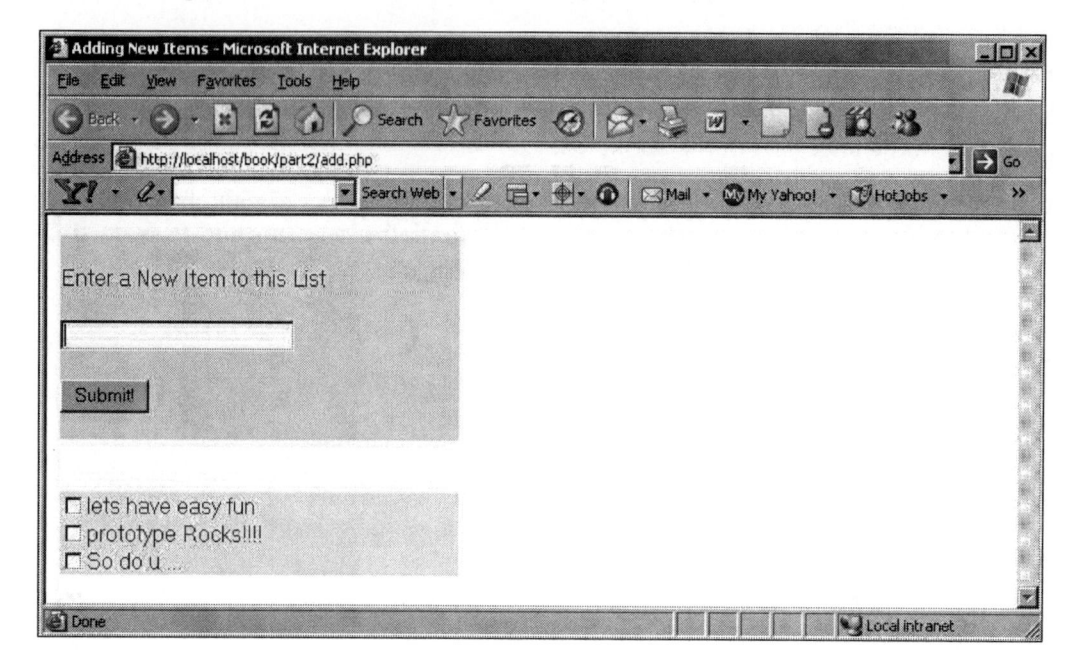

Summary

In this chapter we have learned about the wonderful Prototype library. We have also
explored various features such as DOM, AJAX, and event handling.

A quick recapitualtion of all the features we explored in this chapter is as follows:

- Helper functions
- AJAX components
- Handling events and forms

In the next chapter we will learn the server-side techniques using PHP—our new
best friend.

3
Server-side Techniques with PHP and MySQL

Finally, we have reached a point where we can connect the dots. We have learned about the fantastic Prototype, have seen an overview of script.aculo.us, and in this chapter we will explore the server-side techniques.

Some of the key topics that we will cover in this chapter are:

- Server-side scripting with PHP
- Database management using MySQL
- User login management system
- Creating tag clouds

Basic requirements

In this section, we will be looking at some of the basic and key requirements for working on web applications in Windows and Linux operating systems.

We will be learning about the PHP, MySQL, WAMP server (only for Windows), and phpMyAdmin applications.

> Throughout the book we will work with various browsers to make sure that our code is consistent and compatible with them. We will be using Mozilla Firefox, Internet Explorer, and Google Chrome.

A word about PHP 5.0 or above

PHP is undoubtedly a powerful server-side scripting language, which has powered new age web applications. With PHP 5 or above, we also get a standard set of object-oriented programming methodologies. Web applications can be created in a structured manner by classifying their components into classes and objects using different features such as inheritance, constructors, and so on. It's so much fun to work with!

With loads of features, libraries, and documentation, we get complete support from the lovely community as well.

While we are at it, it is recommended that you download the latest stable version 5.2.6 from the official PHP web site at http://php.net.

A word about MySQL 5.0

Ask any open-source developer who hacks with PHP, the database (s)he loves to work with, and the answer will be simple—MySQL. What makes MySQL so special?

MySQL has a lot of inbuilt functions, which are very useful and engaging for a beginner or an expert. MySQL has native support for the PHP scripting language, which makes it the most preferable database to work with in the backend. Not to forget, the supportive community help and documentation that comes in handy all the time.

You can grab the latest copy of MySQL from the official web site: http://mysql.com.

> Most of the Linux distributions come with pre-packaged PHP and MySQL installations. So if you are using any of the leading Linux distributions, you don't have to install PHP and MySQL packages separately. They should come by default. Please check with your distribution manual for more help.

The WAMP server: A must-have for Windows users

There are people like me who don't necessarily swear by the Linux operating system; but yes, they surely swear by PHP and MySQL. If you are one amongst them, then you should have a WAMP server. WAMP is the abbreviation of *Windows/Apache/MySQL/PHP*. It is a platform stack for Windows, which can be downloaded, pre-packaged with PHP and MySQL.

You can grab a free copy of WAMP from the official web site at `http://www.wampserver.com/`.

It comes with the latest version of PHP and MySQL, and so we don't have to worry about the version history.

phpMyAdmin

The official site of phpMyAdmin describes phpMyAdmin as *A tool written in PHP intended to handle the administration of MySQL over the Web*.

It is indeed very simple and powerful. Working with phpMyAdmin will make working with the MySQL database easy and highly interactive. You can do everything from the browser that you can otherwise do at the console.

You can download the latest version of phpMyAdmin from the web site at `http://phpmyadmin.net`.

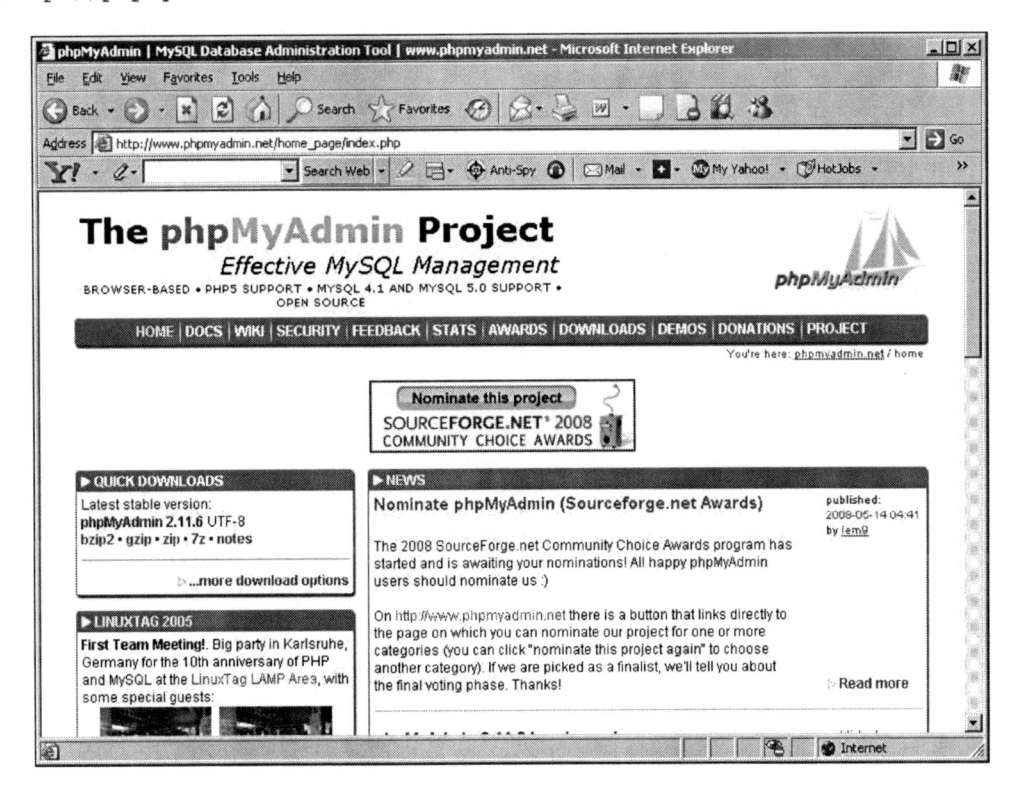

Now that all the required pieces are in place, I know you are excited to get your hands dirty with code. So what are we waiting for? Let the party begin!

Getting the playground ready

Since you have installed PHP, MySQL, or WAMP as a package, try performing some basic procedures to check that the required software is up and running properly.

Checking the PHP installation using the WAMP server

Fire up your browser and type **http://localhost/** in the URL bar. You should be able to see the `index.php` file up and running. If not, then we should check the configurations in the `httpd.conf` and `php.ini` files. Some of the key points you should check are:

- The port should not be in use already
- You have started the WAMP server

> Please refer to the installation manual or documentation of WAMP for further help.

If the installation is a success, we should be able to see the page shown in the following screenshot:

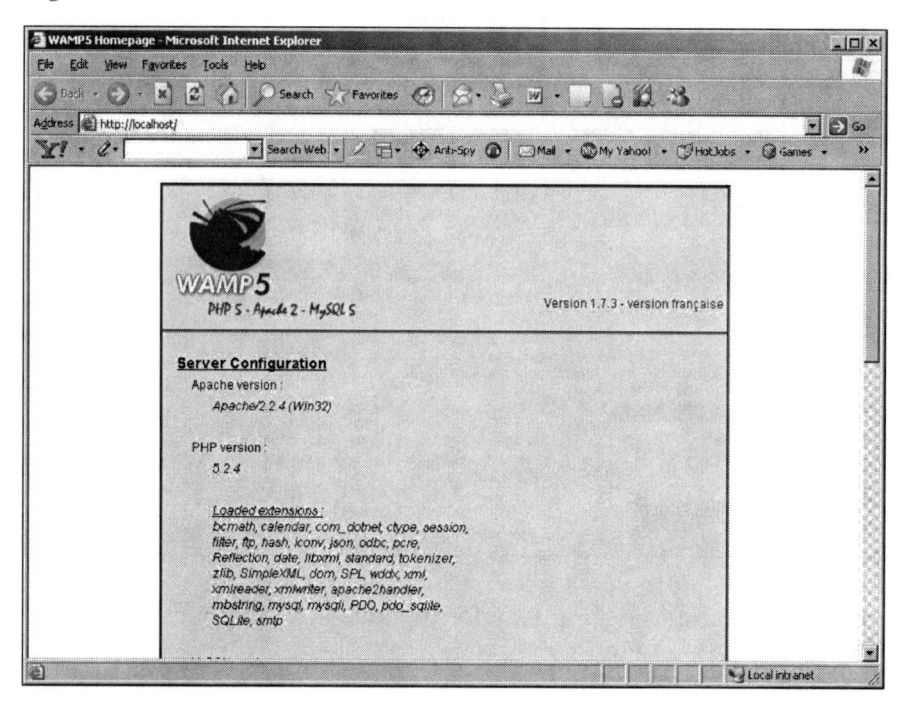

Checking the MySQL installation using the WAMP server

Now, we need to test the MySQL connection using the phpMyAdmin tool.

Fire up your browser and type in the following URL: `http://localhost/phpmyadmin/index.php`.

On success, you should be able to see a screen similar to the screenshot that follows:

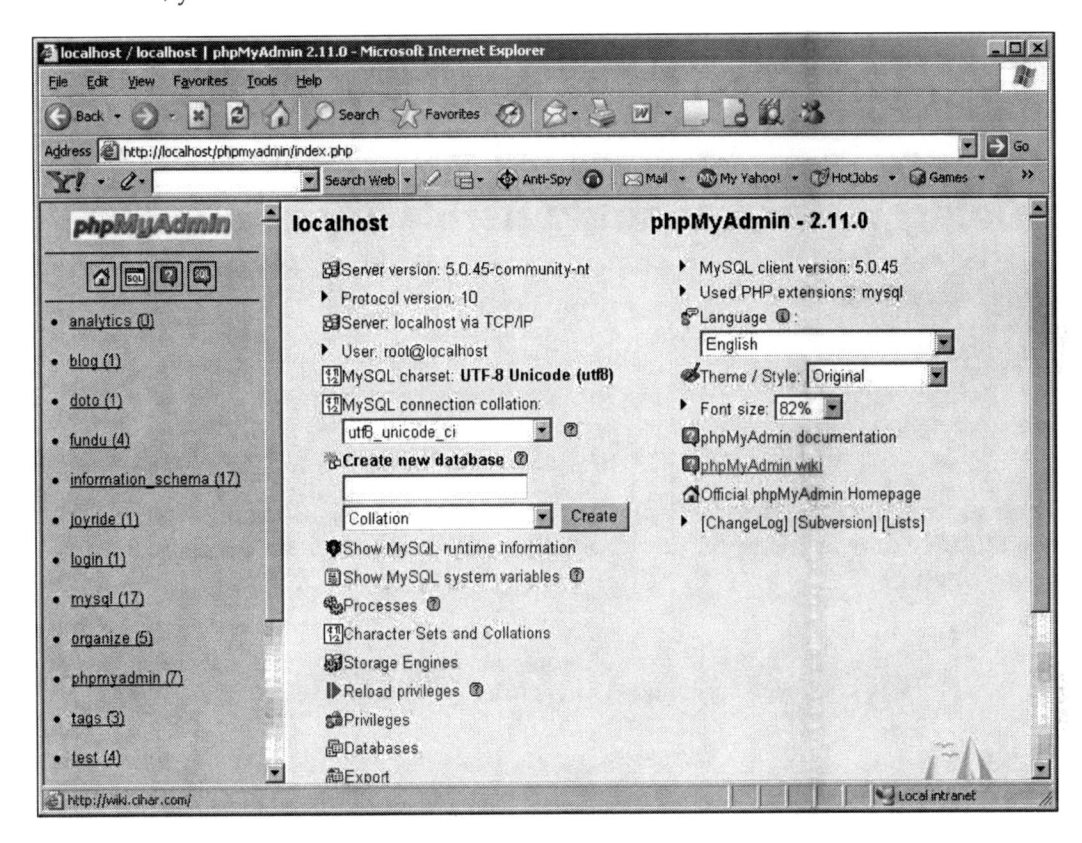

OK, a pat on your back. We have successfully configured all the required server-side software to create our dynamic and powerful web applications. We have seen how to include the Prototype library and the script.aculo.us library in Chapter 2. Let's quickly revise that front and get started with the code.

Adding Prototype library in our code

Before we start exploring the features of Prototype, we need to tell our browser to include the library in our code.

Take a quick look at the folder structure to know where the files should be placed:

webroot | application name | javascript files | prototype library

Let's place our Prototype library inside our `js` folder.

```
<script type="text/javascript" src="js/prototype.js"></script>
```

Just one line pointing towards the path of the source of the library, and we are done.

No, I am serious! We are done.

Adding the script.aculo.us library in our code

Once we have added the Prototype library to our application, we then have to add script.aculo.us too.

Let's do it.

```
<script type="text/javascript" src="src/scriptaculous.js">
</script>
<script type="text/javascript" src="src/effects.js"></script>
```

These are just the basic files that have been included for demonstration. If we need to have drag and drop, controls, or slider, we need to include the respective JavaScript files.

> The script.aculo.us library is dependent on the Prototype framework, so don't forget to add both the libraries.

Basic classes

No developer wants to rewrite the same code again and again. So it is best to create basic classes, which we will use throughout our applications.

> You can create and place all these basic class files under the `includes` folder. Alternatively, you can also place them in the `current application` folder in `webroot`.

For any web-driven application, we need a strong backend support. So, let's first create the `DBConfig` file.

DBConfig.php

In the code that follows, we will create a simple class where the variables and login credentials will be declared. It really makes the task of developing web applications easy at a later stage.

If at some point of time you need to point the application to a different database, all you need to do is change the settings in the DBConfig file.

```php
<?php
   class DBConfig {
   var $settings;
      function getSettings() {
      // Database variables
         $settings['dbhost'] = 'localhost';
         $settings['dbusername'] = 'root';
         $settings['dbpassword'] = '';
         $settings['dbname'] = 'book';
      // return all the db settings required
      return $settings;
      }
   }
?>
```

We need to pass the hostname, username, password, and the name of the database. In the above example, we are pointing to our localhost as the host and root as username, with no password (a bad idea). We are also using a database called book, which will contain all the tables that we will create for our examples.

DBClass.php

In the code that follows, we are creating a simple class where we will be creating various functions to work with our database. Some of these functions in the class are:

- Reading settings from the DBConfig class
- Querying
- Reading the data
- Closing the connection

Throughout the examples explained in the book, we will be making use of these functions to read settings, query, fetch the data, and close the connection.

These are generic functions and we need to pass parameters to these functions. We don't have to write the code again. Instead, we can just call these functions. Code re-usage is the best thing we developers can learn while building web applications.

```php
<?php
require_once 'DBConfig.php';
class DbClass extends DBConfig{
    var $theQuery;
    var $link;
    //DbClass, Purpose: Connect to the database
    function DbClass(){
    // Load settings from parent class
        $settings =DBConfig::getSettings();
    // Get the main settings from the array we just loaded
        $host = $settings['dbhost'];
        $db = $settings['dbname'];
        $user = $settings['dbusername'];
        $pass = $settings['dbpassword'];
    // Connect to the database
        $this->link = mysql_connect($host, $user, $pass);
        mysql_select_db($db);
        register_shutdown_function(array(&$this, 'close'));
    }
//execute the query, Purpose: Execute a database query
    function query($query) {
        $this->theQuery = $query;
        return mysql_query($query, $this->link);
    }
    // fetch results in the array
        function fetchArray($result) {
        return mysql_fetch_array($result);
    }
    function close() {
        mysql_close($this->link);
    }
}
?>
```

Secure.php

The main purpose of this file is to clean up the data to prevent SQL injections, data validations, and so on.

It is important to clean the data before entering or manipulating with the server.

```php
<?php
/*
Class: Secure.php
*/
class Secure {
function clean_data($value, $handle) {
   if (get_magic_quotes_gpc()) {
       $value = stripslashes($value);
   }
   if (!is_numeric($value)) {
       $value = "'" . mysql_real_escape_string($value, $handle) . "'";
   }
   return $value;
}
} // class ends here
?>
```

Hands-on examples: Common scripts

In the following examples, we will see how to script some modules that are commonly used while creating web applications. We will also be making use of these modules in our examples throughout the book.

User login management system

Now that we are ready with our powerful open-source artillery, let's get to the serious business of having fun with raw code.

In this example we will create a simple yet powerful login management system.

This module will help us achieve the following:

- Register new users
- Log in existing users
- Log out

For any web application, this module is the basic requirement. Rarely will you find interactive web applications that do not have authentication and authorization modules.

The login management system is an essential feature that we will be integrating in all the projects covered in the chapters to come.

Before we get into actual PHP coding, it would be a nice idea to familiarize ourselves with the database schema.

```
CREATE TABLE `users` (
  `userID` int(11) NOT NULL auto_increment,
  `Username` varchar(40) NOT NULL,
  `Password` varchar(40) NOT NULL,
  PRIMARY KEY  (`userID`)
) ENGINE=InnoDB DEFAULT CHARSET=latin1 AUTO_INCREMENT=1;
```

Here we have a table called `users`. It has `userID` as an `auto_increment` along with `Username` and `Password`. In this, `userID` acts as the `PRIMARY KEY` for the table. `Username` would be `varchar`. `Password` would also be `varchar`, and in order to protect our passwords we would also apply **Message Digest 5** (**MD5**) or **Secure Hash Algorithm** (**SHA**) encryption techniques. In our application, we are using MD5.

Let's move on to the `Signup` page details.

Signup.php

This is pretty much a simple user interface layout in HTML. It builds a simple form with two fields: **Username** and **Password**. Remember the schema? A new user enters the username and password. If everything looks fine with the system, we add the user to the table and return the values.

```
<html>
<head>
   <title>New User. Sign Up!!!</title>
   <link rel="stylesheet" href="style.css" >
   <script type="text/javascript" src="scripts.js"></script>
   <script type="text/javascript" src="prototype.js"></script>
</head>
<body>
   <h4>New User? Sign-up!!!!</h4>
   <FORM NAME ="form1" METHOD ="POST" ACTION ="signup.php"
      class="signup-form">
   <table class="signup-table">
   <tr>
```

```
            <td>Username: </td>
            <td><INPUT TYPE = 'TEXT' Name ='username' id="username"
                value="<?PHP print $uname;?>" maxlength="20">
            </td>
        </tr>
        <tr>
            <td>Password:</td>
            <td><INPUT TYPE = 'TEXT' Name ='password'  value="<?PHP print
                $pword;?>" maxlength="16">
            </td>
        </tr>
    </table>
<P>
    <INPUT TYPE = "Submit" Name = "Submit1"  VALUE = "Register">
    </FORM>
<P>
<?PHP print $errorMessage;?>
</body>
</html>
```

Now let's add the PHP power to our `signup.php` script with the following code:

```
<?PHP
$uname = "";
$pword = "";
$errorMessage = "";
$num_rows = 0;
require_once 'DBConfig.php';
require_once 'Secure.php';
if ($_SERVER['REQUEST_METHOD'] == 'POST'){
    $uname = $_POST['username'];
    $pword = $_POST['password'];

    $uname = htmlspecialchars($uname);
    $pword = htmlspecialchars($pword);

    if ($errorMessage == "") {

    $settings = DBConfig::getSettings();
    // Get the main settings from the array we just loaded
    $server = $settings['dbhost'];
    $database = $settings['dbname'];
    $user_name = $settings['dbusername'];
    $pass_word = $settings['dbpassword'];

    $db_handle = mysql_connect($server, $user_name, $pass_word);
```

```php
            $db_found = mysql_select_db($database, $db_handle);
            if ($db_found) {
                $secure = new Secure();
                $uname = $secure->clean_data($uname, $db_handle);
                $pword = $secure->clean_data($pword, $db_handle);
                $SQL = "INSERT INTO users (userID,Username,password) VALUES
                    (NULL,$uname, md5($pword))";
                $result = mysql_query($SQL);
                mysql_close($db_handle);
                if($result)
                {
                // start a session for the new user
                session_start();
                $_SESSION['login'] = "1";
                header ("Location: index.php");
                }
                else
                {
                    $errorMessage ="Somethign went wrong";
                }
            }
            else {
                $errorMessage = "Database Not Found";
            }
        }
    }
?>
```

Let's break down the code into functionality, as this helps us to understand it better.

- Include the common scripts such as `DBConfig.php` and `Secure.php`.
  ```
  require_once 'DBConfig.php';
  require_once 'Secure.php';
  ```

- Check if the data has been posted.
  ```
  if ($_SERVER['REQUEST_METHOD'] == 'POST')
  ```

- Read the DB settings to get `dbhost`, `dbname`, `dbuser`, and `dbpassword`.
  ```
  $settings = DBConfig::getSettings();
  ```

- Clean the user input.
  ```
  $secure = new Secure();
  $uname = $secure->clean_data($uname, $db_handle);
  $pword = $secure->clean_data($pword, $db_handle);
  ```

- Run the INSERT query to add users and get the results.

  ```
  $SQL = "INSERT INTO users (userID,Username,password) VALUES
  (NULL,$uname, md5($pword))";
  ```

- If a user is added successfully, set SESSION['login'] as 1, which will tell our system that the user is logged in. We can also prompt the user with errors that were caused during operations.

- Prompt the errors.

  ```
  $errorMessage = "Database Not Found";
  ```

Finally, the sign-up page should be like the screenshot that follows:

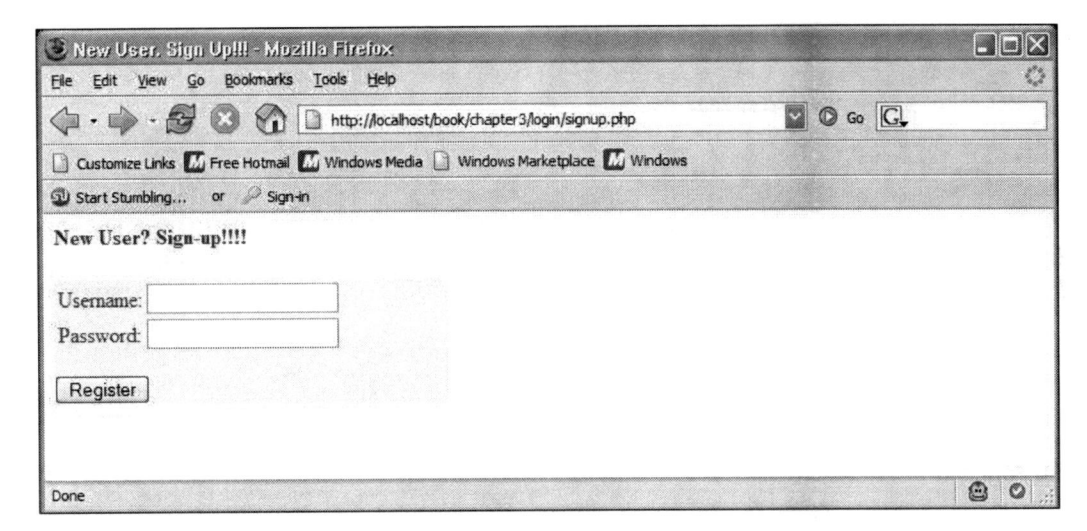

Now, let's move on to the login.php page details. We have added the user successfully to our user's table. It's probably a good idea to cross-check. Fire up the web browser, open phpMyAdmin, and navigate to the user table under the books database.

Alternatively, we can also check through the login.php page.

Login.php

Again, we are creating a simple user interface using HTML to show the user a simple form where he or she will be required to enter a username and password.

```
<html>
<head>
    <title>Login Here!!!</title>
    <link rel="stylesheet" href="style.css" >
```

```
        </head>
        <body>
            <h4>Already Registered? Sign-in!!!</h4>
            <FORM NAME ="form1" METHOD ="POST" ACTION ="login.php"
                class="login-form">
            <table class="login-table">
            <tr>
                <td>Username: </td>
                <td>
                <INPUT TYPE = 'TEXT' Name ='username'  value="<?PHP print
                    $uname;?>" maxlength="20">
                </td>
            </tr>
            <tr>
                <td>Password: </td>
                <td>
                <INPUT TYPE = 'password' Name ='password'  value="<?PHP
                    print $pword;?>" maxlength="16">
                </td>
            </tr>
            </table>
            <INPUT TYPE = "Submit" Name = "Submit1" VALUE = "Login">
            </p>
            </FORM>
            <a href="signup.php">New User? Sign-up</a>
            <p>
            <?PHP print $errorMessage;?>
        </body>
        </html>
```

Let's add some spice with the PHP power. Add the following code to the `login.php` file that we just created:

```
<?PHP
$uname = "";
$pword = "";
$errorMessage = "";
require_once 'DBConfig.php';
require_once 'Secure.php';
// Check if the user has submittied with POST on the form
if ($_SERVER['REQUEST_METHOD'] == 'POST'){
    $uname = $_POST['username'];
```

```php
        $pword = $_POST['password'];
        $uname = htmlspecialchars($uname);
        $pword = htmlspecialchars($pword);
//Can also use a DBclass instead of the code below.
$settings = DBConfig::getSettings();
// Get the main settings from the array we just loaded
$server = $settings['dbhost'];
$database = $settings['dbname'];
$user_name = $settings['dbusername'];
$pass_word = $settings['dbpassword'];
$db_handle = mysql_connect($server, $user_name, $pass_word);
$db_found = mysql_select_db($database, $db_handle);
    if ($db_found) {
    $secure = new Secure();
    $uname = $secure->clean_data($uname, $db_handle);
    $pword = $secure->clean_data($pword, $db_handle);
    $SQL = "SELECT * FROM users WHERE username =$uname AND password=
        md5($pword)";
    $result = mysql_query($SQL);
    $num_rows = mysql_num_rows($result);
        if ($result) {
            if ($num_rows > 0) {
                session_start();
                $_SESSION['login'] = "1";
                header ("Location: index.php");
            }
            else {
                session_start();
                $_SESSION['login'] = "";
                header ("Location: signup.php");
            }
        }
        else {
            $errorMessage = "Error logging on";
        }
    mysql_close($db_handle);
    }
    else {
        $errorMessage = "Error logging on";
    }
}
?>
```

Server-side Techniques with PHP and MySQL

Let's break down the code into functionality once again:

- Include the common scripts such as `DBConfig.php` and `Secure.php`.
  ```
  require_once 'DBConfig.php';
  require_once 'Secure.php';
  ```

- Check if the data has been posted.
  ```
  if ($_SERVER['REQUEST_METHOD'] == 'POST'){
  ```

- Read the database settings to get `dbhost`, `dbname`, `dbusername`, and `dbpassword`.
  ```
  $settings = DBConfig::getSettings();
  ```

- Clean the user input.
  ```
  $uname = $secure->clean_data($uname, $db_handle);
  $pword = $secure->clean_data($pword, $db_handle);
  ```

- Run the `SELECT` query to check if the username and password entered by the user matches to the ones present in the database table, and get the results.
  ```
  $SQL = "SELECT * FROM users WHERE username =$uname AND password= md5($pword)";
  ```

- If `username` and `password` matches, set `SESSION['login']` as 1, which will tell our system the user is logged in; or else prompt him with errors that were caused during operations.

At the end of this part, we should be able to see the application as shown in the following screenshot:

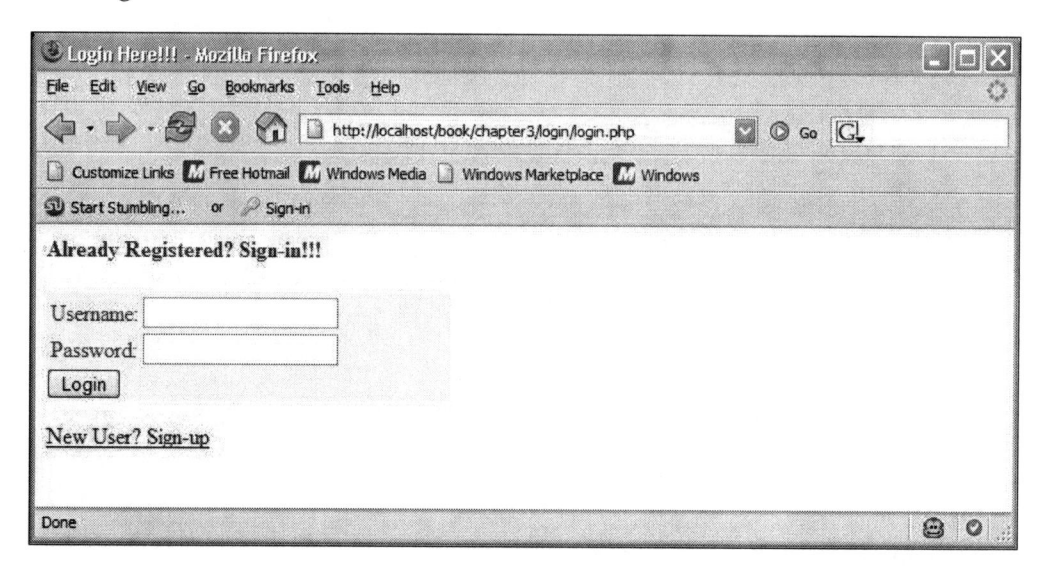

[56]

Index.php

Take a look at the `index.php` file. This is pretty much a straightforward approach. Only users who are logged in will be able to see this data. Using SESSION, we check if the user is logged in or not.

```
<?PHP
session_start();
if (!(isset($_SESSION['login']) && $_SESSION['login'] != '')) {
   header ("Location: login.php");
}
?>
   <html>
   <head>
   <title>Home Page</title>
   </head>
   <body>
   <p>
Thank God.You logged In, system admin was rude...with me!!!!
<p>
   This is where all the protected contents come into picture
<p>
<A HREF = logout.php>Log out</A>
   </body>
   </html>
```

Breaking this code down as per functionality, we do the following:

- Check if the SESSION variable `login` is set.
  ```
  session_start();
  if (!(isset($_SESSION['login']) && $_SESSION['login'] != '')) {
     header ("Location: login.php");
  }
  ```
- If set, show the user the page details.
- Else, redirect him to `login.php`.

Server-side Techniques with PHP and MySQL

We should now have reached a level where our application will look like the following screenshot:

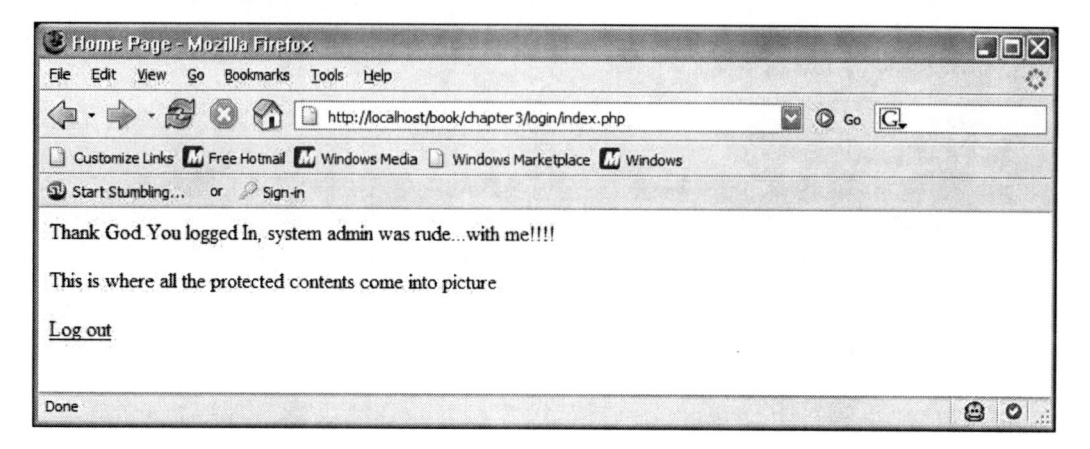

Home Page - Mozilla Firefox
`http://localhost/book/chapter3/login/index.php`

Thank God. You logged In, system admin was rude...with me!!!!

This is where all the protected contents come into picture

Log out

Logout.php

Finally, we come to our last script `Logout.php`.

The purpose of this script is to destroy the sessions that we have set, while logging the user inside the application.

```
<?PHP
   session_start();
   session_destroy();
?>
<html>
<head>
   <title>Logout</title>
</head>
<body>
   Okay, destroyed the sessions of the user. Now try hitting the
      back button. You should be able to see the login page :)
   <p>
      User Logged Out
   <p>
   Want to Login again? <a href="login.php">Login Here</a>
</body>
</html>
```

The logout interface is shown in the following screenshot:

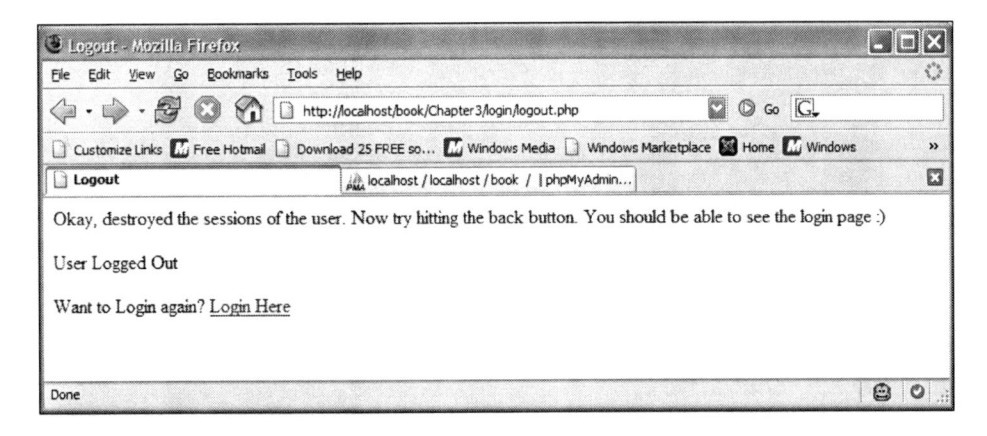

Adding a username availability script to the login management system

In the previous chapter, we saw how to add a username availability script using AJAX. But in those scripts we were using an array to supply our data, not the real database values. So, let's combine the scripts and make something more powerful, beautiful, and agile.

We need to add the `CheckUsername.php` script to our login management system in the `signup.php` file. We used the following form in the `signup.php` file to create a user interface, right?

```
<FORM NAME ="form1" METHOD ="POST" ACTION ="signup.php"
    class="signup-form">
<table class="signup-table">
<tr>
    <td>Username: </td>
    <td>
    <INPUT TYPE = 'TEXT' Name ='username' id="username"
        value="<?PHP print $uname;?>" maxlength="20">
    </td>
</tr>
<tr>
    <td>Password:</td>
    <td>
    <INPUT TYPE = 'TEXT' Name ='password'  value="<?PHP print
        $pword;?>" maxlength="16">
    </td>
</tr>
</table>
<p>
    <INPUT TYPE = "Submit" Name = "Submit1"  VALUE = "Register">
</FORM>
```

Just add the following code to the above form inside the table in `signup.php`. This will make it more interactive.

```
<tr>
    <td></td>
    <td>
    <a href="JavaScript:CheckUsername();">Check Availability
    </a>
    <div class="result" name="result" id="result"></div>
    </td>
</tr>
```

The resulting code is shown here:

```
<FORM NAME ="form1" METHOD ="POST" ACTION ="signup.php"
    class="signup-form">
<table class="signup-table">
<tr>
    <td>Username: </td>
    <td><INPUT TYPE = 'TEXT' Name ='username' id="username"
        value="<?PHP print $uname;?>" maxlength="20">
    </td>
</tr>
<tr>
    <td></td>
    <td>
    <a href="JavaScript:CheckUsername();">Check Availability
    </a>
    <div class="result" name="result" id="result"></div>
    </td>
</tr>
<tr>
    <td>Password:</td>
    <td>
    <INPUT TYPE = 'TEXT' Name ='password'  value="<?PHP print
        $pword;?>" maxlength="16">
    </td>
</tr>
</table>
<p>
<INPUT TYPE = "Submit" Name = "Submit1"  VALUE = "Register">
</FORM>
```

This would invoke the JavaScript function, `CheckUsername()`, when the **Check Availability** link is clicked.

Once we have defined the JavaScript function, we need to include the following JavaScript files to our `signup.php` file. Add them to our code as follows:

```
<script type="text/javascript" src="scripts.js"></script>
<script type="text/javascript" src="prototype.js"></script>
```

Now that we have defined the `scripts.js` file, which will contain all our JavaScript functions required, quickly create it.

Add the `CheckUsername()` function to show the response to our code.

In the code that follows, we are reading the value from the input field name `username`, making an `Ajax.Request`, and passing the value to `Checkuser.php`. On completion of the request, we invoke the `ShowUsernameStatus` function which displays the data.

```
function CheckUsername(){
var user = $('username');
var name = "username='"+user.value+"'";
var pars = name;
new Ajax.Request(
'CheckUser.php',
    {
        method:'post',
        parameters:pars,
        asynchronous:true,
        onComplete: ShowUsernameStatus
    }
);
}
function ShowUsernameStatus(originalRequest) {
    var newData = originalRequest.responseText;
    $('result').innerHTML=newData;
}
```

The following screenshot shows the user availibility script incorporated into the login form:

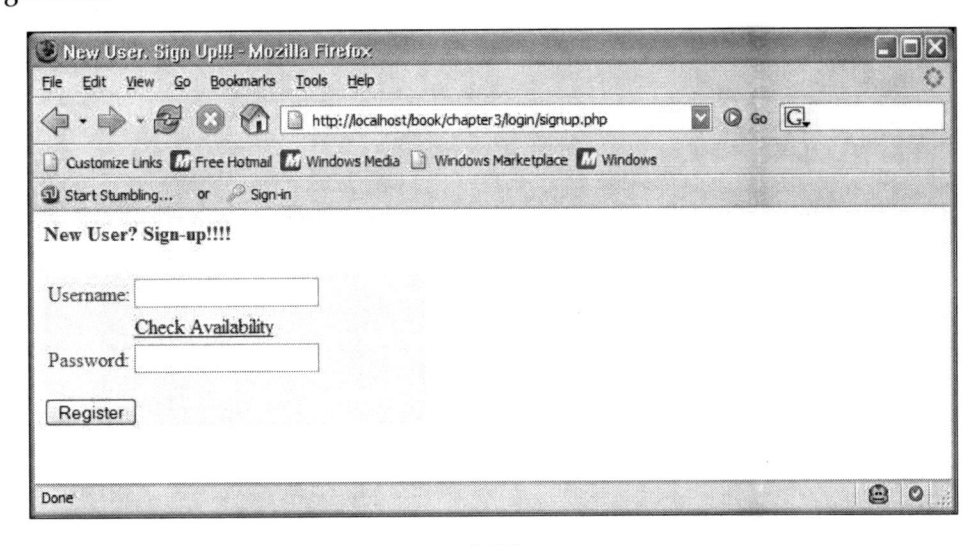

As mentioned in Chapter 3, we have made use of the `Ajax.Request` feature of the Prototype library. You will find it similar to the `Ajax.Request` example we have seen in Chapter 2.

The only difference is in the `CheckUser.php` file.

```php
<?php
require_once "DBClass.php";
    $dbclass = new DBClass();
    $username = $_POST['username'];
    $name= stripslashes($username);
    $sql = "SELECT userID from users where username=".$name."";
    $result= $dbclass->query($sql);
    $num = mysql_num_rows($result);
        if ($num>0) {
            echo 'UserName is NOT avaliable';
        }
        else {
            echo 'UserName is avaliable';
        }
?>
```

Let's break the code as per functionality:

- Connect to the database and tables.

    ```
    require_once "DBClass.php";
    $dbclass = new DBClass();
    ```

- Run the SELECT query to check if the username already exists in the table.

    ```
    $sql = "SELECT userID from users where username=".$name."";
    $result= $dbclass->query($sql);
    ```

- Depending upon the response, update the message in the `signup.php` page.

With this, our login management system is complete.

We will be using it later in the book. Some significant changes will be made in the later part of the projects, as and when required.

The final resulting page will appear like the following screenshot:

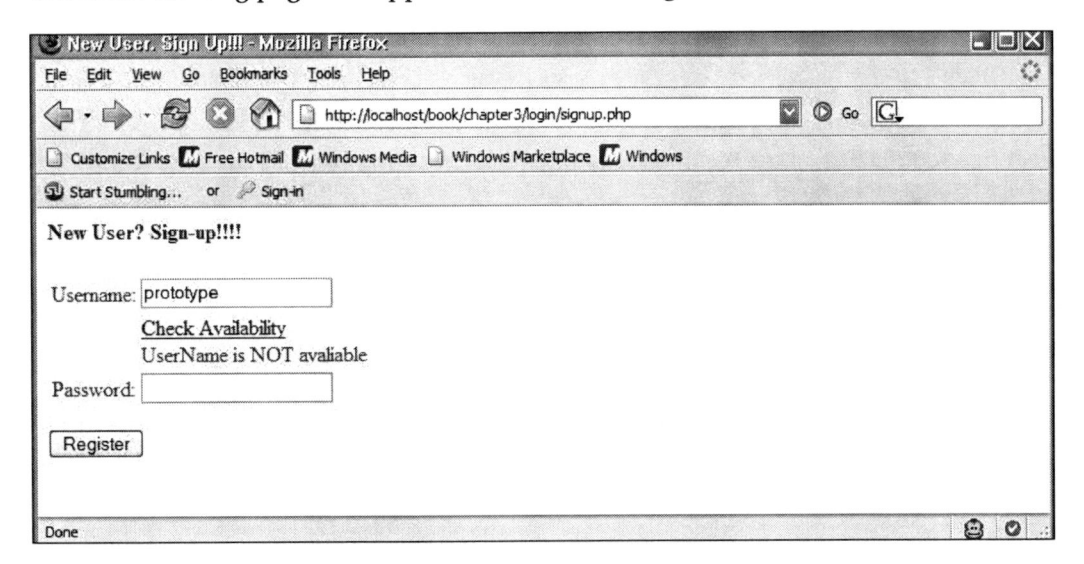

[Screenshot of a Mozilla Firefox browser showing a "New User? Sign-up!!!!" page at http://localhost/book/chapter3/login/signup.php with Username field containing "prototype", a "Check Availability" link showing "UserName is NOT avaliable", a Password field, and a Register button.]

Creating a simple tag cloud

We have our login management system ready, so now we can move on and create a simple tag cloud module.

> Tags are user-generated words, or words that describe functionality of the site. When these tags are displayed based on weight or frequency of usage in the form of clouds, we call them tag clouds.

In every chapter we learned something new to impress your friends, right? So, we don't want to miss out on that in this chapter. This is purely for fun and to make you feel comfortable with PHP and MySQL scripting.

Let's start with the table required for the module, and let's call it `tags`. The table will contain three columns: `tagID`, `tagName`, and `count`. `tagID` will be set to `auto_increment` and will act as the PRIMARY KEY for the table. `count` will be used in real-time projects when we need to create the count of how many times a particular tag was used.

```
CREATE TABLE `tags` (
  `tagID` int(11) NOT NULL auto_increment,
  `tagName` varchar(20) NOT NULL,
  `count` int(11) NOT NULL,
  PRIMARY KEY  (`tagID`)
) ENGINE=InnoDB DEFAULT CHARSET=latin1 AUTO_INCREMENT=1 ;
```

Now that we have our database table `tags` ready, it's time to populate the table with some data. The code to insert a tag in the table is given here:

```
INSERT INTO `tags` ( `tagID` , `tagName` , `count` ) VALUES ( NULL , 'Prototype', '3' );
```

Feel free to add more tags to see a huge tag cloud. Moving on, let's do the coding part of the tag cloud.

```
<?php
require_once 'DBClass.php';

$dbclass = new DBClass();

function tag_info() {
    $result = mysql_query("SELECT * FROM tags GROUP BY tagName ORDER
            BY Rand() DESC LIMIT 0 , 30");
    while($row = mysql_fetch_array($result)) {
        $arr[$row['tagName']] = $row['count'];
    }
    //ksort($arr);
    return $arr;
}
function tag_cloud() {
    $min_size = 20;
    $max_size = 60;
    $tags = tag_info();
    $minimum_count = min(array_values($tags));
    $maximum_count = max(array_values($tags));
    $spread = $maximum_count - $minimum_count;
    if($spread == 0) {
        $spread = 1;
    }
    $cloud_html = '';
    $cloud_tags = array();
    $step = ($max_size - $min_size)/($spread);
    foreach ($tags as $tag => $count) {
        $size = $min_size + ($count - $minimum_count)
            * $step;
//  $size = ($max_size + $min_size)/$spread;
        $cloud_tags[] = '<a style="font-size: '. floor($size) . 'px'
            .'" class="tag_cloud"
                href="http://localhost/content/SearchTag.php?tag=' . $tag
                . '" title="\'' . $tag . '">'
                . htmlspecialchars(stripslashes($tag)) . '</a>';
    }
    $cloud_html = join("\n", $cloud_tags) . "\n";
```

```
        return $cloud_html;
}
?>
<style type="text/css">
.tag_cloud
    {padding: 3px; text-decoration: none;
     font-family: verdana;     }
.tag_cloud:link    { color: #8FC486; }
.tag_cloud:visited { color: #BACC89; }
.tag_cloud:hover   { color: #BACC89; background: #000000; }
.tag_cloud:active  { color: #BACC89; background: #000000; }
div.wrapper{
   position:absolute;
   height:300px;
   width:500px;

}
</style>
<div id="wrapper" class="wrapper">
 <?php print tag_cloud(); ?>
</div>
```

Again, as in the pattern we follow, let's break it down according to the features and functionality.

- Call the `DBClass` class, initiate the object of the database, and connect to the database as well as the table.

    ```
    require_once 'DBClass.php';
    $dbclass = new DBClass();
    ```

- The `Tag_info` function returns the particular tags by querying the `tags` table.

    ```
    function tag_info() {
       $result = mysql_query("SELECT * FROM tags GROUP BY tagName
                ORDER BY Rand() DESC");
       while($row = mysql_fetch_array($result)) {
          $arr[$row['tagName']] = $row['count'];
       }
       return $arr;
    }
    ```

- When we call the `tag_cloud()` function, we read all the tags and define the maximum and minimum size of the tags we would want to see on our page.

- In the `tag_cloud()` function, we are reading out all the tags and getting their maximum and minimum count. Using a simple calculation, we are able to provide a random value as `font-size`.
- We get the array and just loop through it. Then we put them back in the page by defining various attributes of HTML such as `size`, `width`, `height`, and `color`.

As seen in the following screenshot, this is how it should look when we run the above script in the browser:

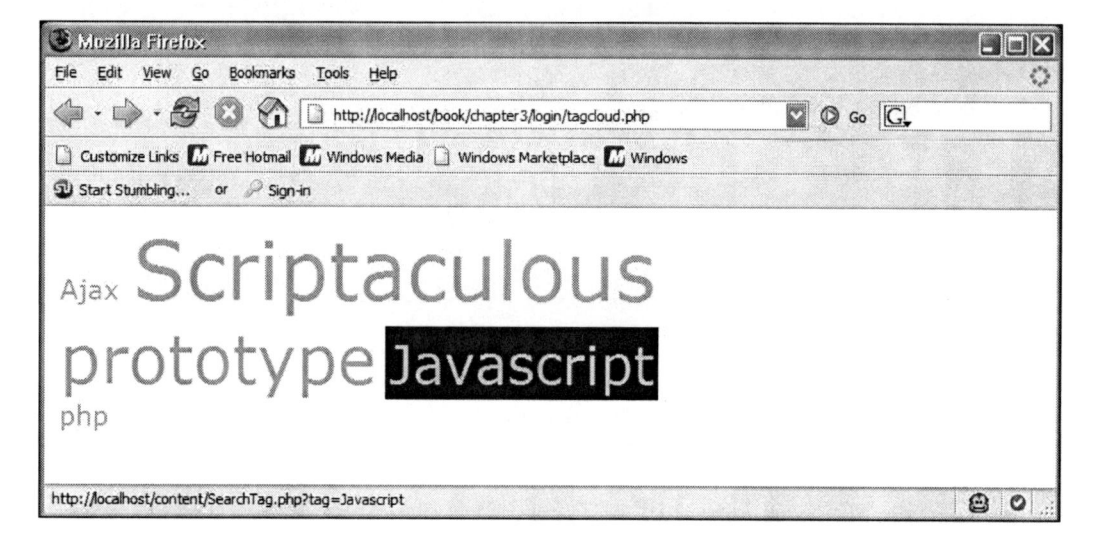

Summary

In this chapter we learned quite a lot of things from the rocking PHP 5 to the lovely MySQL, and from the powerful WAMP server to the exciting phpMyAdmin.

We also got our hands dirty with code while building a complete login management system. We tried to recapitulate the AJAX feature that we have used in a login module.

To impress our friends, we did a small clean hack of the tag cloud.

In the next chapter, we will get into the effects feature of the script.aculo.us library and go through loads of hands-on examples. If you thought that the fun is over, I must tell you the party has only just begun! Read on!

4
Adding Effects and Multimedia to User Interface Design

We finished Chapter 3 on the note that the party has only just begun. So, let your hair down and get ready to play with code! We have learned about the necessities that enable us to dive into the script.aculo.us world and explore it.

In this chapter we will learn how to:

- Add effects and multimedia content
- Use different types of effects such as `morph`, `scale`, `opacity`, `fade`, `appear`, and many more
- Use sounds and play MP3 songs using script.aculo.us from any browser

Introduction to effects

Before we get started, do you remember how we impressed your friends in Chapter 2? Even without knowing much about the effects, you were able to use them.

Effects help us in improving the look and feel of our applications during user interactions. Imagine a situation where a user clicks on the **Delete** button in an application, and an offending item is deleted (using AJAX). Now the user thinks *What just happened?*

The idea, therefore, is to use effects in such a way that the user is kept informed about the various things happening to the page elements and is also presented with an attractive and appealing page.

Adding Effects and Multimedia to User Interface Design

script.aculo.us is highly customizable when it comes to using effects. We can set opacity, colors, different types of effects, and duration. In short, script.aculo.us empowers developers to use their creativity and bring out their best on the page. Effects can be used in many ways. We can make use of effects for specific JavaScript events, on a page load, or on function-calling events—just about anything and everything is possible!

If, for example, you want to let a user hide some portion of the page that is no longer needed, we can use `Fade` or `Dropout`. If you want to inform the user about something important, we can use the `Highlight` effect.

Types of effects

There are various types of effects provided in the script.aculo.us visual library. The `Effects.Methods` contains them, as well as helper methods which can be used to interact with the DOM elements.

There are six core effects, which are:

- `Effect.Opacity`: Affects the translucence of an element.
- `Effect.Scale`: Scales any DOM element in terms of width and height. We can use this effect for smooth transition, or for changing the relative size of any element dynamically.
- `Effect.Morph`: Changes an element's CSS properties smoothly from whatever CSS properties it is currently having. On the fly you can change the font size, background, width, and much more.
- `Effect.Move`: Moves the element around the page.
- `Effect.Highlight`: We can use this to highlight any portion of the page.
- `Effect.Multiple`: Using this we can club effects for different elements. For example, we can apply the `Fade` effect to multiple elements, so that using one event all the elements defined will fade away from the page.

Along with these six core effects, we also have methods for lots of other effects. Here's the complete list of all the additional methods that we can apply to any page element. We have a visual demo treat coming up in the next section.

- `Appear`
- `BlindDown`
- `BlindUp`
- `SwitchOff`
- `SlideDown`

Chapter 4

- `SlideUp`
- `DropOut`
- `Shake`
- `Pulsate`
- `Squish`
- `Fold`
- `Grow`
- `Shrink`
- `Highlight`

Common parameters

There is a set of parameters that we can use with many of the effects mentioned above. These parameters play an important role in customizing the look and feel of the effects.

Some of the common parameters are:

- `Duration`: This parameter helps us in setting the duration of the `Effect`, that is, how long the `Effect` should play
- `to`: Used to set the end time of `Effect`
- `from`: Used to set the start time of `Effect`
- `delay`: Used to determine how much to delay the `Effect`

Code usage

Now that we are (at least in theory) aware of all the effects, let's get into the code and make our page look funky.

First, include the script.aculo.us library and Prototype library in the page. Since we are working with effects, don't forget to add the `effects.js` file too.

```
<script src="../../lib/prototype.js" type="text/javascript"></script>
<script src="../../src/scriptaculous.js" type="text/javascript">
</script>
<script src="../../src/effects.js" type="text/javascript"></script>
```

Now let's save it as `index.php`.

After that, quickly create some `<div>` elements in the page to apply the effects.

```
<div id="mydiv"><div>
This is some random text to amaze u :)
</div>
```

Adding Effects and Multimedia to User Interface Design

OK, here's the magic now.

Add this one line of JavaScript code and open the page in a browser.

```
<a href="#" onClick="new Effect.Fade('mydiv');
return false;">Fade Away my DIV</a>
```

You saw the `<div>` with `id=mydiv` fading away when you clicked on the link we just created above, didn't you?

Yeah, this is very similar to what we saw in Chapter 1. Now, let's make it a little spicier. In the same page, add this piece of code:

```
<a href="#" onClick="new Effect.Highlight('mydiv',
{ startcolor: '#ffff99', endcolor: '#ffffff'});
return false;"">Highlight my DIV</a>
```

Fire up the code in the browser. Did you see something special this time? Did you see the change in colors? Magicians still exist. We are overriding the constructor with the parameters such as `startcolor`. More parameters can be specified depending upon their requirement.

This was pretty straightforward. It would be great if you could just replace the word `Highlight` with `BlindUp`, or any other `Effect` name you like.

What will that result in? Here is the complete code and the corresponding screenshots too:

```
<!DOCTYPE html PUBLIC "-//W3C//DTD XHTML 1.0 Transitional//EN"
"http://www.w3.org/TR/xhtml1/DTD/xhtml1-transitional.dtd">
<html xmlns="http://www.w3.org/1999/xhtml">
<head>
<meta http-equiv="Content-Type" content="text/html;
charset=iso-8859-1" />
<title>Untitled Document</title>
    <style type="text/css">
       #mydiv {
       width: 500px;
       border: 1px green solid;
       background:#FFFFCC;
       }
    </style>
    <script src="includes/scriptaculous/lib/prototype.js"
       type="text/javascript"></script>
    <script src="includes/scriptaculous/src/scriptaculous.js"
       type="text/javascript"></script>
    <script src="includes/scriptaculous/src/effects.js"
```

```
            type="text/javascript"></script>
    <script src="includes/scriptaculous/src/unittest.js"
            type="text/javascript"></script>
</head>
<body>
    <br>
    <a href="#" onClick="new Effect.Fade('mydiv'); return
       false;">Fade</a>
       
    <a href="#" onClick="new Effect.Highlight('mydiv', { startcolor:
       '#ffff99',endcolor: '#DFEDFF' }); return false;"">Highlight</a>
       
    <a href="#" onClick="new Effect.Appear('mydiv'); return
       false;">Reset</a>
    <p>
    <div class="mydiv" id="mydiv">
       This is some random text to amaze u :)
    </div>
</body>
</html>
```

The following screenshot shows how our page looks at this stage:

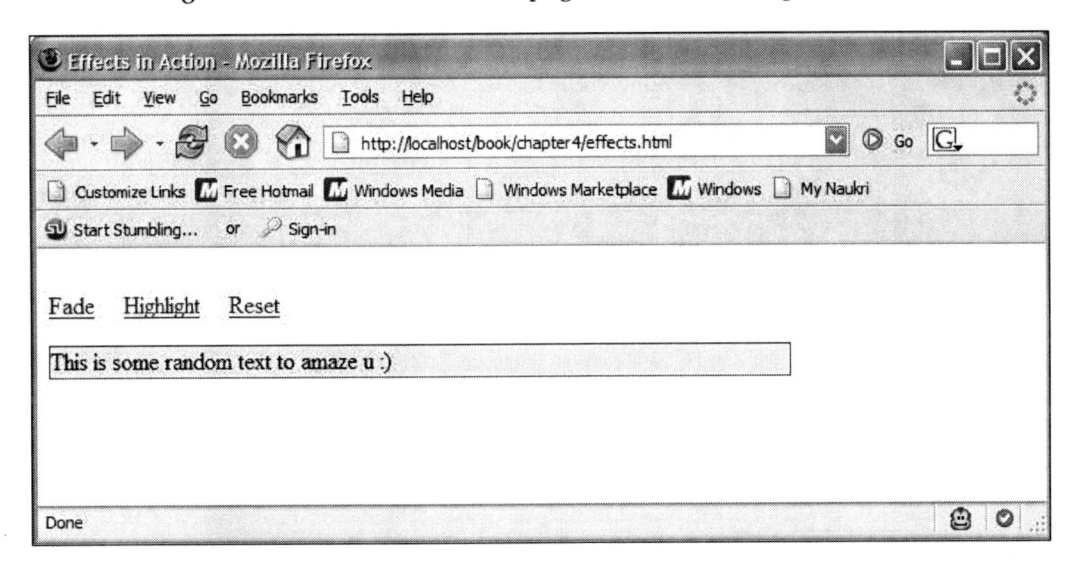

We can also add duration and opacity to the effects.

```
<a href="#" onClick="new Effect.Opacity('mydiv',{from:1.0,to:0.10});
return false;">Change my  DIV with Opacity</a>
```

So, the modified page will look like the following screenshots:

Before applying opacity:

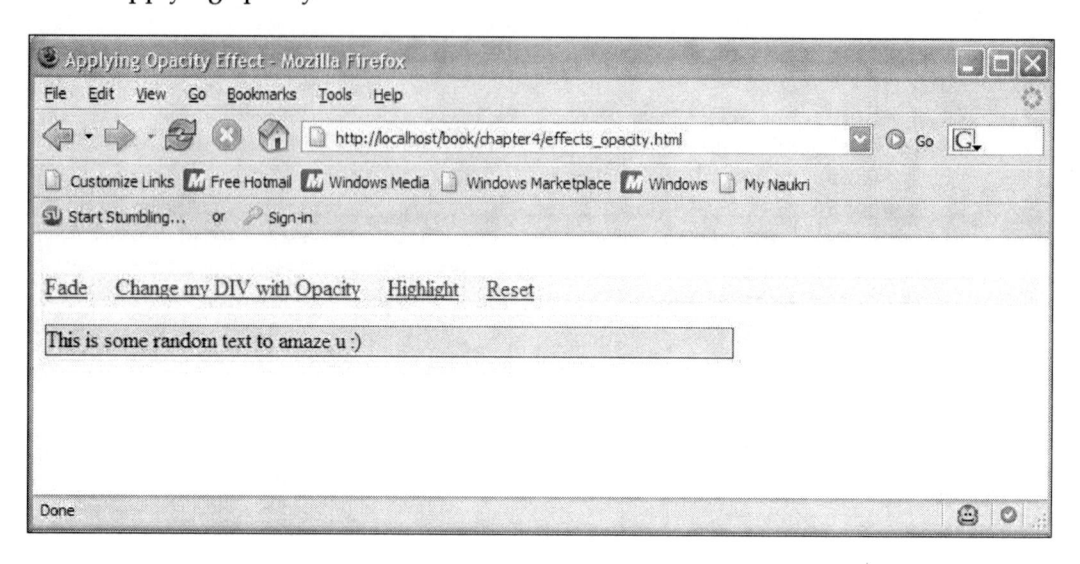

After applying opacity:

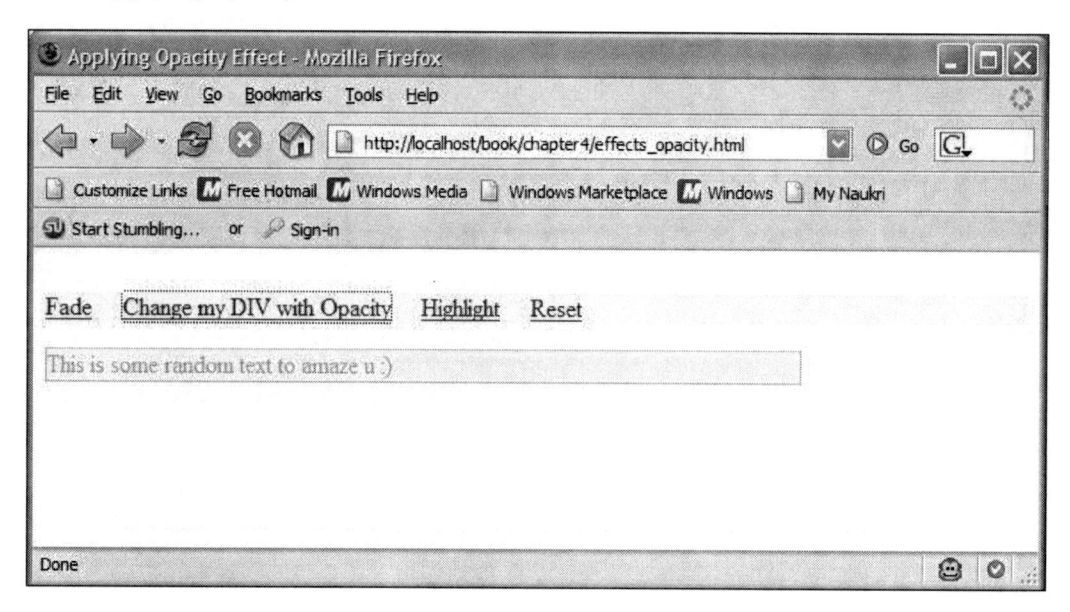

In the piece of code that we just saw, we restricted ourselves to using only text, but feel free to add images and multimedia as well. Use the `<img>` tags to add images in the code to see the effects on the images.

Excited? Want to get more creative? Here we go.

Hands-on examples

The best way to understand, believe, and visualize what script.aculo.us can do for us is by getting our code up and running. Quickly, let's explore some features of script.aculo.us with examples and real-world scenarios before we move on to create the next big thing on the Web.

The core effects

As mentioned above, there are some core effects (`highlight`, `opacity`, `morph`, and `scale`) you will probably want to use. So let's see them in action.

It may seem like a lot of messy code here, but it is the simplest part. Trust me!

Let me give you a walk-through. As we learned, we are adding a link and on click we are adding our JavaScript code for effects. All we are doing here is changing the name of the effect. Simple?

```
<a href="#" onclick="$('mydiv1').morph('background:#CDEDCD;
width:450px;'); return false;">Morph</a>  
```

Similarly, let's just change the name of the effect. Instead of `morph`, change it to `highlight` and see the result. You will find that I have listed out all the effects for you here.

In the following code, we have used several images in BMP format, but feel free to add either text or multimedia to use your own creativity. All the mentioned code can be downloaded as well.

```
<!DOCTYPE html PUBLIC "-//W3C//DTD XHTML 1.0 Transitional//EN"
"http://www.w3.org/TR/xhtml1/DTD/xhtml1-transitional.dtd">
<html xmlns="http://www.w3.org/1999/xhtml">
<head>
<meta http-equiv="Content-Type" content="text/html;
    charset=iso-8859-1" />
<title>Combination of Core Effects</title>
    <style type="text/css">
        #mydiv {
        border: 1px #green solid;
```

```html
            }
            #mydiv1 {
            border: 1px #green solid;
            background:#DFEDFD;
            }
            .toolbar {
            background:#FFFFCC;
            }
        </style>
        <script src="includes/scriptaculous/lib/prototype.js"
            type="text/javascript"></script>
        <script src="includes/scriptaculous/src/scriptaculous.js"
            type="text/javascript"></script>
        <script src="includes/scriptaculous/src/effects.js"
            type="text/javascript"></script>
        <script src="includes/scriptaculous/src/unittest.js"
            type="text/javascript"></script>
    </head>
    <body>
        <div class="toolbar">
        <a href="#" onClick="new
            Effect.multiple(['mydiv','mydiv1'],Effect.Appear); return
            false; ">RESET</a>  
        <a href="#" onClick="new
            Effect.multiple(['mydiv','mydiv1'],Effect.Fade); return
            false;">Multiple</a>  
        <a href="#" onClick="new
            Effect.Opacity('mydiv',{from:1.0,to:0.10}); return
            false;">Opacity</a>  
        <a href="#" onclick="$('mydiv1').morph('background:#CDEDCD;
            width:450px;'); return false;">Morph</a>  
        <a href="#" onClick="new Effect.Highlight('mydiv1', { startcolor:
            '#ffff99',endcolor: '#ffffff' }); return
            false;"">Highlight</a>  
        <a href="#" onClick="new Effect.Scale('mydiv1', 200); return
            false;">Scale</a>  
        </div>
        <p>
        <div class="mydiv" id="mydiv" >
            <img src="wallpaper2.bmp" width="450">
        </div>
        <div class="mydiv1" id="mydiv1" style="background:#DFEDFD;">
            This is some random Text to make u smile. Please say Cheese :)
        </div>
    </body>
</html>
```

Chapter 4

Now, you should be able to see the result before and after applying the core effects as shown in the following screenshots.

Before applying the core effects:

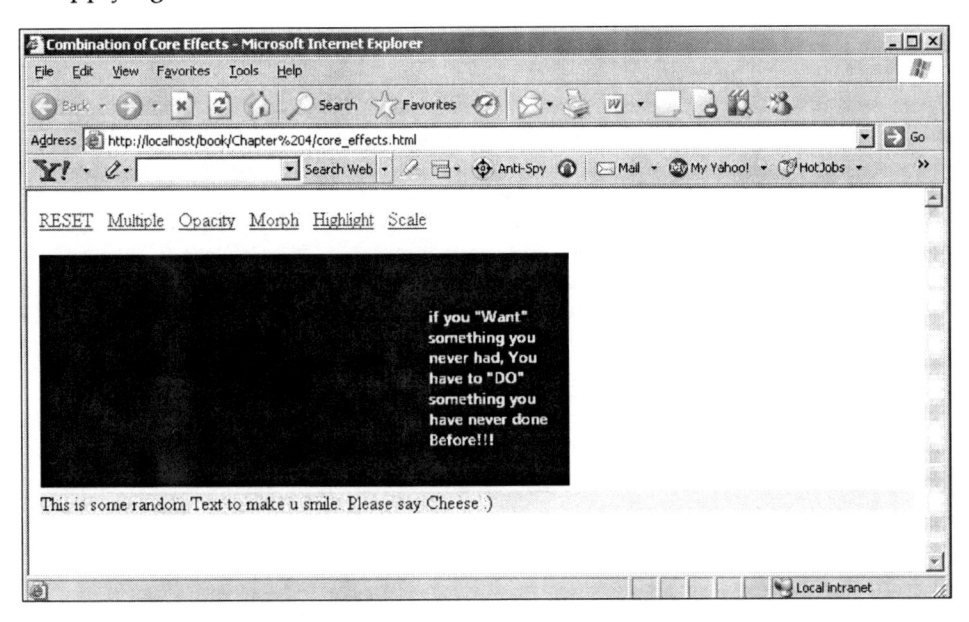

After applying the core effects:

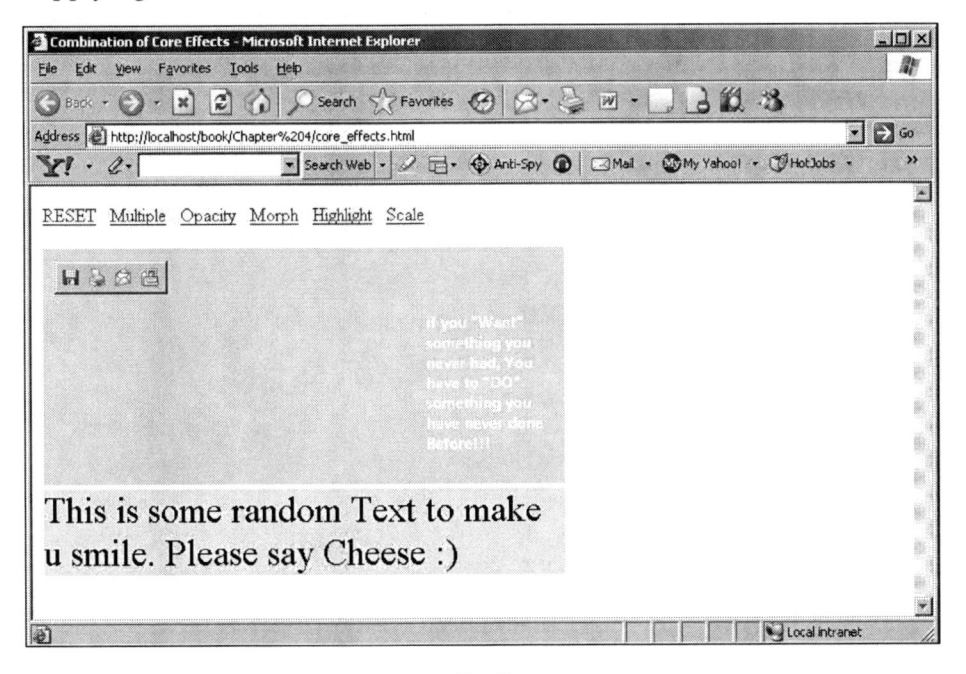

Adding Effects and Multimedia to User Interface Design

Various effects

We are aware of the fact that script.aculo.us provides us with many effects which we can play with in the user interface.

So let's quickly create a complete page with the various effects.

We have mastered the art of adding `morph` and `highlight` in the previous example. We are going to do it again, but this time we will be playing with lots of other effects. We will walk through a few effects; you must have surely hacked the rest already!

To create a shake effect in the page, we will add the following code:

```
<a href="#" onClick="new Effect.Shake('mydiv');
return false;">Shake</a>  
```

Similarly, let's add one more effect. Remember, all you need to do is change the name of the effect you want to use.

```
<a href="#" onClick="new Effect.Shrink('mydiv');
return false;">Shrink</a>  
```

You saw how, on the fly, we added a new effect `Shrink` with one line.

In the code that follows, you will see that we have all the effects listed on the page. We have two `<div>`s, `mydiv` and `mydiv1`, upon which the effects will show their magic.

```
<!DOCTYPE html PUBLIC "-//W3C//DTD XHTML 1.0 Transitional//EN"
"http://www.w3.org/TR/xhtml1/DTD/xhtml1-transitional.dtd">
<html xmlns="http://www.w3.org/1999/xhtml">
<head>
<meta http-equiv="Content-Type" content="text/html;
   charset=iso-8859-1" />
<title>Combination of Various Effects</title>
   <style type="text/css">
      #mydiv {
      border: 1px #green solid;
      }
      #mydiv1 {
      border: 1px #green solid;
      background:#DFEDFD;
      }
      .toolbar {
      background:#FFFFCC;
      }
   </style>
   <script src="includes/scriptaculous/lib/prototype.js"
```

```html
            type="text/javascript"></script>
    <script src="includes/scriptaculous/src/scriptaculous.js"
            type="text/javascript"></script>
    <script src="includes/scriptaculous/src/effects.js"
            type="text/javascript"></script>
    <script src="includes/scriptaculous/src/unittest.js"
            type="text/javascript"></script>
</head>
<body>
    <div class="toolbar">
    <a href="#" onClick="new Effect.Fade('mydiv'); return
        false;">Fade</a>  
    <a href="#" onClick="new Effect.SlideUp('mydiv'); return
        false;">SlideUp</a>  
    <a href="#" onClick="new Effect.SlideDown('mydiv'); return
        false;">SlideDown</a>  
    <a href="#" onClick="new Effect.Puff('mydiv'); return
        false;">Puff</a>  
    <a href="#" onClick="new Effect.DropOut('mydiv'); return
        false;">DropOut</a>  
    <a href="#" onClick="new Effect.Shake('mydiv'); return
        false;">Shake</a>  
    <a href="#" onClick="new Effect.Pulsate('mydiv'); return
        false;">Pulsate</a>  
    <a href="#" onClick="new Effect.Squish('mydiv'); return
        false;">Squish</a>  
    <a href="#" onClick="new Effect.Shrink('mydiv'); return
        false;">Shrink</a>  
    <a href="#" onClick="new
        Effect.multiple(['mydiv','mydiv1'],Effect.Appear); return
        false; ">RESET</a>  
    <a href="#" onClick="new Effect.BlindUp('mydiv'); return
        false;">BlindUp</a>  
    <a href="#" onClick="new Effect.SwitchOff('mydiv'); return
        false;">SwitchOff</a>  
    <a href="#" onClick="new Effect.Fold('mydiv'); return
        false;">Fold</a>  
    <a href="#" onClick="new Effect.Grow('mydiv'); return
        false;">Grow</a>  
    </div>
    <p>
    <div class="mydiv" id="mydiv" >
        <img src="wallpaper2.bmp" width="450">
    </div>
    <div class="mydiv1" id="mydiv1" style="background:#DFEDFD;">
        This is some random Text to make u smile. Please say Cheese :)
    </div>
</body>
</html>
```

Adding Effects and Multimedia to User Interface Design

Finally, this is how it looks when we add the additional effects:

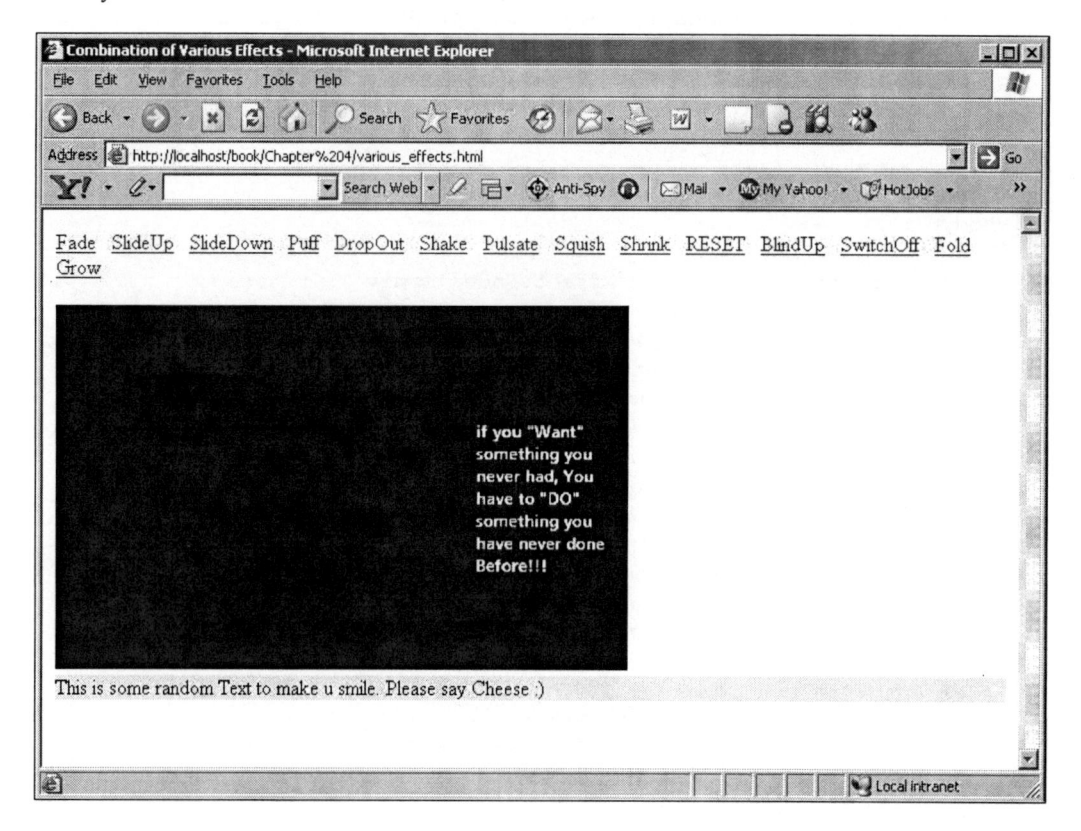

Combining all the effects

Now that we have learned about the different types of effects, why not create a simple page to involve all the possible effects on a single page?

There's nothing new in this code. Just club together the above two snippets and you should be able to see all the effects on one page.

No, I am not giving you the code now, but only the screenshot. This screenshot will help you to understand what the resulting code should contain. This is for you to try out. We will see the solution in the next chapter.

Chapter 4

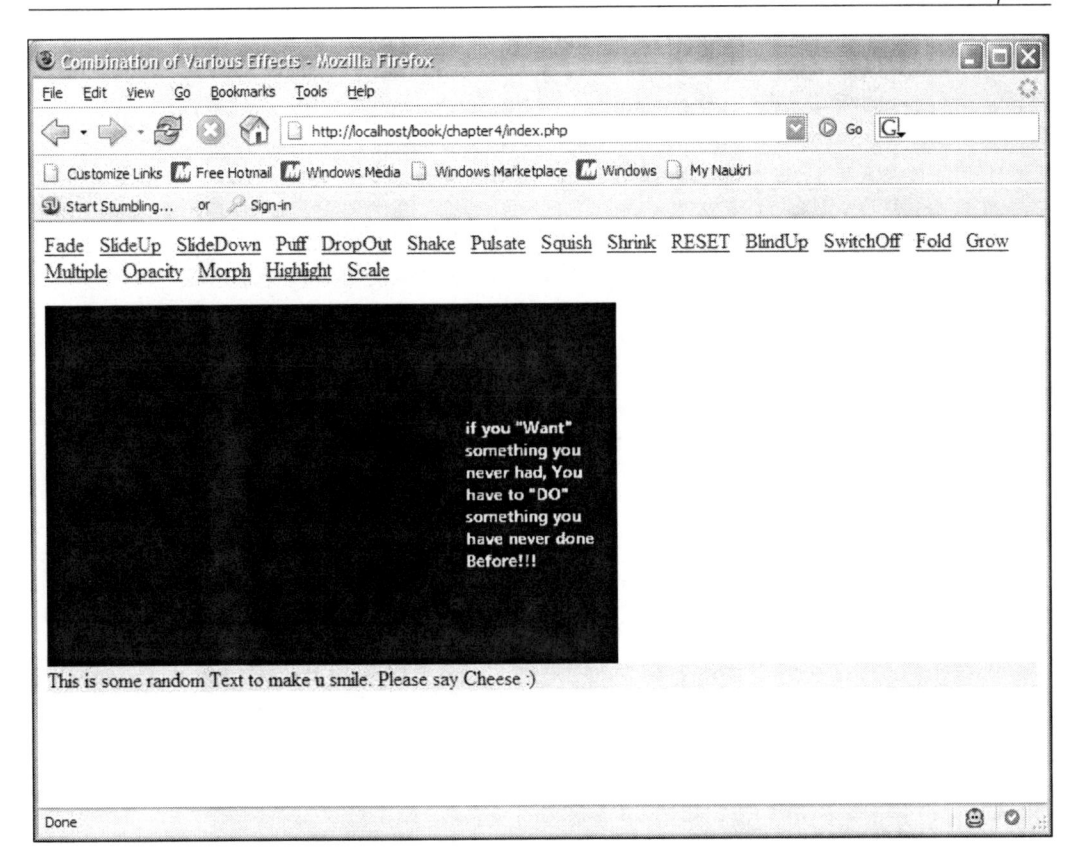

Playing sounds with script.aculo.us

Hey, what is your best friend's favorite song? Wouldn't it be great if you could surprise him/her by playing his/her favorite song from the browser (copyright issues notwithstanding)? Let's see how.

script.aculo.us provides us with the `sounds.js` file through which we can play any song with just one line of code. It is dead simple to play a song from the browser using JavaScript.

Types of sounds

Not to mention, most of us are bitten by music bugs—especially if you like to work late nights with your favorite music playing. Here is a simple tutorial section to quickly create your own playlist and share it with others too. Using this module, we can play music through the browser. Let's see it in action.

Adding Effects and Multimedia to User Interface Design

MP3 sounds

MP3s are supported only in the `sounds.js` file from script.aculo.us 1.8 onwards. This feature is not available in version 1.6. Here are some of the methods we can use while trying to play sounds with script.aculo.us.

- `play`: When this method is invoked, the MP3 file starts playing
- `disable`: We can disable the MP3 playback using this option
- `enable`: The MP3 playback can be enabled using this option

You might want to use this feature for critical events when something goes wrong (maybe introduce a beep). Alternatively, a more positive sound could be played that lets the user know something successful has happened.

Code usage

The syntax for using this feature is pretty simple. But before we get started, let's get all of the necessary files included in a single file and save it as `song.html`.

```
<script src="../../lib/prototype.js" type="text/javascript"></script>
<script src="../../src/scriptaculous.js" type="text/javascript"></script>
<script src="../../src/sounds.js" type="text/javascript"></script>
```

OK, so now quickly add this piece of JavaScript code into the page:

```
<a href="#" onclick="Sound.play('dance_of_dead.MP3');
return false">play sound (parallel)</a>
```

A hands-on example

A simple example is demonstrated here.

To play a song we need to create a link that, on clicking, should play the song.

```
<a href="#" onclick="Sound.play('dance_of_dead.MP3');
return false">Play Song</a>
```

The song path can be on our server side. Alternatively, we can even pass the complete and correct URL of the location of the song.

> We can have the MP3 song residing on our own server space, or we can specify a path for the song. But generally it would require much more engineering work to make the application work fast in a multiuser environment.

To disable the sound being played, we define the following code:

```
<a href="#" onclick="Sound.disable(); return false">Mute</a>
```

Again, to enable the sound we use:

```
<a href="#" onclick="Sound.enable(); return false">Enable</a>
```

Simple? OK. Now that we have our basics ready, let's see the action.

```
<!DOCTYPE html PUBLIC "-//W3C//DTD XHTML 1.0 Transitional//EN"
        "http://www.w3.org/TR/xhtml1/DTD/xhtml1-transitional.dtd">
<html xmlns="http://www.w3.org/1999/xhtml" xml:lang="en" lang="en">
<head>
<title>Let The Music PLay, baby!!!</title>
   <style type="text/css">
      .toolbar {
      background:#FFFFCC;
      }
   </style>
<meta http-equiv="content-type" content="text/html; charset=utf-8" />
   <script src="includes/scriptaculous/lib/prototype.js"
      type="text/javascript"></script>
   <script src="includes/scriptaculous/src/scriptaculous.js"
      type="text/javascript"></script>
   <script src="includes/scriptaculous/src/effects.js"
      type="text/javascript"></script>
   <script src="includes/scriptaculous/src/sound.js"
      type="text/javascript"></script>
</head>
<body>
   <h4>
      Let The Music Play, baby!!!
   </h4>
   <div class="toolbar">
   <a href="#" onclick="Sound.play('dance_of_dead.MP3');
   return false">Play Song</a>  
   <a href="#" onclick="Sound.play('rainmaker.mp3',{replace:true});
   return false">Change The Next Song</a>  
   <a href="#" onclick="Sound.disable();
   return false">Mute</a>  
   <a href="#" onclick="Sound.enable();
   return false">Enable sounds</a>  
   </div>
</body>
</html>
```

When you run the script, you should be able to see the following screenshot and hear the song when you click on the **Play Song** link:

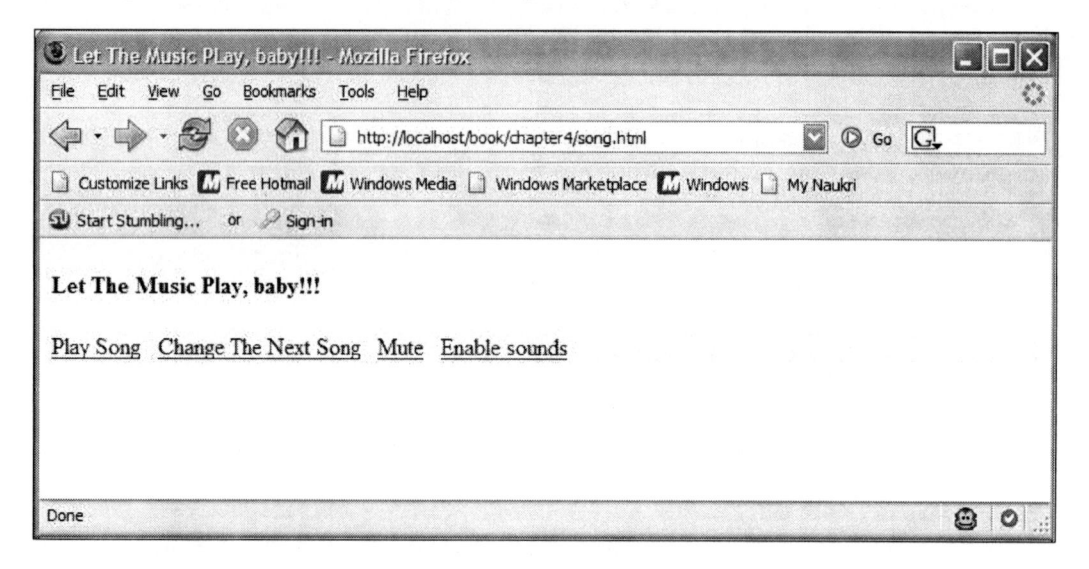

Summary

So far, we have covered various multimedia effects using script.aculo.us.

In this chapter we learned:

- To use different types of effects such as `morph`, `highlight`, `fade`, `blinddown`, and many more
- About the options available with effects
- How to use sounds, and play songs using script.aculo.us from any browser
- To have fun while working with the hands-on examples

In the next chapter, we shall have loads of fun learning to implement the drag and drop functionality using script.aculo.us. Play on!

5
AJAX Drag and Drop Feature using script.aculo.us

In Chapter 4 we saw the various effects provided by the script.aculo.us visual library. At the end of Chapter 4, I also gave you a hands-on task. How did you do it? The solution to the task that combines all the effects in one go, is as follows:

```
<script src="includes/scriptaculous/lib/prototype.js"
        type="text/javascript"></script>
<script src="includes/scriptaculous/src/scriptaculous.js"
        type="text/javascript"></script>
<script src="includes/scriptaculous/src/effects.js"
        type="text/javascript"></script>
<script src="includes/scriptaculous/src/unittest.js"
        type="text/javascript"></script>
</head>
<body>
   <div class="toolbar">
   <a href="#" onClick="new Effect.Fade('mydiv');
   return false;">Fade</a>  
   <a href="#" onClick="new Effect.SlideUp('mydiv');
   return false;">SlideUp</a>  
   <a href="#" onClick="new Effect.SlideDown('mydiv');
   return false;">SlideDown</a>  
   <a href="#" onClick="new Effect.Puff('mydiv');
   return false;">Puff</a>  
   <a href="#" onClick="new Effect.DropOut('mydiv');
   return false;">DropOut</a>  
   <a href="#" onClick="new Effect.Shake('mydiv');
   return false;">Shake</a>  
   <a href="#" onClick="new Effect.Pulsate('mydiv');
   return false;">Pulsate</a>  
   <a href="#" onClick="new Effect.Squish('mydiv');
   return false;">Squish</a>  
```

```html
<a href="#" onClick="new Effect.Shrink('mydiv');
    return false;">Shrink</a>  
<a href="#" onClick="new
    Effect.multiple(['mydiv','mydiv1'],Effect.Appear);
    return false; ">RESET</a>  
<a href="#" onClick="new Effect.BlindUp('mydiv');
    return false;">BlindUp</a>  
<a href="#" onClick="new Effect.SwitchOff('mydiv');
    return false;">SwitchOff</a>  
<a href="#" onClick="new Effect.Fold('mydiv');
    return false;">Fold</a>  
<a href="#" onClick="new Effect.Grow('mydiv');
    return false;">Grow</a>  

<a href="#" onClick="new
    Effect.multiple(['mydiv','mydiv1'],Effect.Fade);
    return false;">Multiple</a>  

<a href="#" onClick="new
    Effect.Opacity('mydiv',{from:1.0,to:0.10});
    return false;">Opacity</a>  

<a href="#" onclick="$('mydiv1').morph('background:#CDEDCD;
    width:450px;'); return false;">Morph</a>  

<a href="#" onClick="new Effect.Highlight('mydiv1', { startcolor:
    '#ffff99',endcolor: '#ffffff' }); return
    false;"">Highlight</a>  

<a href="#" onClick="new Effect.Scale('mydiv1', 200);
    return false;">Scale</a>  
</div>
<p>
<div class="mydiv" id="mydiv" >
<img src="wallpaper2.bmp" width="450">
</div>

<div class="mydiv1" id="mydiv1" style="background:#DFEDFD;">
    This is some random Text to make u smile. Please say Cheese :)
</div>
```

Here is the screenshot for how it should look:

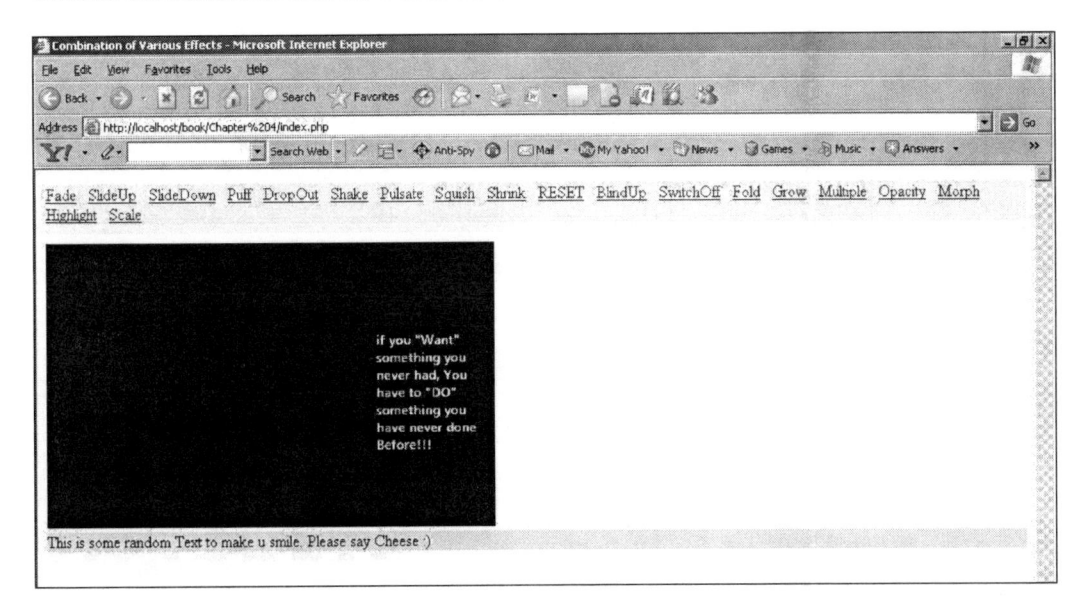

I am sure you got it right in one go!

Let's move on to yet another appealing Web 2.0-ish feature—Drag and drop using script.aculo.us. In this chapter we will learn the following:

- Drag and drop—an introduction and explanation
- The functionality of code usage
- Getting started quickly with an example
- Creating a multifunctional drag and drop application

Introduction to the drag and drop feature

We all have used the drag and drop feature many times. Let me give you some examples. If you've used any of the applications such as iGoogle, Blogger, Wordpress, Backpackit, and Yahoo Mail, then chances are you will have come across drag and drop. See the next screenshot taken from the **iGoogle** application where we can drag various widgets provided by Google. We can also customize the whole layout and rearrange the whole user interface as we want.

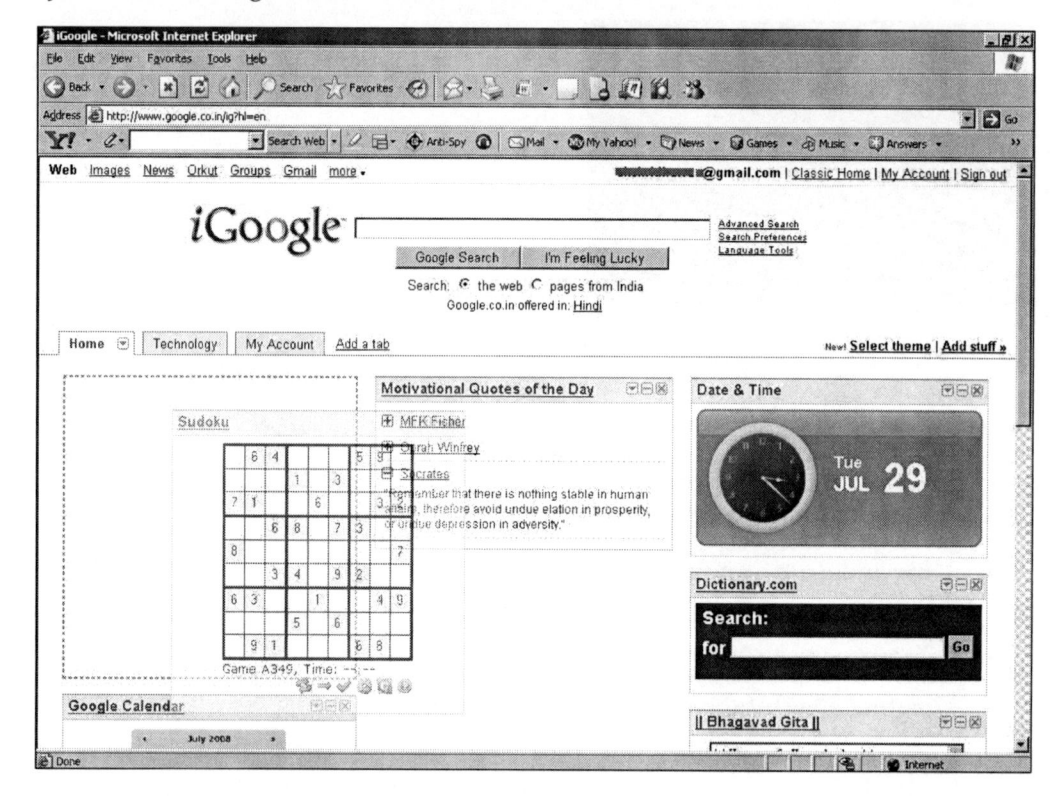

You will find that we can do a lot just by dragging the widgets into a certain portion on the interface, and the application's behaviour changes with it. As the name suggests, we can make the elements of the page draggable and apply functionality to the behavior.

Explanation of the drag and drop feature

We can easily make any element draggable just by creating a draggable class instance from the drag and drop module of the script.aculo.us library. We can also add various options to the element that we want to make draggable, to add greater interactivity as well as functionality.

A simple way of initializing the draggable element is shown here:

```
new Draggable(element, options );
```

Some of the available options that we can explore with drag and drop are:

- `revert`: When set to true, the element returns to the original position when the drag ends. By default, this is set to false.
- `snap`: This is used to form a draggable area or grid. It constrains the movement of the element.
- `ghosting`: When you are dragging the element, a clone of the original element will be in the starting position until the drag ends.
- `constraint`: Using this option we can restrict the movement of the element on horizontal and vertical planes.
- `handle`: Using this option, we can handle the movement and drag of an element using some other element. This is rarely used because of the fact that every draggable element will have its own handle by default.
- `startEffect`: This option changes the behavior of the element on the user interface when the drag begins. We can change opacity, colors, and so on to make flexible user interface changes.
- `endEffect`: This option defines what effects should be shown when the drag ends in the page.
- `revertEffect`: This option is valid only with the `revert` feature. When an element is applied with the `revert` option, this particular `revertEffect` is called. When the drag action ends, the effect changes (reverts) to the initial effect, or the default effect, specified.

There are various callback options that we can use along with drag and drop:

- `onStart`: This is called when a drag is initiated
- `onDrag`: This is called while the drag is in progress, with every mouse movement
- `change`: This is the same as the `onDrag` callback option, but is used mostly with every mouse movement
- `onEnd`: This is called when a drag is ended

We have learned about dragging things in the page, but hang on—where are we going to drop them? Yes, this is yet another interesting feature with script.aculo.us—Droppables.

Droppables is a namespace where we can drop the dragged element by making a call to the `add()` method inside this namespace. The droppables namespace has two methods to work with:

- `Add`: Calling this will add the dragged and dropped element to the target area
- `Remove`: Calling this will remove the element from the target area

This namespace also comes with certain useful callbacks. They are:

- `onHover`: When the mouse is rolled over the target area and its elements
- `onDrop`: When a particular element is dropped inside the target area

If you feel this was a heavy dose of theory, just relax! We will see in detail each and every option mentioned above in the next section of code usage.

Code usage of the drag and drop feature

To get started with drag and drop, the obvious thing to do is to include the drag and drop module. We will also include the effects module to add more beauty to our user interface.

```
<script type="text/javascript" src="src/scriptaculous.js"></script>
<script type="text/javascript" src="src/effects.js"></script>
<script type="text/javascript" src="src/dragdrop.js"></script>
```

We know that to initialize the draggable element we have to call the instance of the draggable class:

```
new Draggable(element,options );
```

The first parameter is the ID of the element which we want to make draggable. The other parameters are optional, like fading effect, revert, and the others that we have covered above.

Now, let's learn to add different options step-by-step.

- Add the `revert` option

  ```
  new Draggable(element,{revert:true} );
  ```

- Add the `snap` option

  ```
  new Draggable(element,
      {
        revert:true,
        snap: [x,y]
  } );
  ```

- Add the ghosting option
  ```
  new Draggable(element,
      {
        revert:true,
        snap: [x,y],
        ghosting:true
  } );
  ```

- Add the constraint option
  ```
  new Draggable(element,
      {
        revert:true,
        snap: [x,y],
        ghosting:true,
        constraint:"horizontal"
  } );
  ```

- Add the handle option
  ```
  new Draggable(element,
   {
    revert:true,
    snap: [x,y],
    ghosting:true,
    constraint:"horizontal",
    handle: 'dragHandle'
  } );
  ```

- Add the startEffect option
  ```
  new Draggable(element,
      {
        revert:true,
        snap: [x,y],
        ghosting:true,
        constraint:"horizontal",
    handle: 'dragHandle',
        startEffect: CallFunction('element')
  } );
  ```

- Add the endEffect option
  ```
  new Draggable(element,
      {
        revert:true,
        snap: [x,y],
        ghosting:true,
        constraint:"horizontal",
  ```

AJAX Drag and Drop Feature using script.aculo.us

```
    handle: 'dragHandle',
        startEffect: CallFunction('element'),
    endEffect: EndcallFunction('element')
} );
```

- Add the `revertEffect` option

```
new Draggable(element,
    {
      revert:true,
      snap: [x,y],
      ghosting:true,
      constraint:"horizontal",
    handle: 'dragHandle',
        startEffect: CallFunction('element'),
    endEffect: EndcallFunction('element'),
    revertEffect:callrevertFunction('element')
} );
```

Well, this was all about the draggable options. Let's quickly define the callback functions (in one go) as well.

```
new Draggable(element,
    {
        onStart: callFunctionOnStart(),
        onDrag: callFunctionOnDrag(),
        onEnd: callFunctionOnEnd()
});
```

Now, let's not forget the droppables. After all, that's where we're going to drop things, right? As mentioned before, droppables mainly has two methods:

- Adding a new element in the target area

    `Droppables.add(element, options );`

- Removing an element from the target area

    `Droppables.remove(element);`

When we drop elements in the droppable area, they become a part of the new droppable section. Hence, we can add a couple of callbacks and functions within the same.

Let's add some callback functions to the droppables.

```
Droppables.add(
    element,
    {
        onDrop:callDropFunction
    }
);
```

We have approached things differently in this section, adding options step-by-step to make it clear that we can actually do a lot of things with the drag and drop functionality. Having said that, let's move on and play with some code. Again, we shall start with the simplest possible example and convert it step-by-step into a monster.

Hands-on example: Creating a drag and drop sample in one line of code

We can achieve the drag and drop functionality in just one line of JavaScript code. That's how simple script.aculo.us makes it for us.

All we did above was—we created a simple `<div>` and added some text to it. As suggested earlier, let's also add the required `.js` files of script.aculo.us.

```
<script type="text/javascript" src="src/prototype.js"></script>
<script type="text/javascript" src="src/scriptaculous.js"></script>
<script type="text/javascript" src="src/dragdrop.js"></script>
```

Let's quickly add some flesh in our HTML code.

```
<body>
    <h4>This part wont move..come what may!!!!</h4><p>
    <div id="myDiv">
        Drag me to Next level...<p>
        And, Next level is where you drag me
    </div>
</body>
```

Now comes the magic scripting part of JavaScript.

```
window.onload = function() {
    new Draggable('myDiv');
}
```

And we are done! The next screenshot shows what the application looks like:

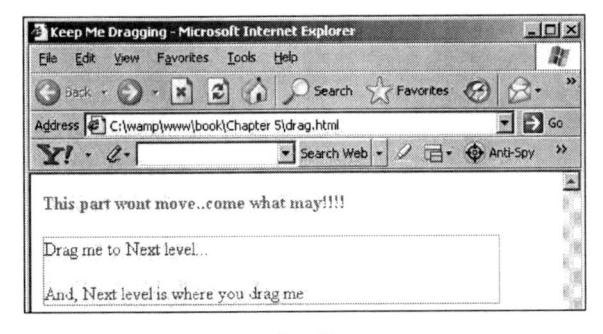

You will have to figure out what the `<div>` box does here. OK, so now that you have learned the art of moving elements in the page, it's our duty as well to send it back to the original place. So, let's modify the above JavaScript code and send the `<div>` box back to the original place using the `revert` option. The updated script is shown here:

```
window.onload = function() {
    new Draggable('myDiv',{revert:true});
}
```

When you drag the `<div>` box and then release the mouse (that is, when a drag is complete), the `<div>` box goes back to the original place.

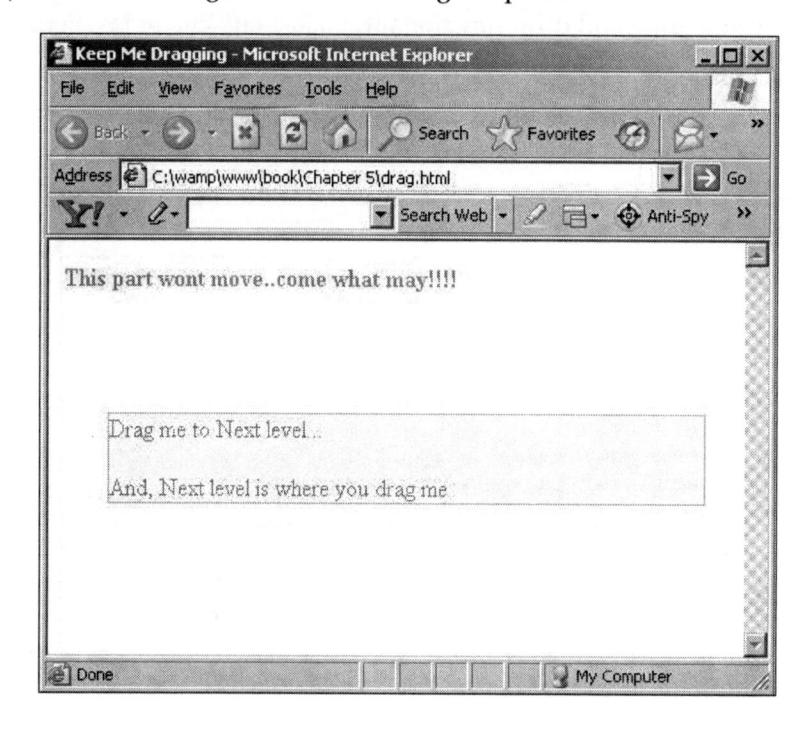

I am sure loads of ideas are running around in your mind about all the possibilities of using the drag and drop feature. Let's walk through some of them. While dragging the element from the page, why not show a clone of the original in its place (and yes, doing it many times results in chaos)?

```
window.onload = function() {
    new Draggable('myDiv',{ghosting:true});
}
```

This is how it might look. Oops! Does it look ugly? You can see why people call it ghost!

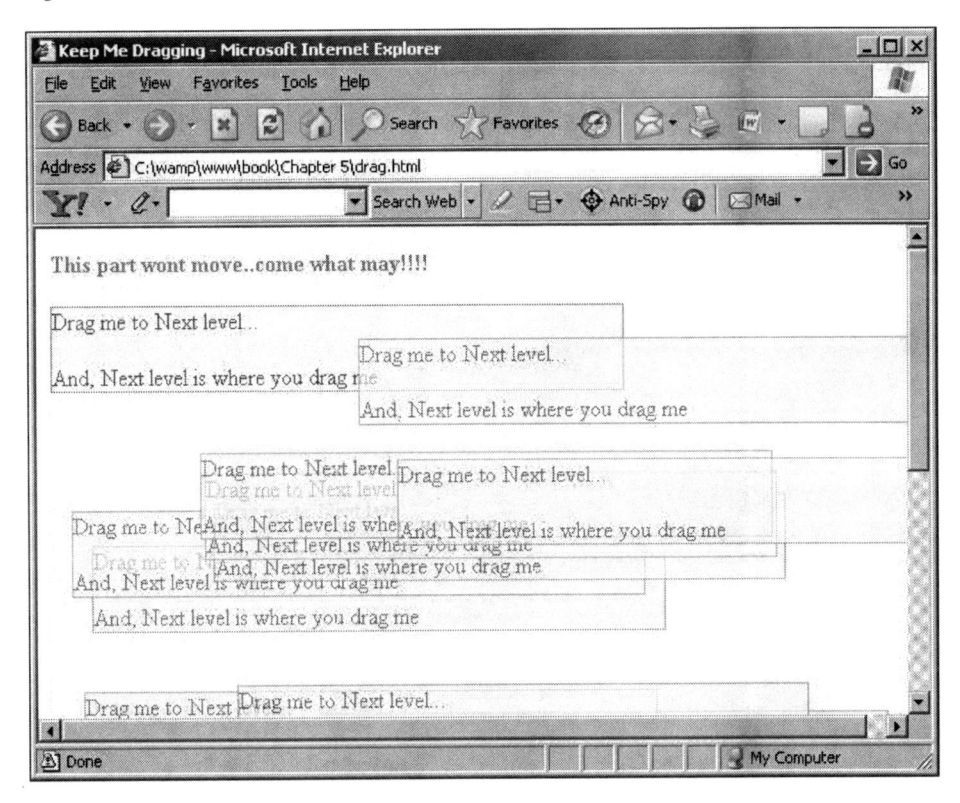

Hands-on example: Advanced drag and drop tutorial

Now that the concepts of drag and drop are clear, we are well set to work out an advanced drag and drop module. Imagine a product cart. As users, we need to select products and then check out. Wouldn't it be simple if a user can just drag the products (s)he wants to buy, drop them in the selected cart, and then check out? On top of that, we will try to keep our user interface pretty neat and clean.

Let's get started with the code. First, add the script.aculo.us libraries to our code in the `<head>` section.

```
<script type="text/javascript" src="src/prototype.js"></script>
<script type="text/javascript" src="src/scriptaculous.js"></script>
<script type="text/javascript" src="src/effects.js"></script>
<script type="text/javascript" src="src/dragdrop.js"></script>
```

AJAX Drag and Drop Feature using script.aculo.us

We will add some effects to our module. We will also need to add some products. For now we are just creating `<div>`s. But in the later part of the book, we will create the same module through a database-driven module too.

Let's create a simple `<div>` and give some name to the product.

```
<div id="myProduct1" align="center">
iPhone <p>
</div>
```

Similarly, let's add a few more `<div>`s and (to give a neat user interface) embed them inside a table. The code now looks like this:

```
<div id="container">
Select products and just drag them!!!
   <table>
   <tr>
      <td>
         <div id="myProduct1" align="center">
         iPhone <p>
         </div>
      </td>
      <td>
         <div id="myProduct2" align="center">
         Ipod Nano<p>
         </div>
      </td>
      <td>
         <div id="myProduct3" align="center">
         MacPro Airbook <p>
         </div>
      </td>
   </tr>
   </table>
   <p>
</div>
   <p>
<div id="myDiv">
   Drag Some products to my menu<p>
</div>
   <p>
<div id="note">
</div>
```

We need to keep our user informed as to what is happening in the module. Therefore, we have added a `<div>` with `id=note`. We will use this to update the user with whatever is happening on the page.

Now moving on to coding, let's first initialize the draggables and droppables of the page.

```
window.onload = function() {
    new Draggable('myProduct1',{revert:true});
    new Draggable('myProduct2',{revert:true});
    new Draggable('myProduct3',{revert:true});
    Droppables.add(
        'myDiv',
        {
            onDrop: addItem
        }
    );
    Droppables.add(
        'container',
        {
            onDrop: removeItem
        }
    );
}
```

We have added all three product `<div>`s as draggable. We have added our myDiv `<div>` as a droppable, as we're dragging the products from the container to myDiv. Similarly, we have also added container as droppables, since we want the user to remove the products as well if (s)he wants to.

We learned about the callbacks in the previous hands-on section. Let's make use of them. We are calling the function addItem and removeItem for the onDrop event. This means when a user drags the product `<div>` and drops it in the droppable area, the functions get called. Now, let's define the functionality for addItem and removeItem. In addItem, we are simply appending the draggable elements to myDiv.

```
function addItem(draggable) {
    myDiv.appendChild(draggable);
    $('note').innerHTML="Added"+draggable.innerHTML;
    new Effect.Highlight($('note'));
}
```

In removeItem, we are appending the draggable elements back to our container.

```
function removeItem(draggable, droppable) {
    container.appendChild(draggable);
    $('note').innerHTML="Removed"+draggable.innerHTML;
    new Effect.Highlight($('note'));
}
```

We are also adding the product name to the `<div>` *note* along with the Highlight effect to help the user understand what is happening on the screen.

AJAX Drag and Drop Feature using script.aculo.us

Now, a little bit of CSS styling for our application. This is how it looks when we add colors to our module:

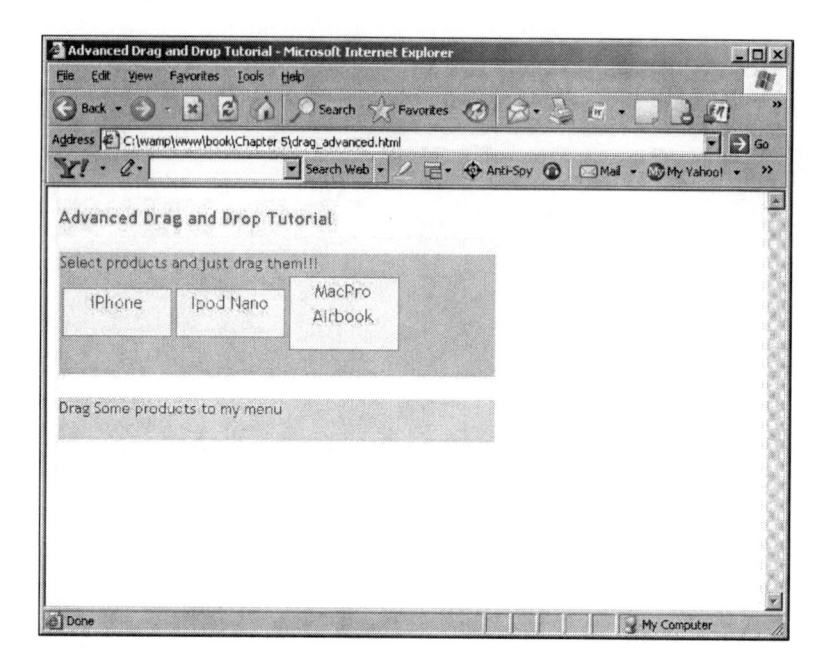

When we drag a product to our menu, we get the following screenshot of the application:

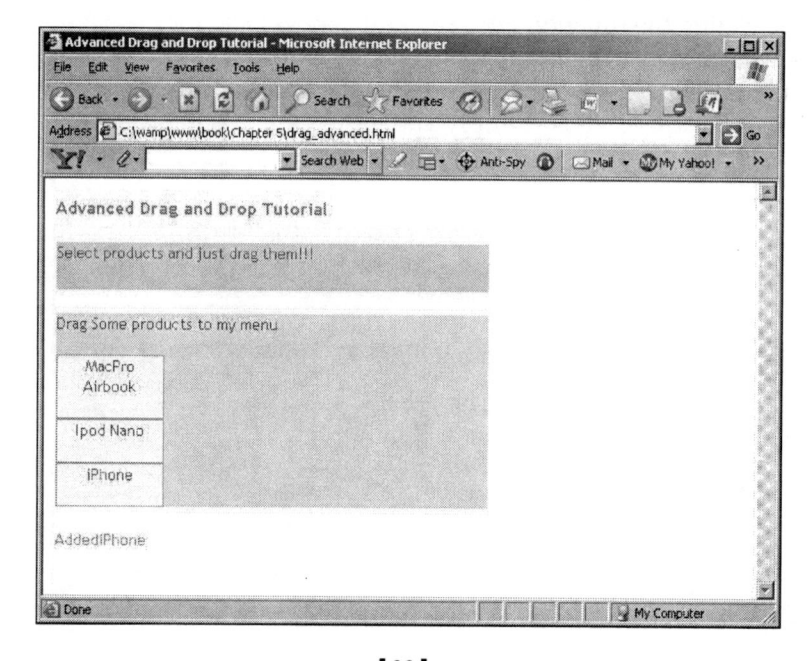

We have also added some effects to the module. Let's see how they look in the application:

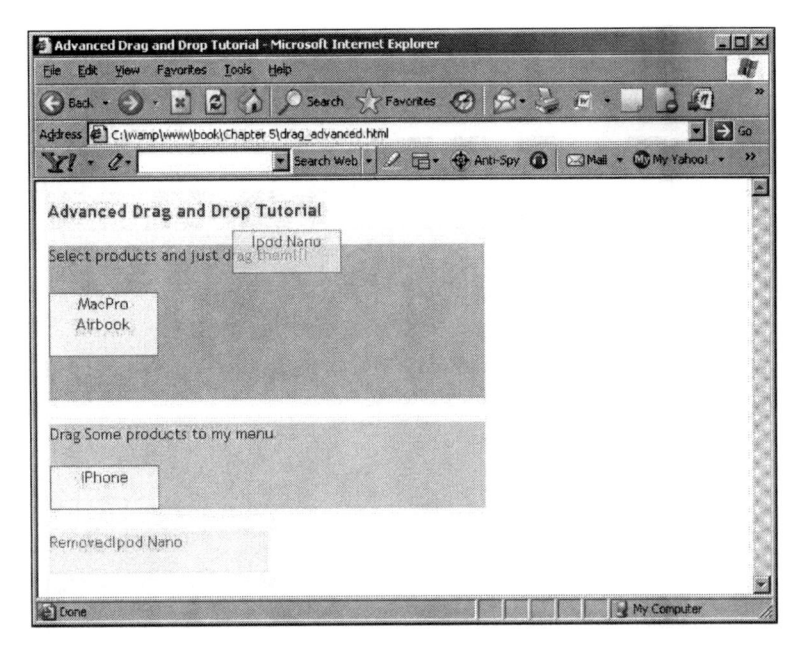

The idea of using `Highlight` here is to showcase that we can use our own creativity and the power of AJAX functionality on the page. We are updating the status without refreshing the page. We can do a lot of things such as fetching data from server or passing data to the server on every event.

Summary

With this happy, clean, and beautiful user interface we come to the end of the drag and drop section. So far we have learned:

- Drag and drop—an introduction and explanation
- Code usage
- Various options and hands-on examples
- Advanced drag and drop module to get comfortable with AJAX

In the next chapter we will learn everything about in-place editing using script.aculo.us. By the way, what is your favourite color? You will need it in the next chapter.

6
In-place Editing using script.aculo.us

In Chapter 5 we learned about the drag and drop features of the script.aculo.us library. We created elements, which we could move around the page, and also tried adding some AJAX functionality to them.

In this chapter, we will learn about editing the content in the page without moving, dragging, or dropping it. This feature is called *in-place* editing. The key topics that we are going to explore in this chapter are:

- Introduction to in-place editing
- In-place editing: Definition and attributes
- Code usage in examples
- Tips and tricks involving in-place editing
- Hands-on example: Handling at the server-side
- Hands-on with `InPlaceCollectionEditor`

An introduction to the in-place editing feature

In-place editing means making the content available for editing just by clicking on it. We hover on the element, allow the user to click on the element, edit the content, and update the new content to our server.

In-place Editing using script.aculo.us

Sounds complex? Not at all! It's very simple. Check out the example about `www.netvibes.com` shown in the following screenshot. You will notice that by just clicking on the title, we can edit and update it.

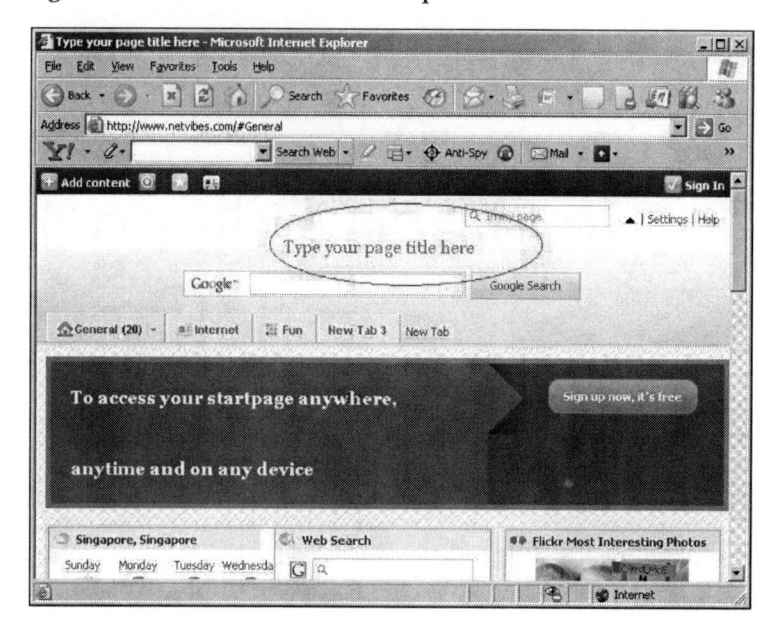

Now, check out the following screenshot to see what happens when we click on the title.

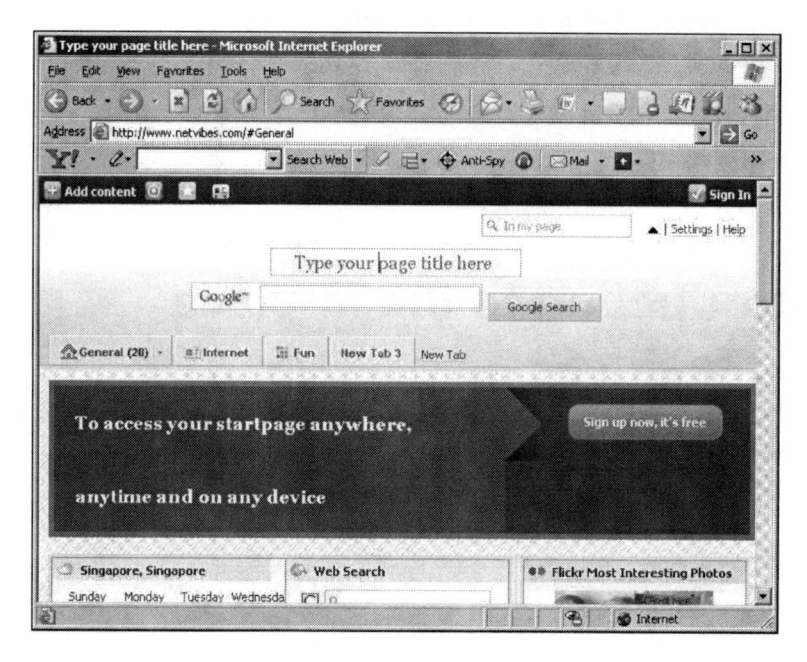

In simple terms, in-place editing is about converting the static content into an editable form without changing the place and updating it using AJAX.

Getting started with in-place editing

Imagine that we can edit the content inside the static HTML tags such as a simple `<p>` or even a complex `<div>`.

The basic syntax of initiating the constructor is shown as follows:

```
New Ajax.InPlaceEditor(element,url,[options]);
```

The constructor accepts three parameters:

- `element`: The target *static* element which we need to make editable
- `url`: We need to update the new content to the server, so we need a URL to handle the request
- `options`: Loads of options to fully customize our `element` as well as the in-place editing feature

We shall look into the details of `element` and `url` in the next section. For now, let's learn about all the options that we will be using in our future examples.

The following set of `options` is provided by the script.aculo.us library. We can use the following `options` with the `InPlaceEditor` object:

- `okButton`: Using this option we show an **OK** button that the user clicks on after editing. By default it is set to true.
- `okText`: With this option we set the text value on the **OK** button. By default this is set to true.
- `cancelLink`: This is the button we show when the user wishes to cancel the action. By default it's set to true.
- `cancelText`: This is the text we show as a value on the **Cancel** button. By default it's set to true.
- `savingText`: This is the text we show when the content is being saved. By default it's set to **Saving**. We can also give it any other name.
- `clickToEditText`: This is the text string that appears as the control *tooltip* upon mouse-hover.
- `rows`: Using this option we specify how many rows to show to the user. By default it is set to 1. But if we pass more than 1 it would appear as a text area, or it will show a text box.

- `cols`: Using this option we can set the number of columns we need to show to the user.
- `highlightColor`: With this option we can set the background color of the element.
- `highlightendColor`: Using this option we can bring in the use of effects. Specify which color should be set when the action ends.
- `loadingText`: When this option is used, we can keep our users informed about what is happening on the page with text such as **Loading** or **Processing Request**.
- `loadTextURL`: By using this option we can specify the URL at the server side to be contacted in order to load the initial value of the editor when it becomes active.

We also have some callback options to use along with in-place editing.

- `onComplete`: On any successful completion of a request, this callback option enables us to call functions.
- `onFailure`: Using this callback option on a request's failure, we can make a call to functions.
- `Callback`: This option calls back functions to read values in the text box, or text area, before initiating a save or an update request.

We will be exploring all these options in our hands-on examples.

Code usage of the in-place editing features and options

Now things are simple from here on. Let's get started with code.

First, let's include all the required scripts for in-place editing:

```
<script type="text/javascript" src="src/prototype.js"></script>
<script type="text/javascript" src="src/scriptaculous.js"></script>
<script type="text/javascript" src="src/effects.js"></script>
<script type="text/javascript" src="src/controls.js"></script>
```

Once this is done, let's create a basic HTML page with some `<p>` and `<div>` elements, and add some content to them.

```
<body>
<div id="myDiv">
    First move the mouse over me and then click on ME :)
</div>
</body>
```

Chapter 6

> In this section we will be learning about the options provided with the in-place editing feature. In the hands-on section we will be working with server-side scripts of handling data.

Now, it's turn to add some spicy JavaScript code and create the object for `InPlaceEditor`.

In the following piece of code we have passed the element ID as `myDIV`, a fake `URL`, and two options `okText` and `cancelText`:

```
Function makeEditable() {
new Ajax.InPlaceEditor(
    'myDIV',
    'URL',
    {
        okText: 'Update',
        cancelText: 'Cancel',
    }
);
}
```

We will be placing them inside a function and we will call them on page load. So the complete script would look like this:

```
<script>
function makeEditable() {
new Ajax.InPlaceEditor(
    'myDIV',
    'URL',
    {
        okText: 'Update',
        cancelText: 'Cancel'
    }
);
}
</script>
<body onload="JavaScript:makeEditable();">
<div id="myDiv">
    First move the mouse over me and then click on ME :)
</div>
</body>
```

In-place Editing using script.aculo.us

Now, save the file as `Inplace.html`. Open it in a browser and you should see the result as shown in the following screenshot:

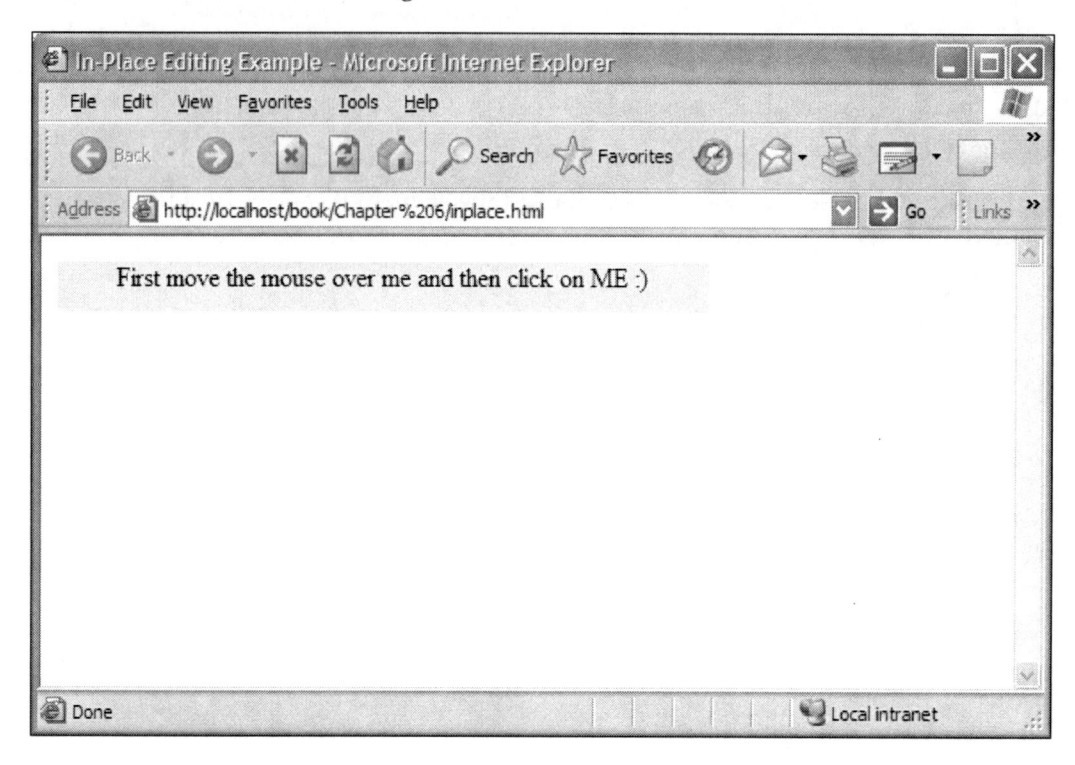

![Screenshot of In-Place Editing Example showing "First move the mouse over me and then click on ME :)" in a browser window]

Now, let's add all the options step-by-step.

> Remember, whatever we are adding now will be inside the definition of the constructor.

1. First let's add rows and columns to the object.

   ```
   new Ajax.InPlaceEditor(
      'myDIV',
      'URL',
      {
         okText: 'Update',
         cancelText: 'Cancel',
         rows: 4,
         cols: 70
      }
   );
   ```

2. After adding the rows and cols, we should be able to see the result displayed in the following screenshot:

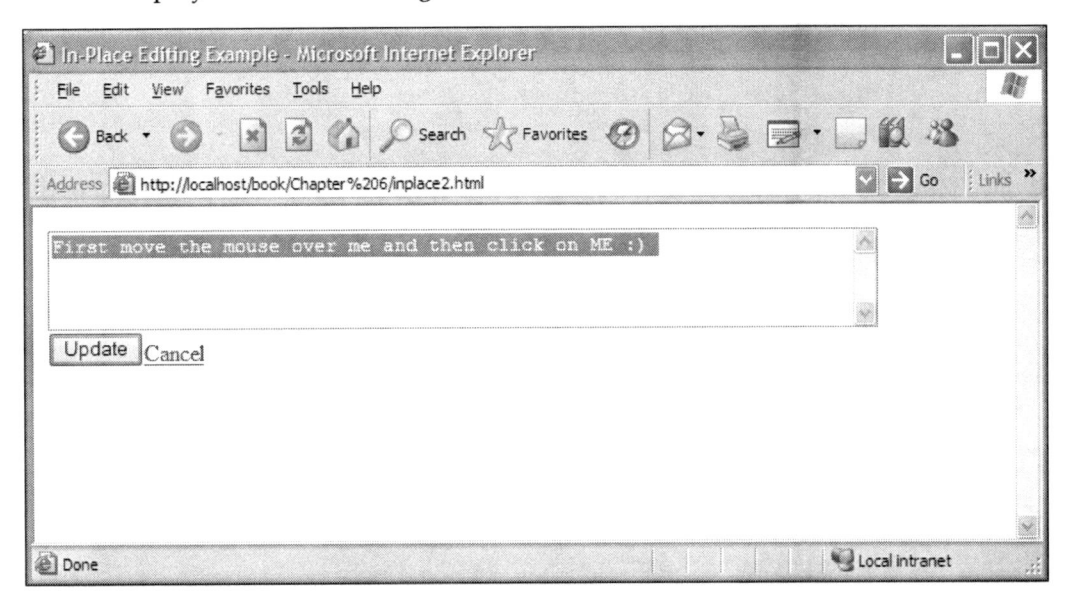

3. Now, let's set the color that will be used to highlight the element.

   ```
   new Ajax.InPlaceEditor(
       'myDIV',
       'URL',
       {
          okText: 'Update',
          cancelText: 'Cancel',
          rows: 4,
          cols: 70,
          highlightColor:'#E2F1B1'
       }
   );
   ```

4. Drag the mouse over the element. Did you notice the change in color? You did? Great!

5. Throughout the book we have insisted on *keeping the user informed*, so let's add more options to make this more appealing. We will add `clickToEditText`, which will be used to inform the user when the mouse hovers on the element.

   ```
   new Ajax.InPlaceEditor(
       'myDIV',
       'URL',
       {
   ```

```
            okText: 'Update',
            cancelText: 'Cancel',
            rows: 4,
            cols: 70,
            highlightColor:'#E2F1B1',
            clickToEditText: 'Click me to edit'
        }
    );
```

Tips and tricks with in-place editing

Now that we have learned how to use in-place editing, we can take a look at some cheat codes. Here are some tips and tricks to get you on a fast track with using in-place editing.

Disabling the element for the in-place editing functionality

We may need to disable the in-place editing functionality of an element after a certain action in the application. In the real world (say a project management application), where to-do lists are shared, we can disable the functionality of certain items based on the user access roles. This is just a teaser; you can think of more. For now, let's quickly learn the art of disabling.

The functionality can be disabled on the fly.

```
Element.dispose();
```

Now, let's try this with the myDIV element created above. To disable it, add this line of code:

```
myDiv.dispose();
```

Disabling the editing functionality certainly comes in handy and can be called after a particular event, or as a callback.

Entering into the edit mode

Now that we have disabled the element, chances are that we may also need to bring back the sanity and make the element editable. Again, making an element editable is as simple as disabling it.

The element can be made editable with a brute force method.

```
Element.enterEnterMode();
```

Chapter 6

We need to invoke the element ID with the `enterEnterMode()` function. To make the `myDiv` element editable, we need to add this line of code:

```
myDiv.enterEnterMode();
```

We can make certain functionality on an application editable only to the administrator, and not to the general users. We can disable in-place editing for general users and allow the admin to do in-place editing.

Submitting on Blur

There may be a lot of places where we don't want to show the user `okButton` or `cancelLink` along with our text box or field.

The following code shows the constructor definition for submitting the data on Blur.

```
new Ajax.InPlaceEditor(
   'theElement',
   'Server-Side Script',
   {
      okButton: false,
      cancelLink:false,
      submitOnBlur :true,
      ajaxOptions: {method: 'post'}
   }
);
```

The resulting user interface is shown in the following screenshot:

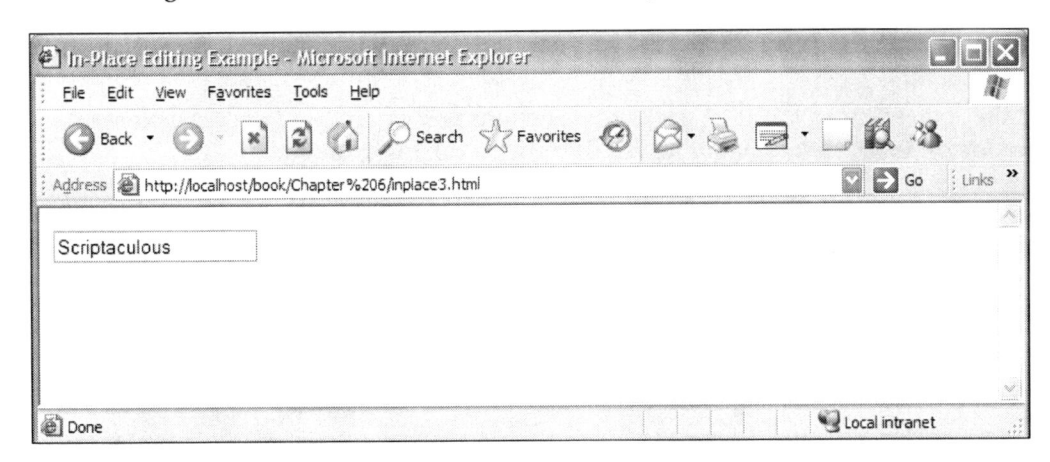

A simple example is the Gtalk status message. We can add our own title and the messenger updates it at runtime, without showing the user the **Submit** and **Cancel** buttons.

There are lots of uses of this particular option. It's not a good practice to present the user with the **Submit** and **Cancel** buttons every time, mainly, from the user interface perspective. So the next time you plan to show the user a **Submit** button, think about the `submitOnBlur` option.

Callbacks for onEnterEditMode and onLeaveEditMode

We can customize callbacks based on the behavior of the user while using applications. We can create callbacks when a particular element is made editable, or when a particular element leaves the edit mode.

These callbacks can be very useful and powerful in keeping the user informed, and also while changing the behavior of the application based on user inputs.

Invoking the callbacks is pretty neat and simple. Don't believe it? Check this code.

```
onEnterEditMode:f1(),
onLeaveEditMode: f2();
```

These options will come with the callback functions in the constructor definition. The complete code snippet will look like this:

```
new Ajax.InPlaceEditor(id, url, {
    callback: function(form, value) { return value},
    onEnterEditMode: f1(form, value),
    onLeaveEditMode: f2(form, value)
});
```

In the code snippet, the `f1()` and `f2()` functions will be invoked once the element becomes editable and when it leaves the edit mode, respectively.

Hands-on example: In-place editing with server-side handling

In the previous section, we saw different uses for the client-side options. In this section we will be working with the server-side processing.

Most of our web applications are database-driven. When the user edits and submits the data, we need to update the database with the new content. Server-side handling comes into the picture here.

Let's go straight into making an in-place editing module. We are not going to write the module from scratch, but we will be extending the above example. In the story so far, we have added a simple `<div>` element to the page, initiated the `InPlaceEditor` constructor, and added a few options to it. We have clubbed together the above pieces of code and the complete code is given here:

```
<html>
<head>
<title>In-Place Editing Example</title>
<script type="text/javascript" src="src/lib/prototype.js"></script>
<script type="text/javascript"
        src="src/src/scriptaculous.js"></script>
<script type="text/javascript" src="src/src/effects.js"></script>
<script type="text/javascript" src="src/src/controls.js"></script>
<style>
Body
 {
    color:black;
 }
 #myDiv
 {
    background-color:#BCE6D6;
    width:400px;
    height:30px;
    text-align:center;
 }
</style>
<script>
window.onload = function() {
    new Ajax.InPlaceEditor(
        'myDiv',
        'URL',
        {
            okText: 'Update',
            cancelText: 'Cancel',
            highlightColor:'#E2F1B1',
            clickToEditText: 'Click me to edit',
            loadingText: 'Loading..',
            savingText: 'Saving..'
        }
    );
}
</script>
<body>
<div id="myDiv">
```

In-place Editing using script.aculo.us

```
    First move the mouse over me and then click on ME :)
</div>
</body>
</html>
```

Let's look closely into the constructor definition.

```
new Ajax.InPlaceEditor(
    'myDiv',
    'URL',
    {
        okText: 'Update',
        cancelText: 'Cancel',
        highlightColor:'#E2F1B1',
        clickToEditText: 'Click me to edit',
        loadingText: 'Loading..',
        savingText: 'Saving..'
    }
);
```

Here, we have given a proxy URL in the option. We now need to create a script at the server side to handle the request sent through this constructor. Let's name it `readValue.php`.

```
<?php
$value = $_REQUEST['value'];
echo $value;
?>
```

That's it! It takes just these two lines to read the value. This is because, by default, it uses REQUEST to send the value. We can also overwrite it by passing our own `ajaxOptions`. We can also replace `$_REQUEST` with `$_POST` and it will still work.

Try it out to believe me. Just replace the URL with `readValue.php`. The new definition of the constructor now looks like this:

```
new Ajax.InPlaceEditor(
    'myDiv',
    'readValue.php',
    {
        okText: 'Update',
        cancelText: 'Cancel',
        highlightColor:'#E2F1B1',
        clickToEditText: 'Click me to edit',
        loadingText: 'Loading..',
        savingText: 'Saving..'
    }
);
```

Open the file in a browser. Click on the `<div>` element and add some new content. It should show you the following result:

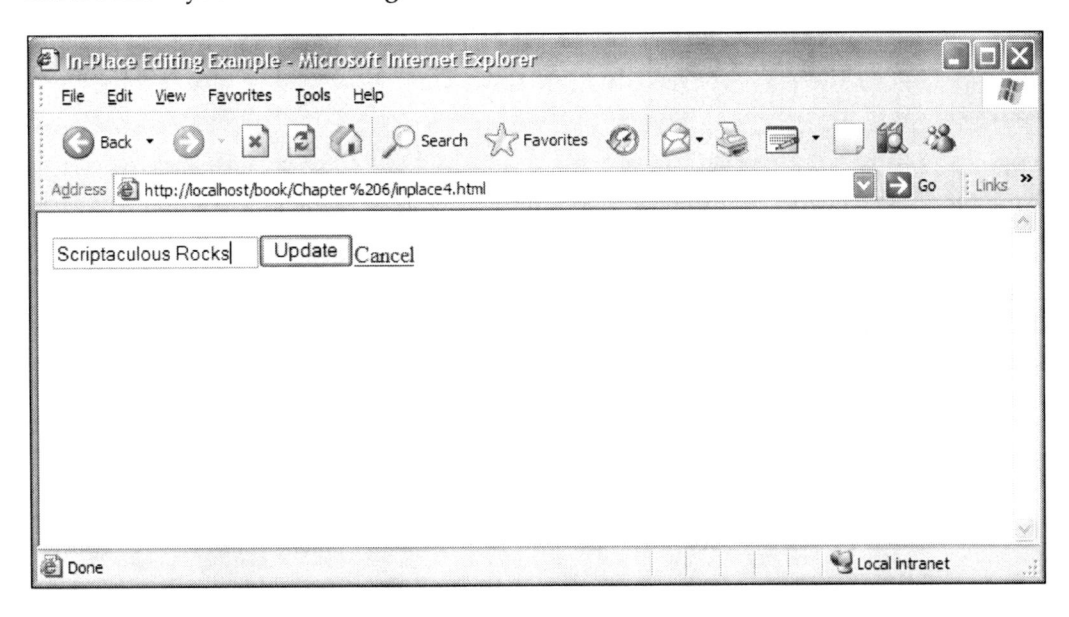

After we edit the text, check out the resulting output:

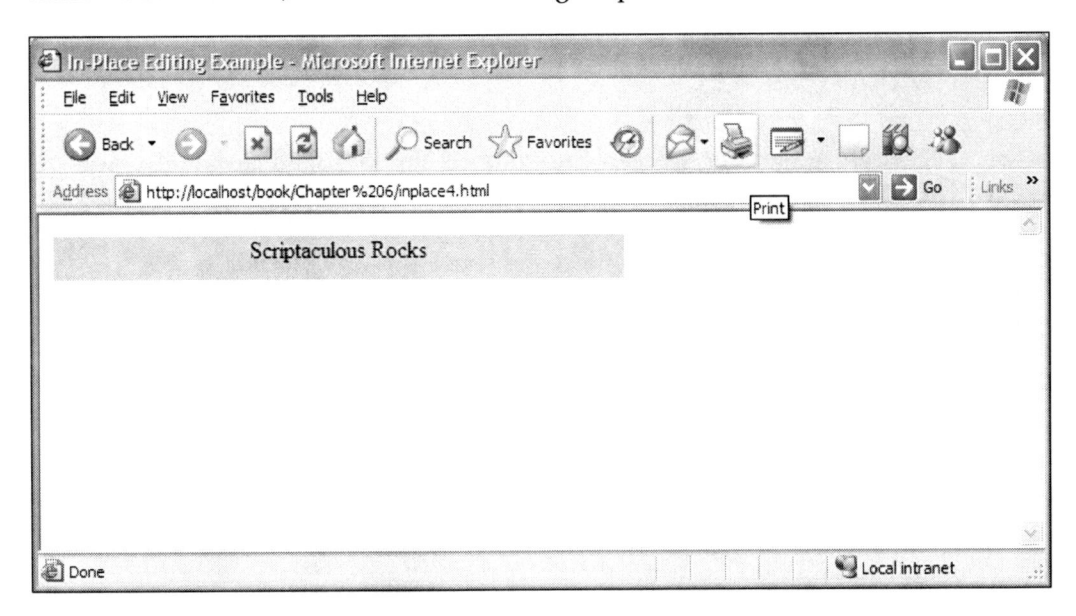

We were able to read the value at the server-side script. We can do a lot of things with the value such as edit it, add it to a database, or print it back.

Hands-on example: InPlaceCollectionEditor

We have covered the `InPlaceEditor` up to now. There is one more nice feature we need to learn while we are at in-place editing—`InPlaceCollectionEditor`.

After clicking on the editable element, the user sees a text box or a text area. In some cases, we need to provide the user with *fixed* values, which they will have to choose between.

A simple example can be—being asked what your favourite programming language is. Instead of entering any value, you would be prompted with fixed values in a drop-down menu.

Firstly, we have to define the element to initiate the `InPlaceCollectionEditor` constructor.

```
new Ajax.InPlaceCollectionEditor(
    'myDIV',
    'URL',
    {
        okText: 'Update',
        cancelText: 'Cancel',
        collection: ['php','mysql','Javascript','C++']
    }
);
```

If you look closely at the code snippet, the syntax is similar to the `InPlaceEditor` syntax. The only major difference is the new option—`collection`. The `collection` option takes multiple values in the form of an array and prompts them in a drop-down menu for the user. We can use the above server-side code as it is.

Leave this as a part of a hands-on exercise, and try it out! You will be provided the complete code in the next chapter. In the following screenshot, check out how it should behave when you convert `InPlaceEditor` to `InPlaceCollectionEditor`:

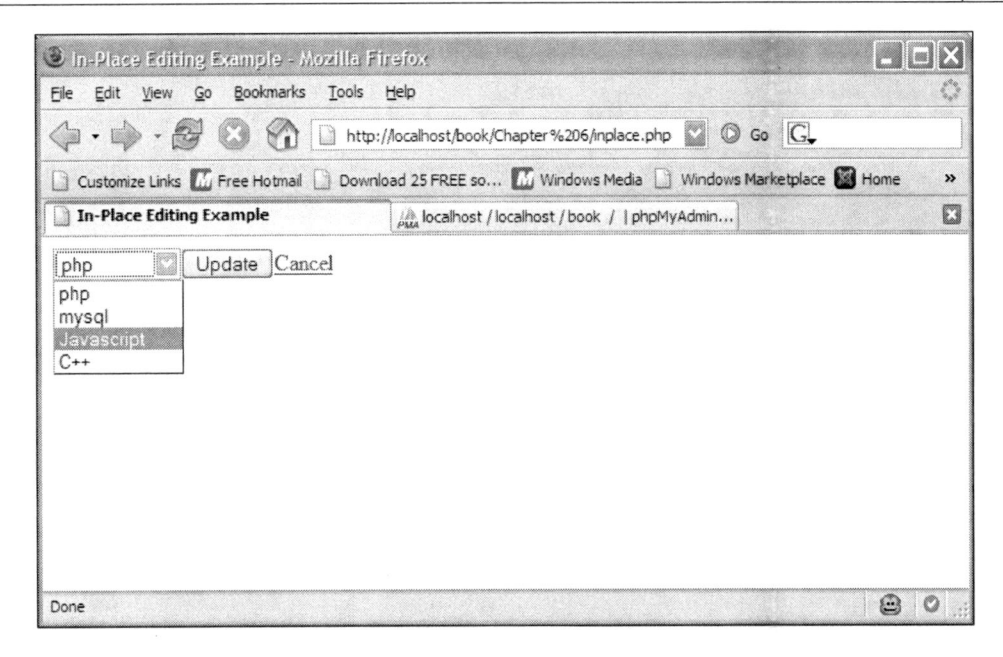

After selecting the **JavaScript** option and clicking on **ok**, we get:

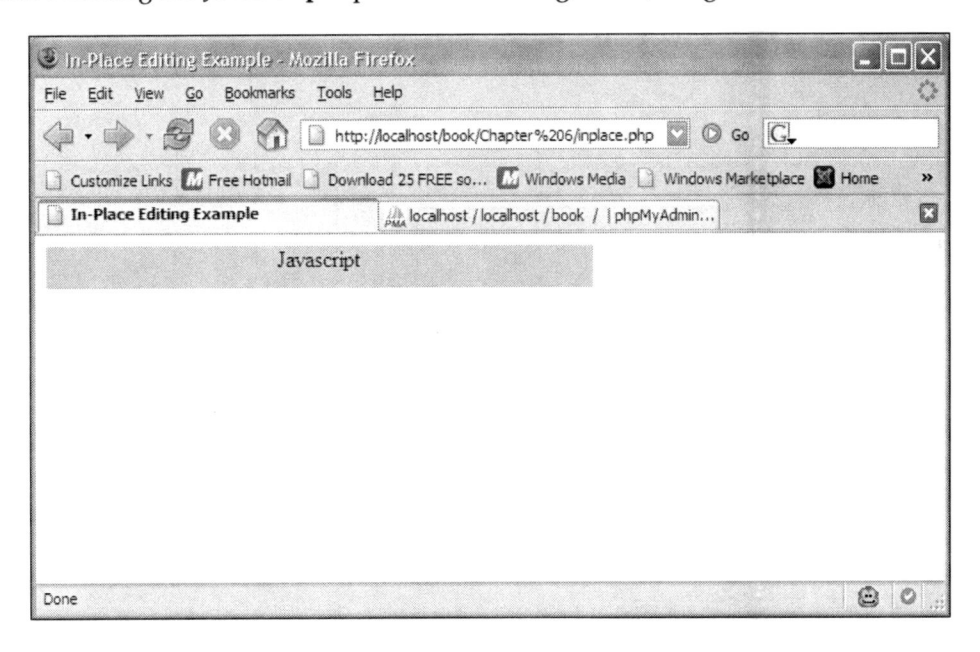

In short, `InPlaceCollectionEditor` is an extension to `InPlaceEditor` providing the user with a set of fixed, predefined values. These values are shown in the form of a drop-down menu.

Summary

We have almost edited everything on the page using `InPlaceEditor` and `InPlaceCollectionEditor`. So far we have:

- Learned about `InPlaceEditor`
- Seen the explanation and code usage for `InPlaceEditor`
- Learned some tips and tricks with in-place editing
- Seen hands-on modules for `InPlaceEditor` at the server-side handling
- Learned about `InPlaceCollectionEditor`

In the next chapter, we will be learning about autocompletion using script.aculo.us. We call this feature a *must* for the Web 2.0 applications. It makes the applications sleek and robust. You have possibly used it in the Yahoo! homepage, or in a Gmail contact list.

7
Creating Autocompletion using script.aculo.us

Having learned the in-place editing functionality, we now move to some *serious* fun. We will discuss yet another power functionality of autocompletion using script.aculo.us. Some of the key topics we will cover are:

- Introduction to autocompletion
- Explanation, types, and options of autocompletion
- Code usage for autocompletion
- Hands-on example using local and remote sources

Introduction to autocompletion

As the end user of an application, we would expect the system, as a whole, to be user-friendly and to help us achieve the desired results faster. It's always good to suggest to users possible matches for the results while the input is being entered, thus enabling the user to select a result if it satisfies his/her criteria. This not only makes the application faster, but also makes it more efficient.

Creating Autocompletion using script.aculo.us

Let me start by giving you a very basic example of Yahoo! search. Look at the following screenshot:

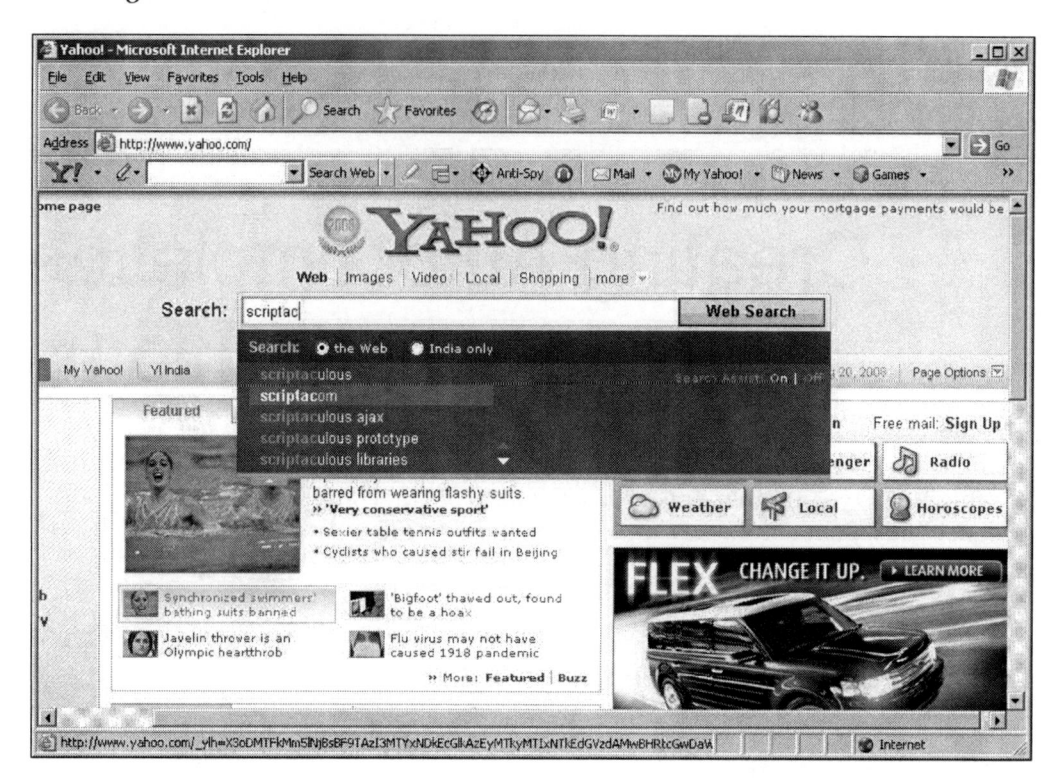

In this screenshot, when we type **scriptac** in the text box we see a drop-down list suggesting some of the relevant topics such as **scriptaculous**, **scriptacom**, and so on.

Imagine that if a user is searching for effects, then (s)he just has to click on the link shown through suggestions and search results would be displayed accordingly.

As a user we don't have to type complete words. Above all, it helps us in refining our criteria which makes it more relevant.

From a developers' point of view, autocompletion is not necessarily used only with web searching, but from our local database as well. It can be used with a string of arrays too. In short, we can apply autocompletion in any project where we need to suggest quick options to the users.

Let me give you another quick example and then we can move to the creation of our own autocompletion modules using script.aculo.us.

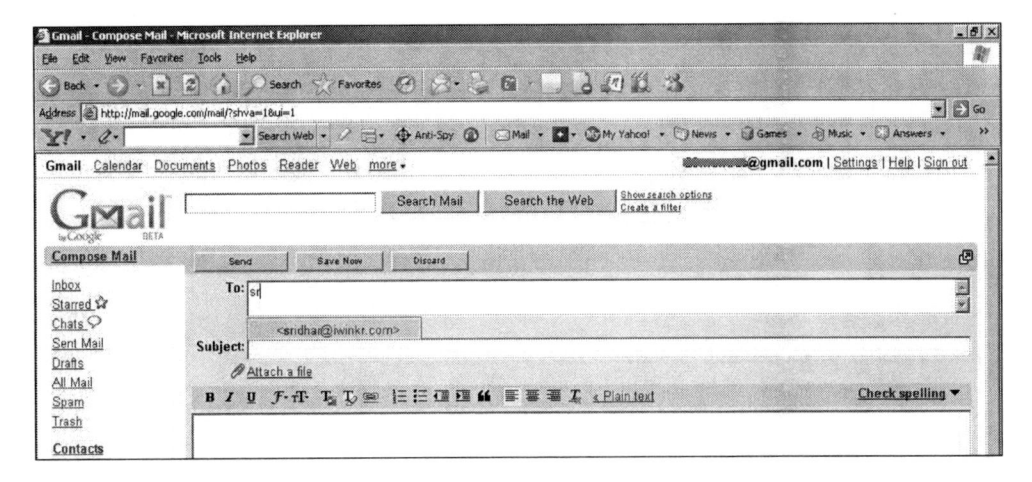

Google has introduced this powerful usage of autocompletion in various features of Gmail. In the **Compose Mail** feature, on typing the name of the contact we see a list showing the related names from the entire contact list. The same applies to some other features such as adding a contact.

I must admit, these features save a lot of time and memory as well (else we would be compelled to remember or add exclusively).

OK! So, we are clear about the real-world usage of the autocompletion feature. We will now move on to learn and build our own modules.

Explanation of the autocompletion feature

Like all the other features, script.aculo.us offers powerful, customizable, and developer-friendly options for implementing autocompletion in our projects.

To invoke the constructor for autocompletion, we need to pass four parameters with options as optional parameters. They are as follows:

- **Element**: This is the reference to the element name or reference of the text field.
- **Container**: This is the reference to the element which would be the host for the options being suggested.

- **Source**: Earlier, in the introduction, I mentioned that we can use autocompletion with a local database or with arrays. This is where we mention our sources. It can be from a server-side script using AJAX or as simple as an array. We will be looking into the details about them in the next section.
- **Options**: We can fully customize our autocompletion feature by adding more callbacks and functions.

Types of autocompletion sources

script.aculo.us provides us with two principle sources for autocompletion. They are:

- Remote sources
- Local sources

Remote sources

Remote sources are used to fetch data from outside sources in real time.

User enters a particular character and on every keyup event the autocompletion feature is called. The entered text is then sent to the server, gets refined in terms of matching words, and is displayed on the page.

On the technical front, an AJAX call is being made to fetch the relevant data from the server side.

The syntax for the constructor is shown below:

```
new Ajax.Autocompleter(ElementID, Container, source URL, [options]);
```

We need to pass `ElementID` or reference, the `Container` element, `Source URL`, and `options`.

A real-world example code usage is shown below:

```
new Ajax.Autocompleter('myDIV','suggestDIV','readSuggests.php', {
updateElement: function(){alert("posted");} } );
```

Local sources

One obvious thought that comes to mind at this point of time is *What is the difference between remote and local sources, when both of them fetch data and prompt the relevant values?*

The difference lies in the sources. Local sources are passed as *an array of strings without making any AJAX calls,* and remote sources take *server-side scripts with AJAX calls.*

This is also useful from the performance point of view. Accessing local sources would result in high performance and using remote sources needs extra care, since it requires querying in the database. But care has to be taken in optimizing the results, either at the database level or at server side.

Now, let's see the syntax for invoking the constructor using local sources.

```
new Autocompleter.Local(element, container, "array"[ , options ] );
```

Real-world example code usage is shown here:

```
var cities= [
'Illinois',
'Idaho',
'Indiana'
];
new Autocompleter.Local('city', 'cityList', cities);
```

Options for autocompletion sources

In this section, we will learn about the options available to explore with the autocompletion feature. We will learn about the options available for remote as well as local sources.

Options for remote sources

script.aculo.us provides various options, which can be used along with autocompletion objects using remote sources. They are:

- `paramName`: When we post our data, that is, through the text field, we can add our own parameter name to the query string. By default it takes the name of the text field. It can be particularly useful for naming the parameter if we are taking our parameter as criteria in the database query.
- `minChars`: We mentioned before that the AJAX calls are made on every keyup event. Using this option we can specify how many minimum characters we need as our data. By default it is one character.
- `Frequency`: This is the interval time which is passed to the server-side script. By default it is 0.4 seconds.
- `Indicator`: This is like *Loading* an image or *Requesting* an element in AJAX calls. This element will be displayed while AJAX calls are being processed at the server side.

- `Parameters`: Sometimes it's not sufficient to fetch results only by passing the query string that has passed through text field. We may also need to pass other parameters such as userID, username, or sessionname. We can pass those parameters using this option.
- `callback`: This is used to modify the query string entered through the text field. This is called before the AJAX call is made. We can modify or format the data and make it ready for the AJAX request to be made to the server side.
- `updateElement`: Once a user selects one element out of the list prompted from the server-side script, we can use this callback option to invoke a function to handle what is to be done with that data. It's like a trigger to add more customized functionality.
- `afterUpdateElement`: Using this callback option we can specify our application of what to do after the `updateElement` execution.
- `Tokens`: Tokens, as an option, are mainly used to delimit the entry of multiple elements into the text field.

Options for local sources

script.aculo.us provides various options that can be used along with autocompletion objects using local sources. They are:

- `Choices`: The number of choices to be displayed. By default it is set to 10.
- `partialSearch`: This is a little tricky option. While using the `partialSearch` option, the search operation is performed on the expressions in matching order from left to right. That means if we enter "ab", the choices will be like "abc", "abxyz", and so on.
- `fullSearch`: In the `fullSearch` option, the search is performed on the matching expressions without any constraints of order; which means they may match anywhere in the expression. For example, if we enter *ab*, we will find *abc*, *fab*, and *labs* because the *ab* pattern is matching in all the choices. By default it is false.
- `partialChars`: The number of characters to be typed before going for a `partialSearch`. By default it is 2.
- `ignoreCase`: The name speaks for itself. We will not take into account the case of characters.

Code usage for all the above mentioned sources and options is explained.

Code usage of autocompletion using remote sources

Let's quickly learn how to create a constructor making good usage of the available options, and create a base example for our hands-on example.

The syntax for the autocompletion constructor using remote sources is shown as follows:

```
new Ajax.Autocompleter(ElementID, Container, source URL, [options]);
```

Let's have a quick glance at the usage of the HTML code.

```
<input type="text" id="cityName"/>
<div id="cityChoices"></div>
```

We have just created a simple `text` field and given an `id` to it. We have also created a `<div>` element with `id`, which will be used to populate with the choices we get from the server side.

Now, to invoke the autocompletion feature, we need to add our required files and scripts. We need to add the script.aculo.us modules `effects.js` and `controls.js`, and the Prototype library as well.

```
<script type="text/javascript" src="/src/effects.js"></script>
<script type="text/javascript" src="/src/controls.js"></script>
<script type="text/javascript" src="src/prototype.js"></script>
<script type="text/javascript" src="src/scriptaculous.js"></script>
```

All set. Now, let's write the JavaScript code.

```
window.onload = function() {
 new Ajax.Autocompleter(
 'cityName',
 'cityChoices',
 'viewCities.php'
   );
}
```

We have invoked a function and passed the element ID `cityName`, the container ID `cityChoices`, and the server URL `viewCities.php`.

Let's add some options to our code to make it more flexible.

[121]

Creating Autocompletion using script.aculo.us

Adding options to our constructor

Let's add some options with our constructor definition to enhance the behaviour and functionality.

```
window.onload = function() {
 new Ajax.Autocompleter(
  'cityName',
  'cityChoices',
  'viewCities.php',
 {
 paramName: 'myQuery',
 minChars:2,
 frequency: 3,
 indicator: 'Requesting',
 updateElement: handleRequest
 }
    );
}
function handleRequest(text)
{
alert(text.value);
}
<input type="text" id="cityName"/>
<div id="Requesting">Searching</div>
<div id="cityChoices"></div>
```

In the above snippet we are adding some options such as `paramName`, `minChars`, `frequency`, `indicator`, and `updateElement`.

To use the indicator option we have added a `<div>` element with text `Searching`, which will be shown while the AJAX request is taking place.

We have also defined a function `handleRequest`, which will be called using the callback option `updateElement`.

Similarly, we can add the rest of the options as well.

Code usage of autocompletion using local sources

After learning about autocompletion using remote sources, now it's time to learn autocompletion using local sources.

The syntax for the autocompletion constructor using local sources is shown as follows:

```
new Autocompleter.Local(ElementID, Container,"array of strings",
[options]);
```

Let's include the required modules and libraries. The HTML part of the code remains the same. Remember, we told you the difference lies only in the way the data is fetched from different sources.

```
<script type="text/javascript" src="/src/effects.js"></script>
<script type="text/javascript" src="/src/controls.js"></script>
<script type="text/javascript" src="src/prototype.js"></script>
<script type="text/javascript" src="src/scriptaculous.js"></script>
<input type="text" id="cityName"/>
<div id="cityChoices"></div>
```

So now let's define our constructor using local sources.

```
var citiesList= [
'Indiana',
'Idaho',
'Illinois'
];
new Autocompleter.Local('cityName', 'cityChoices', citiesList);
```

We have created the constructor by passing the text field element's ID—cityName, the <div> element that will contain the matching choices, and finally the array that has some city names.

Adding options to our constructor

Let's add some options with our constructor definition.

```
<script type="text/javascript" src="/src/effects.js"></script>
<script type="text/javascript" src="/src/controls.js"></script>
<script type="text/javascript" src="src/prototype.js"></script>
<script type="text/javascript" src="src/scriptaculous.js"></script>
<script type="text/javascript">
```

Creating Autocompletion using script.aculo.us

```
    var citiesList= [
    'Indiana',
    'Idaho',
    'Illinois
    ];
    window.onload = function() {
     new Autocompleter.Local(
        'autoCompleteTextField',
        'autoCompleteMenu',
         citiesList,
        {ignoreCase:true,
         fullSearch:true
    }
          );
       }
</script>
<input type="text" id="cityName"/>
<div id="cityChoices"></div>
```

The above snippet shows the complete code for implementing autocompletion using local sources.

We have added three options to our constructor definition: `ignoreCase`, `partialSearch`, and `fullSearch`.

Hands-on example: Autocompletion using remote sources

OK! So, to this point we have learned about the theory and code usage for the autocompletion feature using remote sources.

Now let's get straight into code and quickly get a module up and running.

The module is about finding the city names from the database. Simple, right? Yes it is. And in fact it is one of the most used features in most web applications.

The user starts typing the city name in the text field and we provide the options matching with the data entered by the user.

Before we start with the code, check out the following screenshot to get a clear picture of the working module:

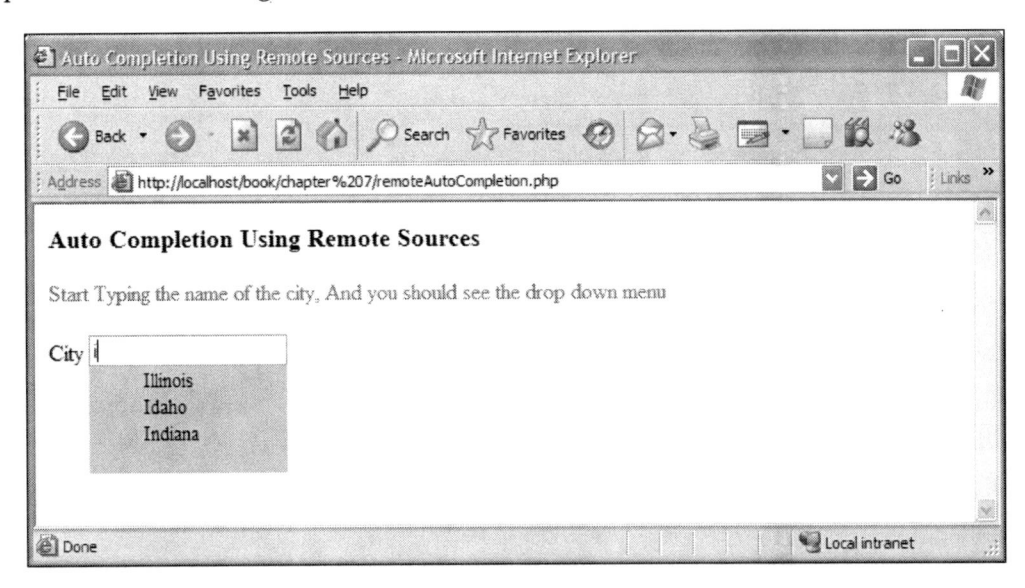

Let's get started and include all the required files and libraries.

```
<script type="text/javascript" src="src/lib/prototype.js"></script>
<script type="text/javascript" src="src/src/scriptaculous.js">
</script>
<script type="text/javascript" src="src/src/effects.js"></script>
<script type="text/javascript" src="src/src/controls.js"></script>
```

Now, let's define the HTML body for our module.

```
<body>
<h3>Advanced Auto Completion Using Remote Sources</h3>
<p>
<span class="intro">Start Typing the name of the city, And you should
see the drop down menu</span><p>
  <div>
      <label>City</label>
      <input type="text" id="city" name="city"/>
      <div id="myDiv"></div>
  </div>
<p>
  <div id="result" name="result"> </div>
</body>
```

Creating Autocompletion using script.aculo.us

We are adding a `text` field named `city`, and a blank `<div>` element `myDIV` which will contain the list of choices prompted from the server.

All set. Let's add the autocompletion constructor to our HTML code.

```
<script type="text/javascript">
    window.onload = function() {
    new Ajax.Autocompleter(
    'city',
    'myDiv',
    'fetchChoices.php'
    );
}
</script>
```

That's right. As you can see we are passing the text field element `city`, container field `myDiv`, and the server-side script URL `fetchChoices.php`.

Before we start with our server-side scripting, let's quickly create a sample test database and a dummy table with some data about cities.

The code for SQL query and dummy data is shown as follows:

```
CREATE TABLE `cities` (
  `cityName` varchar(20) NOT NULL
) ENGINE=InnoDB DEFAULT CHARSET=latin1;
```

Insert some values into the table and make it ready for querying. You can add more values later.

```
INSERT INTO `trial`.`cities` (`cityName`) VALUES ('Lucknow');
```

Now coming back to our server-side script, the complete definition in `fetchChocies.php` is shown as follows:

```
<?php
$value = $_POST['city'];

$dbuser ="root";
$dbpassword = "";
$database = "trial";
$host = 'localhost';

mysql_connect($host, $dbuser, $dbpassword);
mysql_select_db($database) or die("Unable to connect to DB");

$query="SELECT * FROM cities WHERE cityName LIKE '%".$value."%'";
$result=mysql_query($query);

if(!$result) die();
```

[126]

```
echo '<ul class="options" >';
while($row= mysql_fetch_array($result))
{
   echo '<li align="left" name="'.$row["cityName"].'">'
.$row["cityName"].'</li>';
}
echo '</ul>';
?>
```

Now, let's break the code into snippets for easier understanding.

```
$value = $_POST ['city'];
```

script.aculo.us autocompletion recognizes POST by default to read the value.

In `fetchChoices.php` we are getting the value of `city`, which is what the user entered and was posted by our AJAX call.

> We have used the quick method of accessing the database, but we encourage you to use the DBConnector class we created in Chapter 3 and make all necessary security checks.

After having connected to the database—with a valid username and password—we fire a query to fetch the results, which match with the data entered by the user.

```
$query="SELECT * FROM cities WHERE cityName LIKE '%".$value."%'";
```

This means any name that has the matching characters will be shown. Remember the `fullSearch` option?

Now comes the most important part: handling the results returned by the query.

> script.aculo.us autocompletion, using remote sources, should return the values in the form of `ul` elements.

Creating Autocompletion using script.aculo.us

We see the choices returned by the server in our container element. We have also added some style to our results. When the user clicks on any choice, it is selected in the text field.

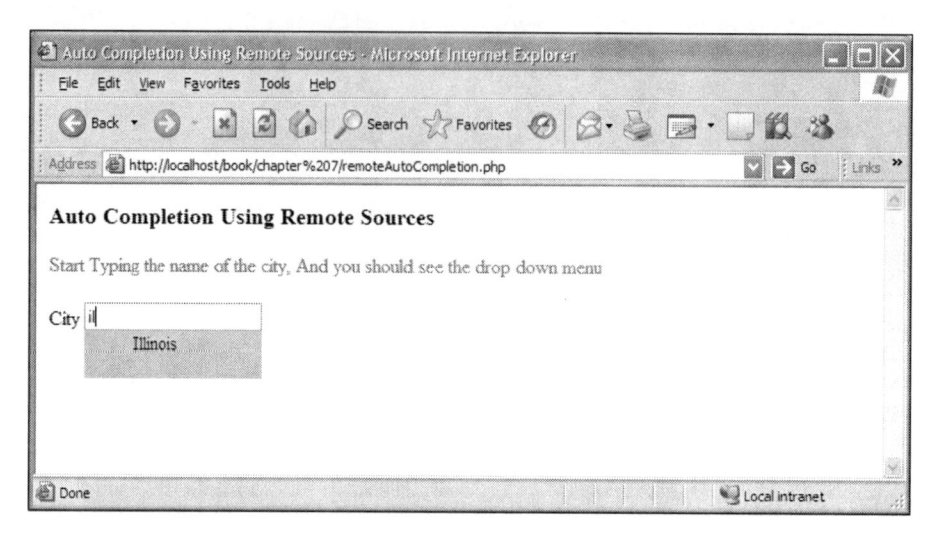

Hands-on example: Advanced autocompletion using remote sources for multiple fields

I am sure you have enjoyed building the city module discussed in the previous hands-on example. At the same time, it must have triggered a couple of thoughts such as:

- How can we edit the data before we display the results?
- Can we read the value selected by the user and format it for other uses?

Well, I must tell you that if you have come across these thoughts, it's simply superb. Questioning is a way to learn more.

Now, let's try to find answers for the same.

Yes, we certainly can edit and format the results before displaying them to users. And, knowingly or unknowingly, we have done it. In the `fetchChoices.php` script, we have created our own `ul` and `li` elements. We were able to format the look and feel. And certainly, a lot more can be done.

The answer to the second question is our advanced hands-on example.

So what will this advanced module do? We were able to display city names to the users, and they will select one choice. Perfect till here.

Now, assuming that we want to show which state the selected city belongs to, we will need to read the value selected by the user and display the results accordingly. We are going to extend the above example.

Remember, our purpose behind this hands-on is to understand and explore the possibilities of using the data the way that we want it for our applications.

Let's create a text field to store our state names. We have also disabled it, so that it gets loaded automatically. The new HTML code is shown here. We have formatted it a little bit by adding all these elements into the table.

```
<body>
<h3>Advanced Auto Completion Using Remote Sources</h3>
<p>
<span class="intro">Start Typing the name of the city, And you should
see the drop down menu</span><p>
   <div>
   <table class="cityForm" cellpadding="5" cellspacing="5">
      <tr><td>City</td><td><input type="text" id="city"
                              name="city"/></td></tr>
      <tr><td></td><td><div id="myDiv"></div></td></tr>
<tr><td>State </td><td><input type="text" id="result" name="result"
                              disabled="true" > </td></tr>
      </table>
   </div>
</body>
```

This would result in the screenshot shown as follows:

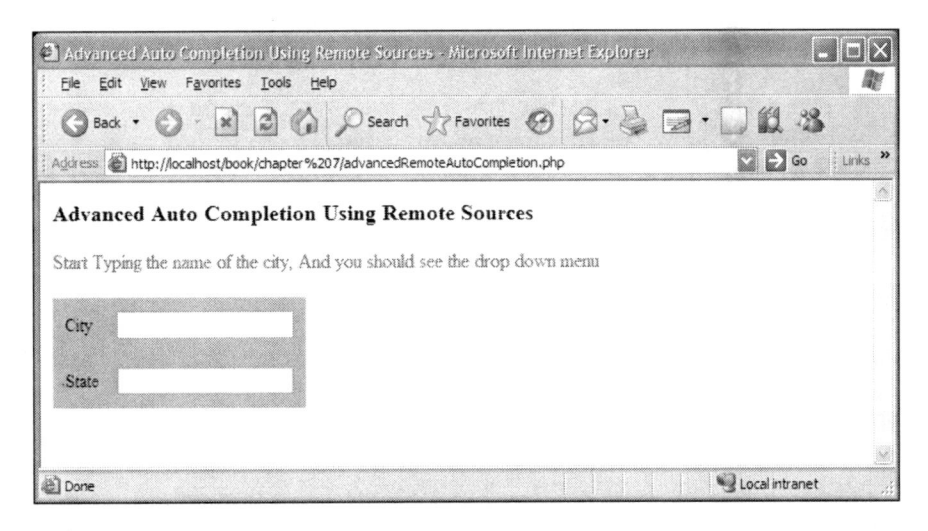

Creating Autocompletion using script.aculo.us

As mentioned earlier, in options for remote sources we can make use of the `afterUpdateElement` callback to do processing after the AJAX call has been made successfully.

Let's modify our constructor definition first and add the callback option `afterUpdateElement`:

```
window.onload = function() {
    new Ajax.Autocompleter(
        'city',
        'myDiv',
        'fetchChoices.php',
        {afterUpdateElement:PostValue}
    );
}
```

We are calling another function named `PostValue` using `afterUpdateElement`. This function would read the value selected by the user and send it back for processing at the server side and display results.

```
function PostValue(text){
var pars = 'cityName='+text.value;
var url = 'getValues.php';
new Ajax.Request(url, {
    method: 'post',
    parameters:pars,
    onSuccess: showResult,
    onFailure:showError
});
}
```

We are reading the value of the choice made by the user. Remember that we learned about using an AJAX request in Chapter 2? Yes, we are making an AJAX call to fetch the values from the database.

We have also defined two more functions, namely, `showResult` and `showError`. For now, let's keep them straight and simple.

```
function showResult(ServerResponse)
{
   alert(ServerResponse.responseText);
    $('result').value=ServerResponse.responseText;
}
function showError() {
   alert("Something Went Wrong");
}
```

We are also calling the `getValues.php` script at the server side to read runtime data. Below is the complete code used in `getValues.php`.

Hey, wait. Before we get into the details of the `getValues.php` script, it's important for us to modify our database table definition. We need to add a state column to the table.

```
ALTER TABLE `cities` ADD `states` VARCHAR( 20 ) NOT NULL ;
```

Insert some values for cities and states as well. OK, now we are all set to create the `getValues.php` script.

```
<?php
$value = $_POST['cityName'];
$dbuser ="root";
$dbpassword = "";
$database = "trial";
$host = "localhost";
mysql_connect($host, $dbuser, $dbpassword);
mysql_select_db($database) or die("Unable to connect to DB");
$query="SELECT states FROM cities WHERE cityName ='".$value."'";
$result=mysql_query($query);
if(!$result) die("Error in fetching results");
while($row= mysql_fetch_array($result))
{
    echo $row["states"];
}
?>
```

We are reading the value of `cityName` through `POST`, and querying the database and fetching the value of the state respectively. We are also passing it back to the `showResult` function.

Open the file in a browser and you will see the result as shown in the following screenshots. When the user starts typing the characters, we prompt the choices.

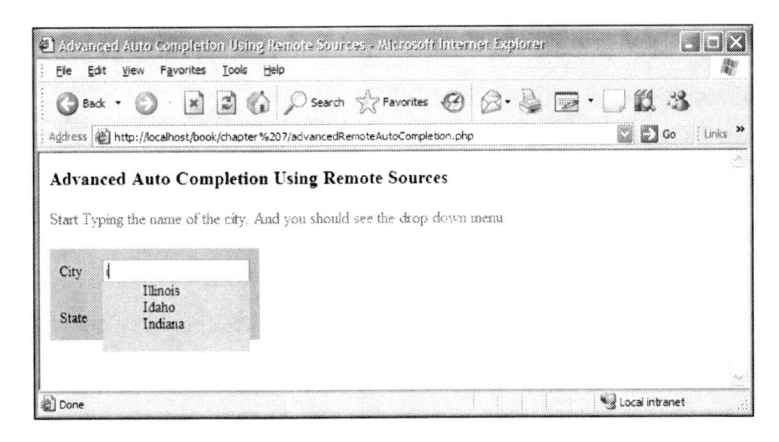

Once the user has selected from one of the choices, the text field for that state gets populated automatically.

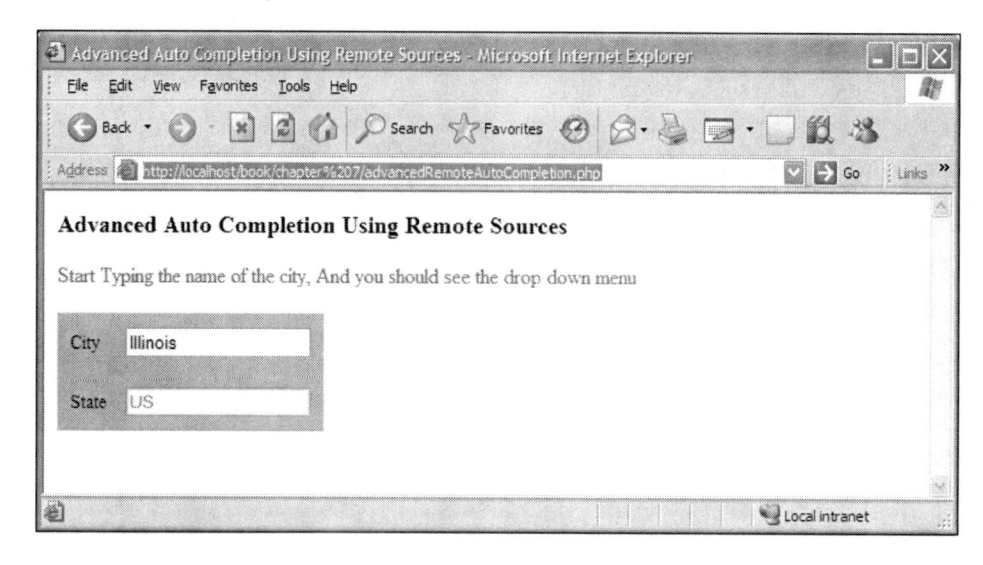

Hands-on example: Autocompletion using local sources

We can even create the same example module using local sources. As mentioned earlier, the difference between autocompletion using remote sources and using local sources is in the source of data.

For local sources, we keep an array of strings with all the values and use the `Autocompleter.Local` constructor.

We will not be using any server-side scripting while working with local sources. I will leave this as a practice example for you at this point of time.

I will give you a step-by-step guide to do it.

- Create a text field and the container `<div>` element in HTML code
- Initiate the `Autocompleter.Local` constructor as described in above code usage
- Create a simple array of strings with some city names in it
- Run the code and check the results. The result should be similar to the above hands-on example

We will give you the complete code for this hands-on in the next chapter.

[132]

Summary

That's all we need to know about the autocompletion feature to get started with more robust and efficient features for 2.0 web sites. In this chapter we have learned about:

- Autocompletion
- Different types of sources of autocompletion
- Different types of options for sources
- Code usage for remote sources and local sources
- A hands-on example with remote sources
- An advanced hands-on example with remote sources

In the next chapter we will be exploring sliders. Sliders are tracks with handles so that the user can drag along the track, and the data gets changed. There are basically two types of sliders: vertical sliders and horizontal sliders. Interesting! We will cover sliders in detail in the next chapter.

Don't forget to work on the hands-on example.

8
Slider for Dynamic Applications using script.aculo.us

Handling, processing, and representing data in the 2.0 era of web applications has become so crucial that designers and programmers are working towards new ways of improving the user interface experience.

Slider is one such killer concept, using which the user can represent and handle data easily.

A slider, according to the dictionary, stands for "the one that slides". Yes, a slider in the web application context stands for holding and sliding values from a fixed given range, or even from an array of values.

The slider is really useful and worthy in places where the user needs to slide through a lot of values and also the application needs to respond to those values and changes.

Some of the key topics we will cover in this chapter are:

- First steps with the script.aculo.us slider
- Types of the slider
- Code usage for the slider
- Tips and tricks with the slider
- Hands-on example with vertical and horizontal slider

Before we start exploring the slider, let me try to give you a complete picture of its functionality with a simple example.

Google Finance uses a horizontal slider, showing the price at a given day, month, and year. Although this particular module is built in Flash, we can build a similar module using the script.aculo.us slider too. To understand the concept and how it works, look at the following screenshot:

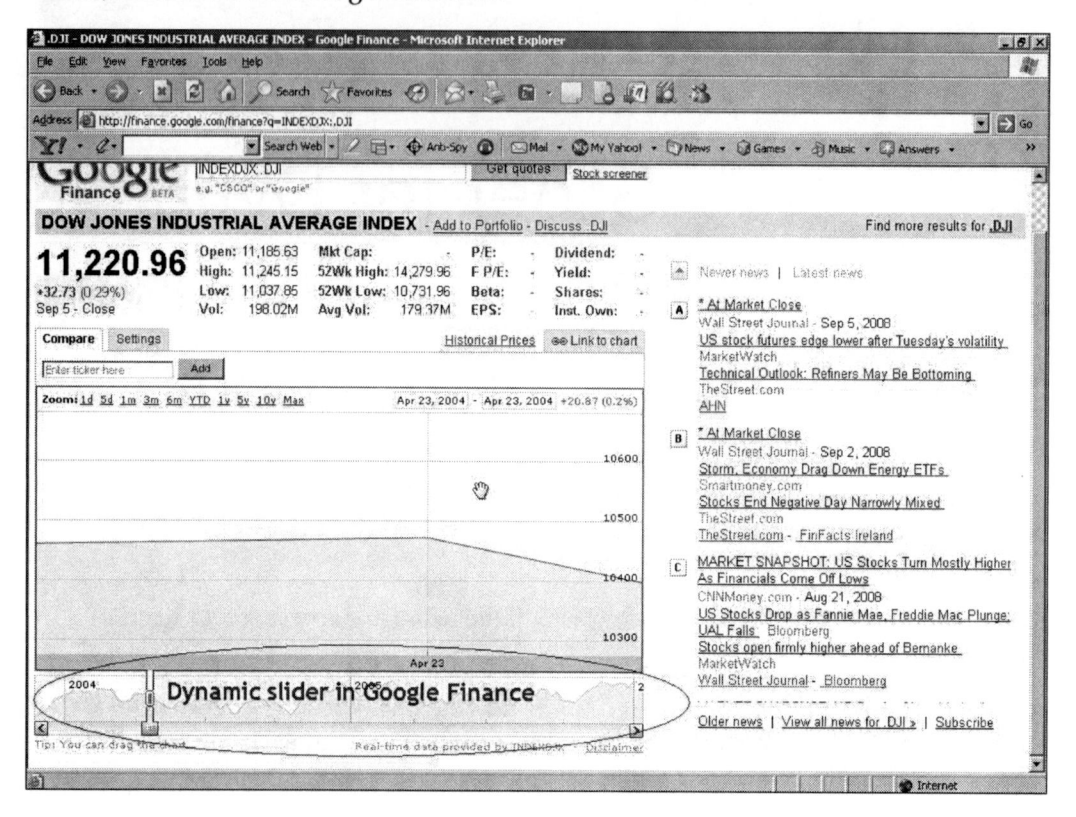

Now that we have a clear understanding of what the slider is and how it appears in user interface, let's get started!

First steps with slider

As just explained, a slider can handle a single value or a set of values. It's important to understand at this point of time that unlike other features of script.aculo.us, a slider is used in very niche applications for a specific functionality.

The slider is not just mere functionality, but is the behavior of the users and the application.

A typical constructor syntax definition for the slider is shown as follows:

```
new Control.Slider(handle, track [ , options ] );
```

Track mostly represents the `<div>` element. Handle represents the element inside the track and, as usual, a large number of options for us to fully customize our slider.

For now, we will focus on understanding the concepts and fundamentals of the slider. We will surely have fun playing with code in our *Code usage for the slider* section.

Parameters for the slider definition

In this section we will look at the parameters required to define the slider constructor:

- `track` in a slider represents a range
- `handle` in a slider represents the sliding along the track, that is, within a particular range and holding the current value
- `options` in a slider are provided to fully customize our slider's look and feel as well as functionality

It's time to put the theory into action. We need the appropriate markup for working with the slider. We have `<div>` for the `track` and one `<div>` for each `handle`. The resulting code should look like the snippet shown as follows:

```
<div id="track"><div id="handle1"></div></div>
```

It is possible to have multiple handles inside a single track. The following code snippet is a simple example:

```
<div id="track"><div id="handle1"></div>
<div id="handle2"></div></div>
```

Options with the slider

Like all the wonderful features of script.aculo.us, the slider too comes with a large number of options that allow us to create multiple behaviours for the slider. They are:

- `Axis`: This defines the orientation of the slider. The direction of movement could be horizontal or vertical. By default it is horizontal.
- `Increment`: This defines the relation between value and pixels.
- `Maximum`: This is the maximum value set for the slider to move to. While using a vertical slider from top-to-bottom, the bottom most value will be the maximum. And for a horizontal slider from left-to-right, the right most value will be the maximum value.

- `Minimum`: This is the minimum value set for the slider to move to. While using a vertical slider from top-to-bottom, the top most value will be the minimum. And for a horizontal slider from left-to-right, the left most value will be the minimum value approach for horizontal slider.
- `Range`: This is the fixed bandwidth allowed for the values. Define the minimum and maximum values.
- `Values`: Instead of a range, pass a set of values as an array.
- `SliderValue`: This sets the initial value of the slider. If not set, will take the extreme value of the slide as the default value.
- `Disabled`: As the name suggests, this disables the slider functionality.

Some of the functions offered by the slider are:

- `setValue`: This will set the value of the slider directly and move it to the value position.
- `setDisabled`: This defines that the slider is disabled at runtime.
- `setEnabled`: This can enable the slider at runtime.

Some of the callbacks supported by the slider are:

- `onSlide`: This is initiated on every slide movement. The called function would get the "current" slider value as parameter.
- `onChange`: Whenever the value of the slider is changed, the called function is invoked. The value can change due to the slider movement or by passing the setValue function.

Types of slider

script.aculo.us provides us the flexibility and comfort of two different orientations for the slider:

- Vertical slider
- Horizontal slider

Vertical slider

When the axis orientation of a slider is defined as vertical, the slider becomes and acts as a vertical slider.

Horizontal slider

When the axis orientation of a slider is defined as horizontal, the slider becomes and acts as a horizontal slider.

So let's get our hands dirty with code and start defining the constructors for horizontal and vertical slider with options. Trust me this will be fun.

Code usage for the slider

As a developer, I am sure you must have got a little bored reading *only* explanation. But hey hang on, we are getting into code!

Let's start with our HTML code and then the basic constructor definition of the slider.

The HTML code snippet is shown as follows:

```
<div id="track"><div id="handle1"></div>div>
```

Here, we have defined our track and handle as `<div>` elements.

The handle element should be placed inside the `track` element.

Good. So let's define the constructor for the slider here:

```
new Control.Slider('handle1', 'track1');
```

That's it! No, wait. We are missing something. Although the code is perfect, when we fire it up in the browser we can't see anything. That's because we need to style it.

The complete code with CSS is shown as follows:

```
<script type="text/javascript">
   window.onload = function() {
       new Control.Slider('handle1', 'track1'
       );
}
</script>
<style type="text/css">
h4{ font: 13px verdana }
#track1 {
   background-color:#BCE6D6;
   height: 1em;
   width: 150px;
}
```

```
#handle1 {
    background-color:#30679B;
    height: 1em;
    width: 6px;
}
</style>
<body>
<h4>Basic Slider Example</h4>
<div id="track1">
    <div id="handle1"></div>
</div>
```

And the resulting output is shown in the following screenshot:

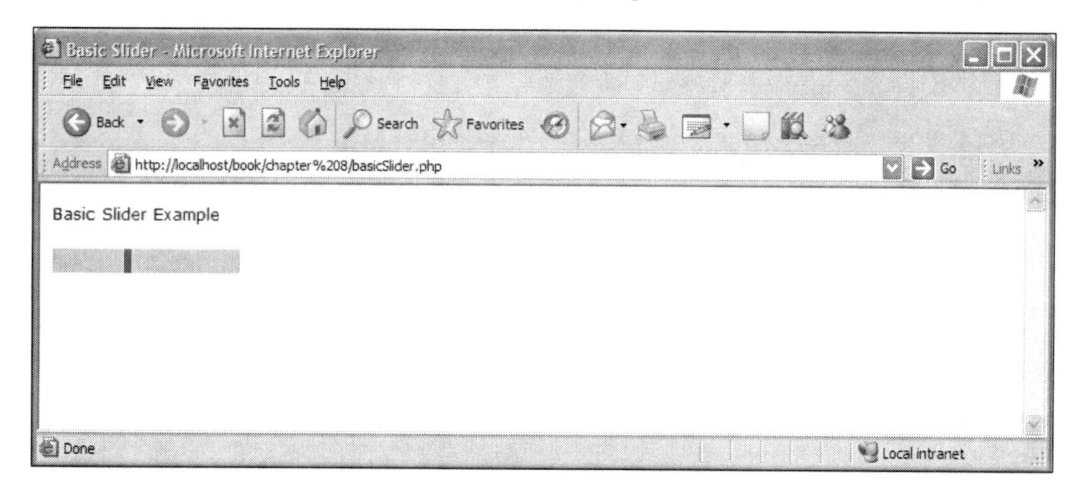

That's the most basic slider we created. And I am sure you are not content with that. We need to explore more.

Code usage for the vertical slider

Moving on, we will now create a vertical slider and add some options to enhance our slider feature.

Most of the code remains from the above example. We will focus on the required changes to be made in the above code.

As mentioned in the explanation above, we need to define the axis orientation as `vertical` in our options to make a slider vertical.

```
axis: 'vertical'
```

Chapter 8

So, the new constructor looks like the snippet shown as follows:

```
window.onload = function() {
  new Control.Slider('handle1', 'track1',
    {
    axis:'vertical'
    }
   );
}
```

And yes, since we are trying to make our slider vertical we need to change the CSS properties of height. The new CSS code will look like the following snippet:

```
#track1 {
   background-color:#BCE6D6;
   height: 10em;
   width: 15px;
}
#handle1 {
   background-color:#30679B;
   height: 1em;
   width: 15px;
}
```

So, the final script for the vertical slider is shown as follows:

```
<script type="text/javascript">
   window.onload = function() {
       new Control.Slider('handle1', 'track1',
         {
       axis:'vertical'
         }
         );
}
</script>
<style type="text/css">
h4{ font: 13px verdana }
#track1 {
   background-color:#BCE6D6;
   height: 10em;
   width: 15px;
}
#handle1 {
```

[141]

```
        background-color:#30679B;
        height: 1em;
        width: 15px;
}
</style>
</head>
<body>
<h4>Basic Vertical Slider Example</h4>
<div id="track1">
    <div id="handle1"></div>
</div>
```

And, the beautiful vertical slider is here! Check out the following screenshot:

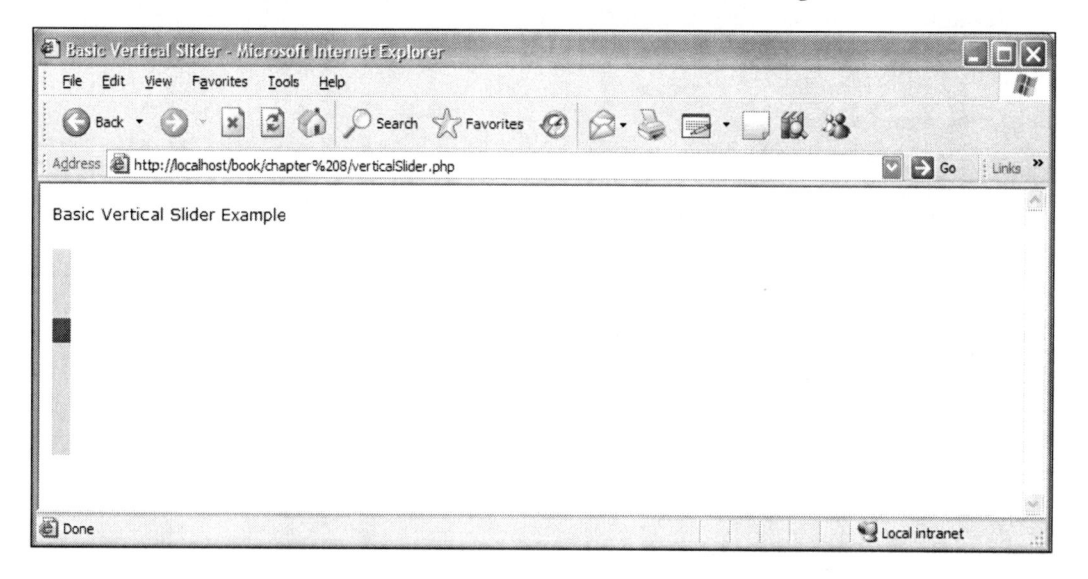

Code usage for the horizontal slider

We have seen how to create a vertical slider. We want you to have a wild guess of how to make a horizontal slider. Let me give you two hints:

- We don't have to struggle to make a slider horizontal. It's the default axis option.

- We can make a horizontal slider by passing the "horizontal" option to axis.

Which one would you prefer?

I am not going to give you code for this one though. But yes, I will guide you for doing the same. The code will be given in the next chapter.

We have already created one horizontal slider in the *Code usage for the horizontal slider* section. That was one approach. Now try changing the axis option to `horizontal` in the above code for the vertical slider.

You may also need to change some CSS properties for height and width, and I am sure you would love doing them. It's so much fun! After you make changes to the height and width parameters of the CSS properties, the screenshot of slider should look like the following:

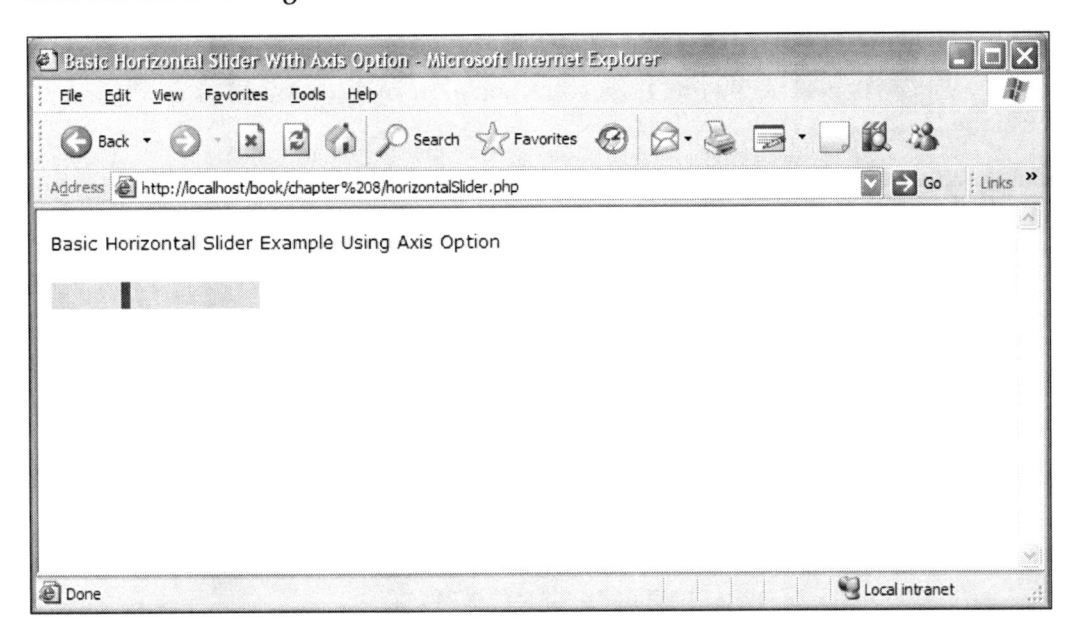

Code usage for sliders with options

We are now done with the most important part of the slider: the implementation of the slider in our applications.

But wait, we need the slider to suit our applications, right? So let's customize our slider with options.

Slider for Dynamic Applications using script.aculo.us

We have mentioned earlier that `track` is the range of values. So let's first define the range for our slider.

```
window.onload = function() {
      new Control.Slider('handle1', 'track1',
          {
    axis:'vertical',
    range:$R(1,100)
    }
```

The range option uses the Prototypes' `objectRange` instance. Hence, we declare it using

`$R (minimum, Maximum)`.

Everything looks neat until here. Let's add some more options to our constructor, `onSlide()`.

Using the `onSlide()` callback every time, we drag the slider and the callback is invoked. The default parameter passed to `onSlide()` is the current slider value.

```
window.onload = function() {
      new Control.Slider('handle1', 'track1',
          {
    axis:'vertical',
    range:$R(1,100),
    onSlide: function(v) { $('value1').innerHTML = "New Slide
                                                  Value="+v;}
    }
```

We have added a div called `value1` in our HTML code. On dragging the slider, we will update the `value1` with the current slider value.

OK, so let's see what happened to our slider uptill now. Check out the following screenshot:

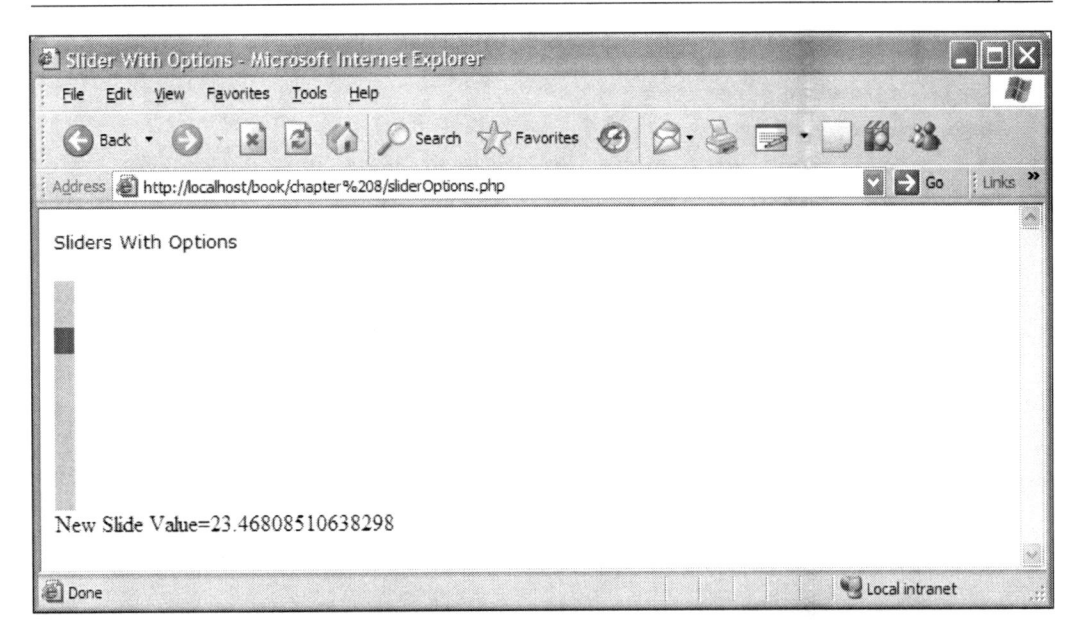

Impressed? And, we are not done yet. Let's add more options to the slider now.

You may ask me, what if the slider in the application needs to be at a particular value by default? And I will say use the `sliderValue` option. Let's make our slider value `10` by default. Here is the snippet for the same:

```
window.onload = function() {
      new Control.Slider('handle1', 'track1',
      {
        axis:'vertical',
        range:$R(1,100),
        sliderValue: 10,
        onSlide: function(v) { $('value1').innerHTML =
                         "New Slide Value="+v;}
      }
}
```

And, you should see the slider value at `10` when you run the code.

Now your dear friend will ask, what if we don't want to give the range, but we need to pass the fixed set of values? And you proudly say, use the `values` option.

Check out the usage of the values options in the constructor.

```
window.onload = function() {
 new Control.Slider('handle1', 'track1',
 {
    range:$R(1,25),
    values:[1, 5,10,15,20,25],
    onSlide:function(v){ $('value1').innerHTML = "New Slide
                                                 Value="+v;}
  }
 );
}
```

We have added a set of values in the array form and passed it to our constructor. Let's see what it looks like.

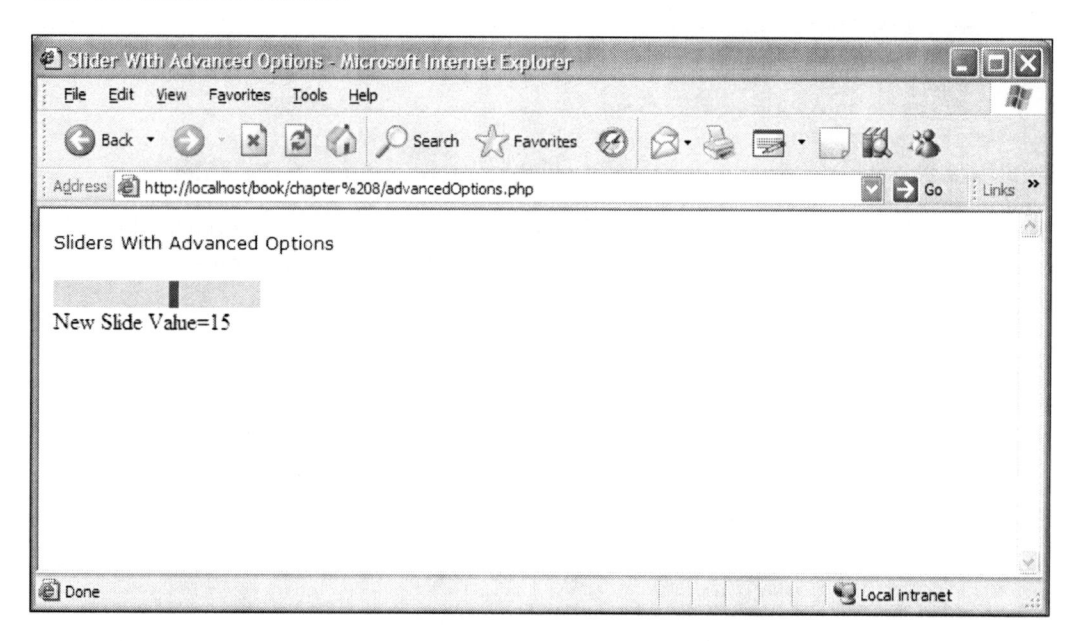

Tips and tricks with the slider

After covering all the aspects of the slider feature, here is a list of simple tips and tricks which we can make use of in our applications with ease.

Reading the current value of the slider

script.aculo.us "genie" provides us with two callbacks for the slider to read the current value of the slider. They are:

- onSlide
- onChange

Both these callbacks are used as a part of options in the slider.

onSlide contains the current sliding value while the drag is on. The callback syntax is shown as follows:

```
onSlide: function(value) {
// do something with the value while sliding. Write or Edit the
//value of current slider value while sliding
}
```

onChange callback will contain the value of the slider while the "sliding" or the drag event ends. After the drag is completed and if the value of the slider has changed then the onChange function will be called. For example, if the slider's current value is set to 10 and after sliding we change it to 15, then the onChange callback will be fired. The callback syntax is shown as follows:

```
onChange: function(value){
    // do anything with the "changed" and current value
}
```

Multiple handles in the slider

Now, a thought comes to our mind at this point: Is it possible for us to have two handles in one track?

And, the mighty script.aculo.us library says yes!

Check out the following code snippet and screenshot for a quick glance of having two handles in one track:

```
HTML code
<div id="track1">
   <div id="handle1"></div>
   <div id="handle2"></div>
</div>
```

JavaScript code for the same:

```
window.onload = function() {
      new Control.Slider(['handle1','handle2'] , 'track1'
      );
}
```

Now, check out the resulting screenshot having two handles and one track:

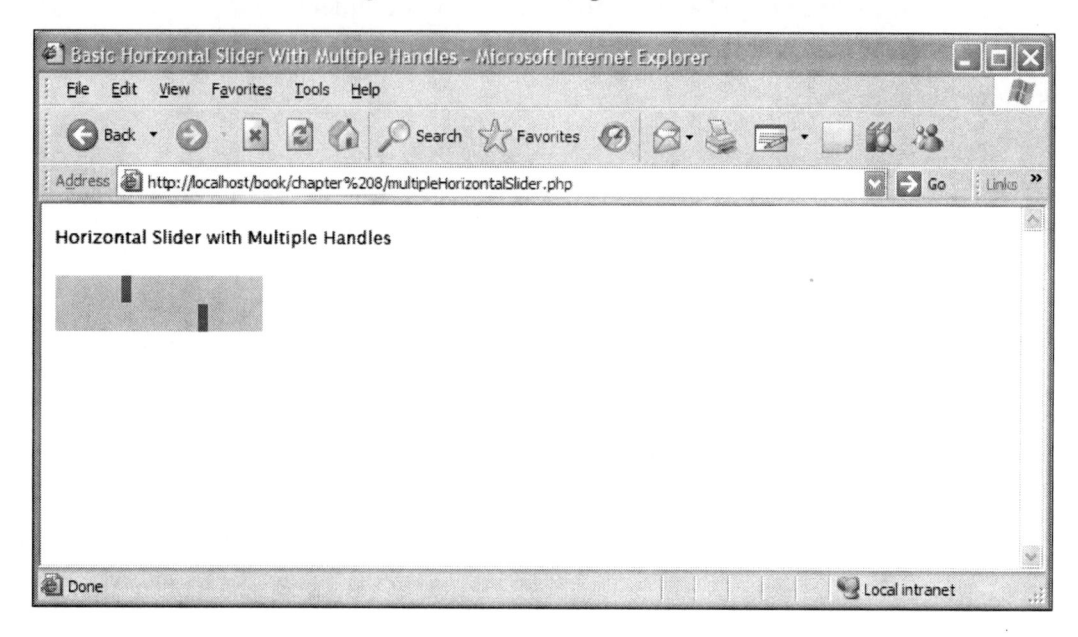

The same can also be applied for the vertical slider too.

Disabling the slider

We can disable our slider element using the option: `disabled`. We need to pass `true` to set the element in the disabled state. By default the value is set to `false`.

Our constructor definition would look like the code snippet shown as follows:

```
window.onload = function() {
 new Control.Slider('handle1', 'track1',
 {
    range:$R(1,25),
    values:[1, 5,10,15,20,25],
     disabled:true,
```

```
                onSlide:function(v){ $('value1').innerHTML = "New Slide
                                                             Value="+v;}
    }
  );
}
```

The `disabled` option will initially make the element's state disabled, and we can change this state using `setDisabled`.

Enabling the slider

As we can disable our slider element using the `disabled` option, we can also enable the element using the same option by passing the value as `false`.

Our constructor definition would look like the code snippet shown as follows:

```
window.onload = function() {
  new Control.Slider('handle1', 'track1',
  {
     range:$R(1,25),
     values:[1, 5,10,15,20,25],
      disabled:false,
      onSlide:function(v){ $('value1').innerHTML = "New Slide
                                                   Value="+v;}
    }
  );
}
```

By default the value of the `disabled` option is `false`. The elements are enabled, and we can change the state using `setEnabled`.

Hands-on example: Using vertical and horizontal slider

Now that we have worked with vertical and horizontal slider, wouldn't it be a great idea to see both types of the slider on the same page? Yes indeed.

Let's get started.

At a very basic level, we can change the `Axis` option of slider and we can get either the horizontal or vertical slider.

So now we will have two slider types on one page, and the only difference is in the axis orientation.

We need to create two tracks and the respective handles for the slider `<div>`s. The HTML part of the code is given as follows:

```
<h4>Mashup of Horizontal + Vertical Sliders</h4>
<div id="track1" class="track">
   <div id="handle1" class="handle"></div>
</div>
<div id="track2">
   <div id="handle2"></div>
</div>
```

This code is pretty simple. We have created a `<div>` as track1 and its respective inner `<div>` to hold the value as handle1. Similarly, we have created one more slider `<div>` as track2 and its handle as handle2.

After a bit of trendy dressing up of, and applying make-up to, the CSS, the basic slider looks like the following screenshot:

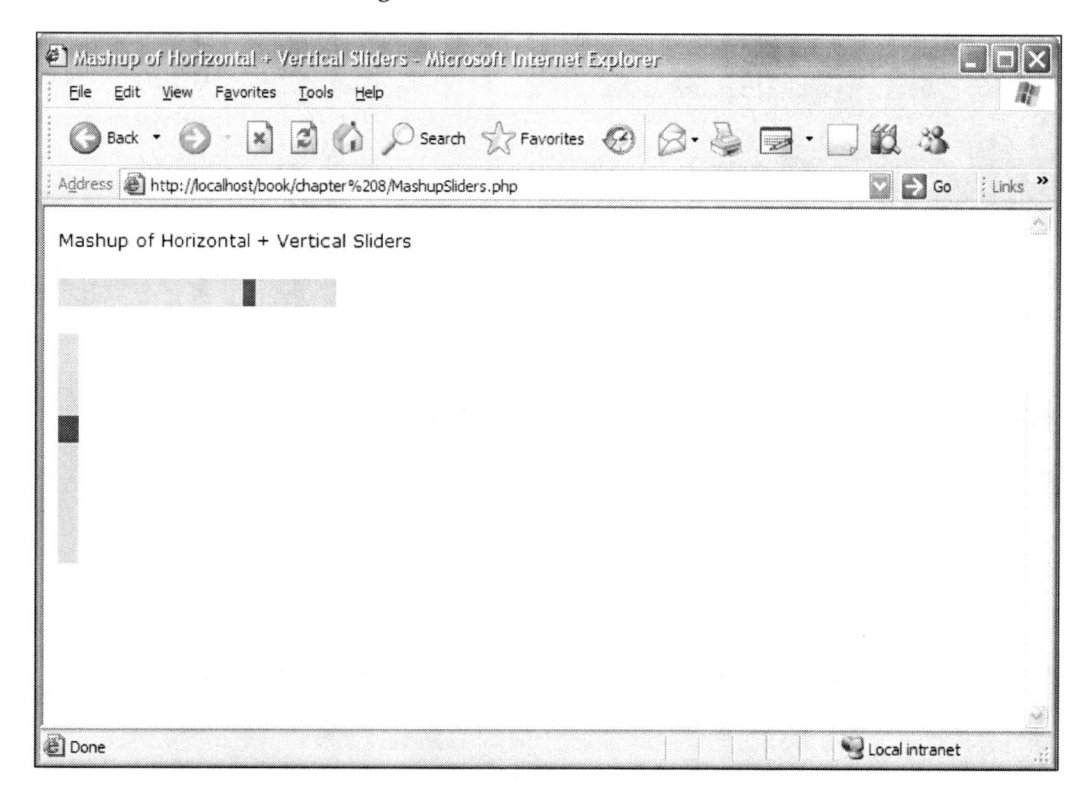

Chapter 8

The CSS code is given here:

```css
h4{ font: 13px verdana }
#track1 {
   background-color:#BCE6D6;
   height: 1em;
   width: 200px;
}
#handle1 {
   background-color:#30679B;
   height: 0.5em;
   width: 10px;
}
#track2 {
   background-color:#BCE6D6;
   height: 10em;
   width: 15px;
 }
 #handle2 {
   background-color:#30679B;
   height: 1em;
   width: 15px;
}
#sliding {
font: 13px verdana;
}
#changed {
font: 13px verdana;
}
```

OK, so now we have our slider in our page. Wait, we are missing something. Are you wondering where is the scripting and functionality?

Before that, let's add two divs, which will help us view the current values using the onChange and onSlide callbacks.

```html
<p id="sliding"></p>
<p id="changed"></p>
```

Now let's first add script.aculo.us power to track1, our first slider.

```javascript
new Control.Slider('handle1', 'track1',
     {
            range: $R(1,50),
            values: [1,5,15,25,35,45,50],
            sliderValue: 1,
            onChange: function(value){
```

[151]

```
            $('changed').innerHTML = 'Changed Value : '+value;
        },
        onSlide: function(value) {
            $('sliding').innerHTML = 'Sliding Value: '+value;
        }
    } );
```

Let's take a closer look at the above code and see what is happening.

We have defined `range`, `values`, and `sliderValue` options for the slider. We have also added two callbacks `onChange` and `onSlide`. As I mentioned earlier, these callbacks get the *current* value of the slider as a parameter.

Hence, we are reading values from both the callbacks and updating the divs' *sliding* and *changed* when the event occurs.

Also, since we did not exclusively mention the axis definition, the default is `horizontal`.

So, the application now looks like the following screenshot:

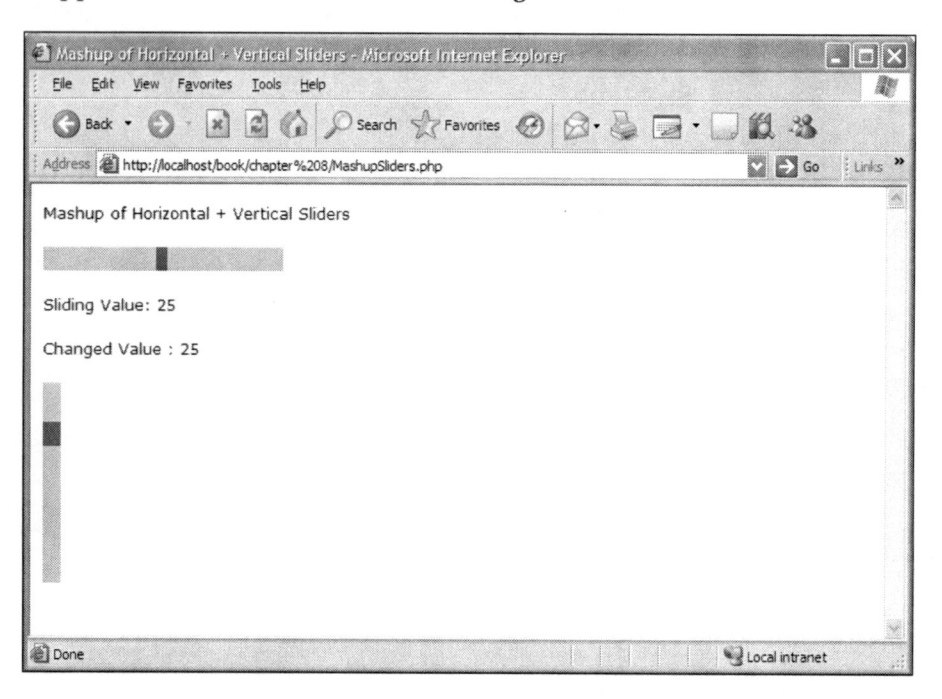

Remember, the values will *only* be updated if we move the horizontal slider. And, nothing happens if we slide through the vertical slider. We have not yet defined the functionality for the vertical slider. Let's do it now.

The code for the vertical slider will also remain mostly similar with only difference of `axis` orientation.

```
new Control.Slider('handle2', 'track2',
     {
          range: $R(1,50),
          axis:'vertical',
          sliderValue: 1,
          onChange: function(value){
               $('changed').innerHTML =
                    'Changed Value : '+value;
          },
          onSlide: function(value) {
               $('sliding').innerHTML =
                    'Sliding Value: '+value;
          }
     } );
```

You can notice the fact that the callback definition remains the same for the vertical slider as well.

So now when we move the vertical slider, the value gets updated in the *sliding* and *changed* `<div>`s. They get updated with the current value.

The complete module with both horizontal and vertical slider is shown as follows:

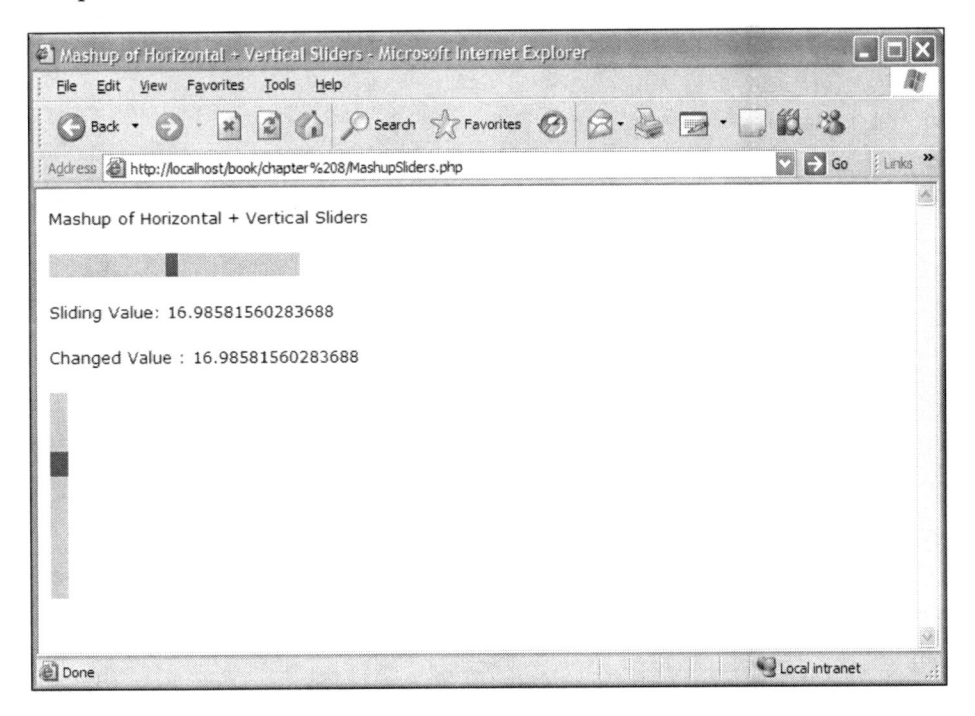

Summary

In this chapter we have learned and explored the following topics:

- Introduction to the slider using script.aculo.us
- Explanation of the slider
- Different types of the slider
- Options provided with the slider
- Code usage for the slider and options
- Tips and tricks with slider
- Hands-on example for the horizontal and vertical slider

So far we have learned all the features of script.aculo.us in detail. We have also worked on some hands-on examples to make us more comfortable using the features of script.aculo.us in our own applications.

But we think it would be nice to have a cheat sheet of all the features in one page. This would act as a reference for us at any point in time. We will cover all this and more in the next chapter!

9
script.aculo.us in One Go

We have explored all the features of script.aculo.us so far. We started with a simple one-line effect to go deep into the Prototype library, which includes everything from PHP techniques to effects, from drag-drop to in-place editing, and finally from autocompletion to slider.

Each of these features has its own significant importance and, when used effectively, can help you in making the next *BIG* thing on the Web.

The script.aculo.us features are very useful, but do we have any quick reference for all of them?

We are going to create one now. At any point if we want to see the feature and its quick implementation, remind yourself of all the quick hands-on examples we will learn in this chapter.

Here's a quick list of the key topics that we will explore in this chapter:

- A hands-on example: Multiple script.aculo.us features mash up
- A quick glance at all of the features of script.aculo.us

Hands-on example: Multiple script.aculo.us features mash up

So far we have worked with features individually. But if we look closely, we will find that some of the features are quite interdependent.

Let's see and work with some of these features. We will aim to get some of the key features of script.aculo.us onto one page.

Adding in-place editing in page

So your friend liked the in-place editing feature? OK! We will start with it.

The basic HTML code for in-place editing is shown as follows:

```
<div id="editme">Click to Edit Me</div>
```

This way we have created a simple `<div>` element, which we will make editable.

Let's make it trendy using CSS.

```
#editme{
    width: 200px;
    font: 13px verdana;
}
```

We have now specified the `width` and `font` for the `<div>` element. You are welcome to add even more CSS style elements to make it even better.

Let's move on to the most interesting part. Yes, you guessed it right, playing with script.aculo.us. Add the required script.aculo.us files here:

```
<script type="text/javascript" src="src/lib/prototype.js">
</script>
<script type="text/javascript" src="src/src/scriptaculous.js">
</script>
<script type="text/javascript" src="src/src/effects.js"></script>
<script type="text/javascript" src="src/src/controls.js"></script>
```

Now, let's make our in-place element editable.

```
new Ajax.InPlaceEditor($('editme'), '/server-side-script.php');
```

That was super cool. Again, we did it just in one line. Wow! Check out how it looks on this page:

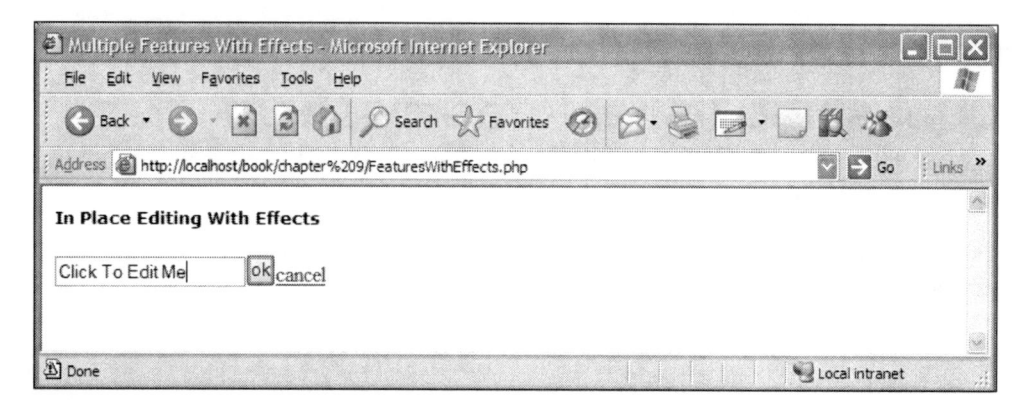

Adding effects to the page

Since we are trying to make use of the script.aculo.us features in a combination, let's add *beauty* to our in-place editing:

```
new Ajax.InPlaceEditor($('editme'), '/server-side-script.php',
    {highlightcolor:'#BCE6D6'});
```

We have added the `highlight` option to our in-place editor. We are overriding the default color with our new color. Now check out how the new in-place editor looks:

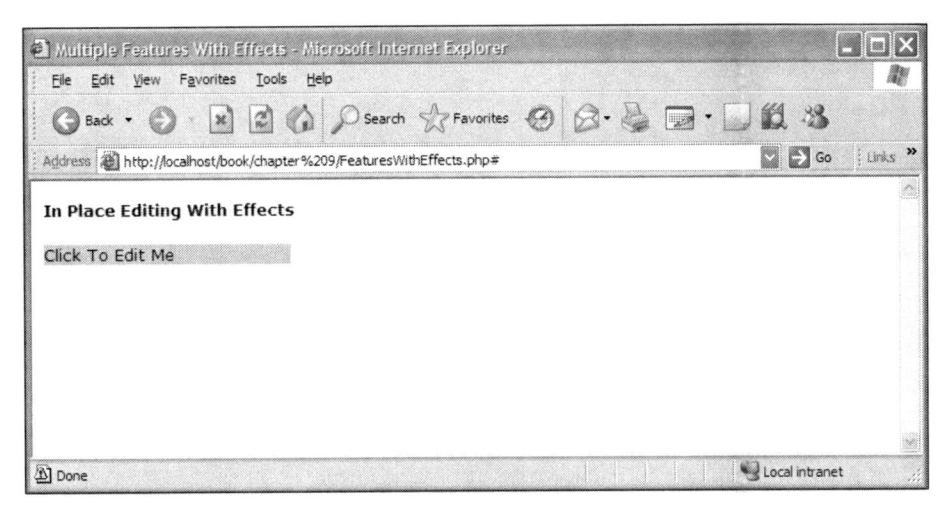

How about adding the drag and drop feature?

We are content with what we just did, but I think we can do much better. Yes, we can add more features to the page. Let's also add the drag and drop feature.

Start with the following basic HTML code:

```
<h4 id="section">Drag & Drop With Effects</h4>
<div id="myDrag">
iPhone <p>
</div>
```

And, let's add some style with CSS as follows:

```
#myDrag {
    font: 13px verdana;
    background-color:#E2F1B1;
    width:300px;
}
```

[157]

We are adding `width`, `font`, and `background-color` style elements to our drag and drop element. Check out the following screenshot:

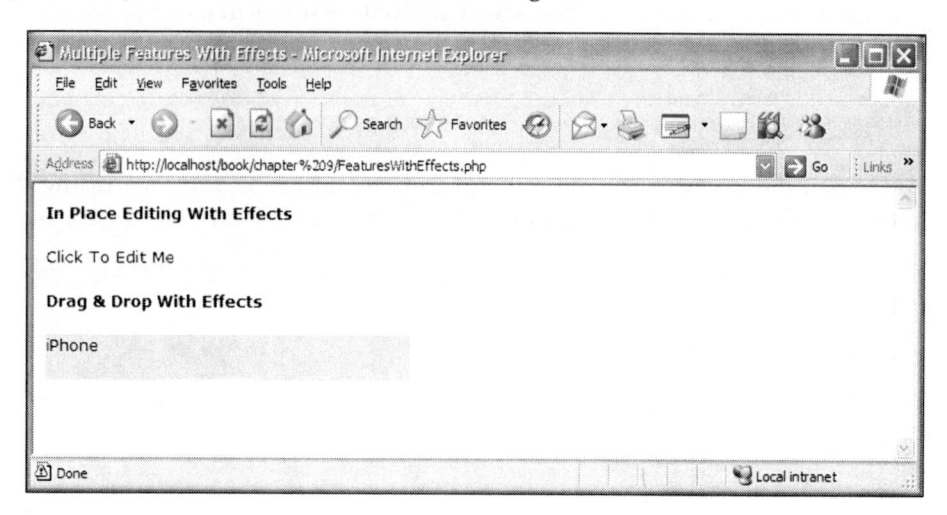

What about the functionality of drag and drop element? Let's spice it up.

```
new Draggable('myDrag',{revert:true});
```

So our element is all set to get dragged and dropped. Check out the following screenshot:

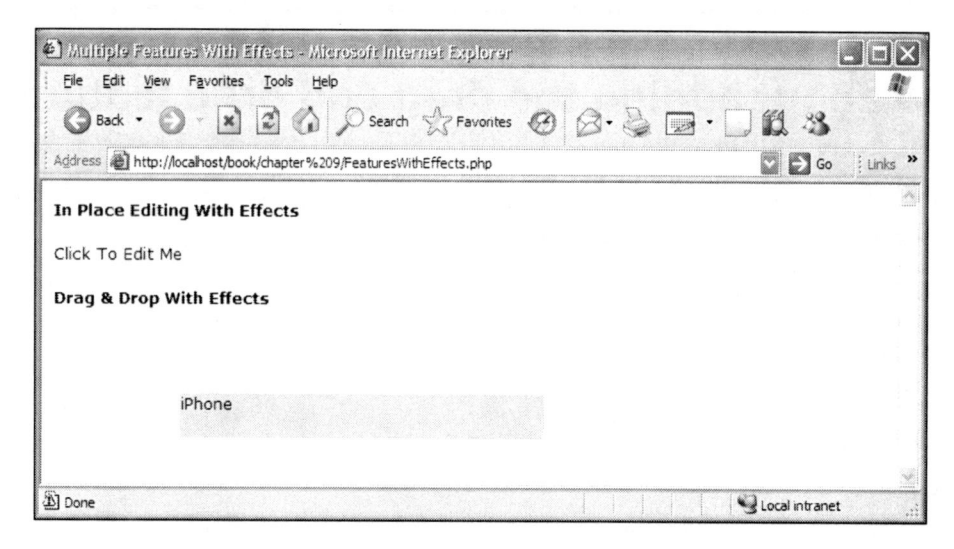

And, how about adding some effects to our element? Yes, your neighbor would love it.

```
new Draggable('myDrag',{revert:true, endeffect: function(element){
                        new Effect.Opacity(element,
                        {from:0, to:1.0, duration:10} )
            }});
```

We have added effects to the `endEffect` option of the drag and drop feature. We are adding the opacity effect and mentioning the time duration for the same. Check out the effects in action after the drag action is complete, in the following screenshot:

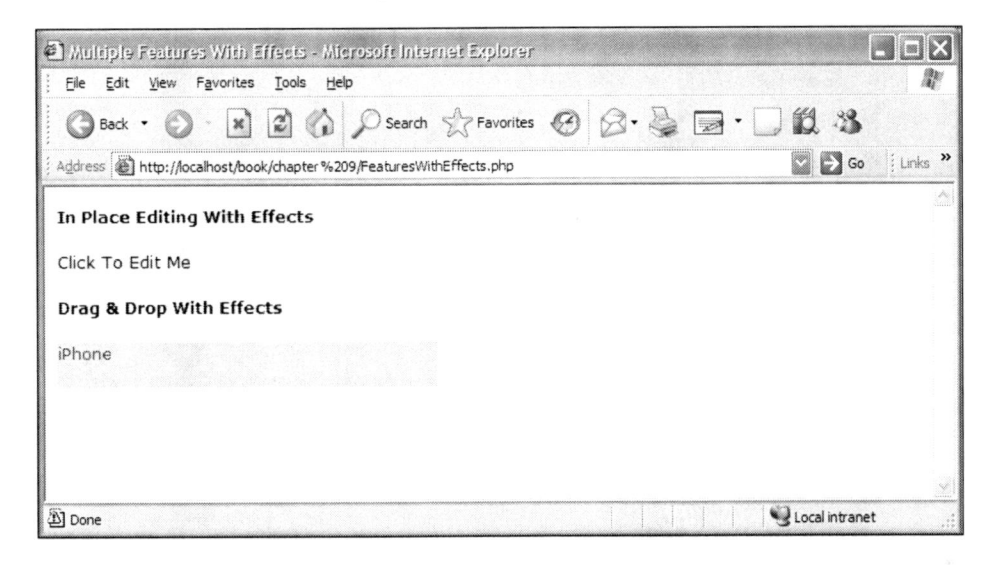

Everything looks fine to this point. Can we please add one more feature? You can add as many features (or users) as you want.

Out of the box thinking—adding multiple features to an element

This has all been the traditional way of using features. In the 2.0 era of application, mash up is the buzz word. So why not mash up these features? Sounds exciting? Good.

Let's call this out of the box thinking.

We are going to have an in-place editing element that can be dragged and dropped, and have effects to inform the user. Here's how we will proceed with it.

The HTML code for creating the element is as follows:

```html
<h4 id="section">(Out Of Box) Drag & Drop + In Place Editing With Effects</h4>
<div id="dragedit">Drag Me Or Click To Edit</div>
<p>
```

We created a simple `<div>` element with `id`.

Some CSS style please!

```css
#dragedit{
    width: 200px;
     font: 13px verdana;
     background-color:#BCE6D6;
}
```

Ok! So we have an element ready to be molded into an in-place editor and drag and drop element. Check out the following screenshot:

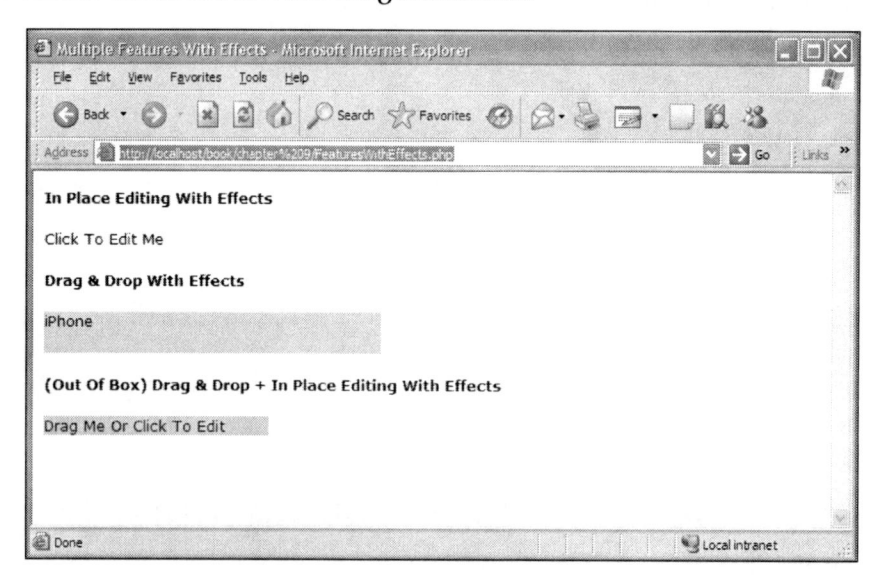

Fine! So now we need to make the element editable.

```
new Ajax.InPlaceEditor($('dragedit'), '/server-side-script.php');
```

Now the element is editable. The user can click on the element and they will see an edit area.

Similarly, let us now also make the element draggable.

```
new Draggable('dragedit', {revert:true});
```

So what does it result in? Check out the screenshots that follow.

We can click on the element and edit the value, since we made it editable.

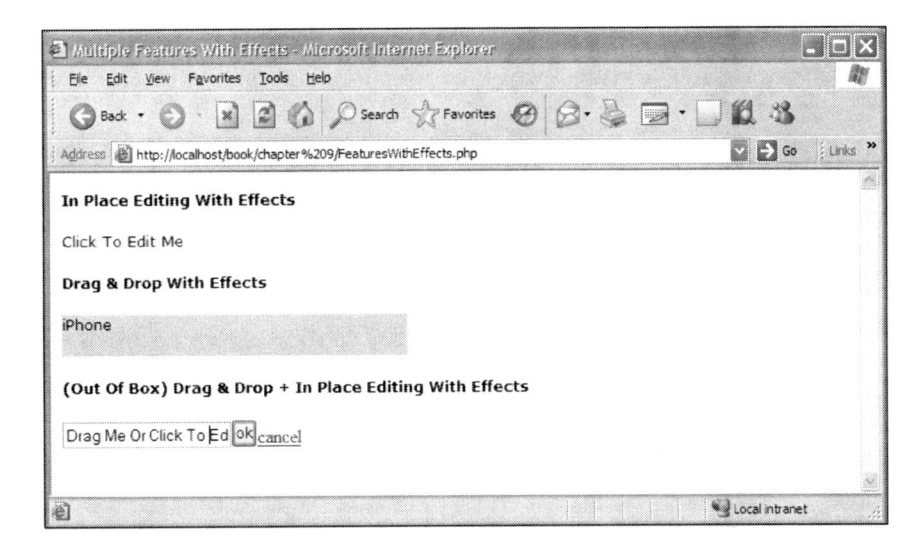

We can also drag the element to any particular location of the page, since we have made it draggable.

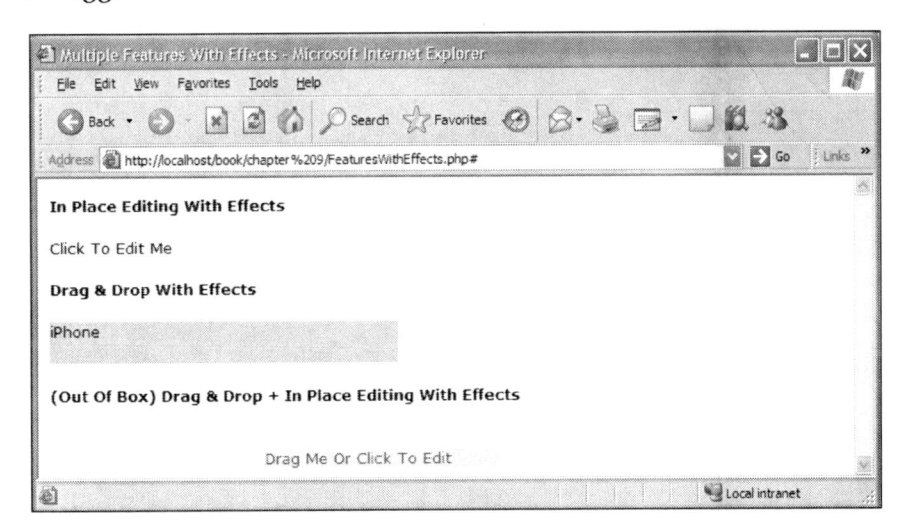

This was just one simple instance of the product of creative cells in the right brain. I am sure you can come up with many more instances.

The idea is to use different features in a clean and clear way to improve functionality as well as the user interface experience. Get your thinking gears on!

Hands-on example: Quick revision of all the features of script.aculo.us in one page

We have worked with multiple features of script.aculo.us. Let's move on to create a full example page to show all the features together on one page. Here we go.

Let's start with effects

We have to admit, effects are something we love to play with in our applications. So let's first play with some effects. But before that, include all the required script.aculo.us files here:

```
<script type="text/javascript" src="src/lib/prototype.js">
</script>
<script type="text/javascript" src="src/src/scriptaculous.js">
</script>
<script type="text/javascript" src="src/src/effects.js"></script>
<script type="text/javascript" src="src/src/controls.js"></script>
```

The HTML code for getting the effects is as follows:

```
<h4 id="section">Effects In Scriptaculous</h4>
<div id="effects">
<div id="dropout" onclick="new Effect.DropOut(this);">
Drop Out Effect</div>
<br>
<div id="fade" onclick="new Effect.Fade(this);">Fade Effect</div>
<br>
<div id="blinddown" onclick="new Effect.BlindDown(this);">
BlindDown Effect</div>
<br>
<div id="ex-highlight" onclick="new Effect.Highlight(this);">
  Highlight Effect</div>
<br>
</div>
<p>
```

We have added four effects here, but feel free to use as many effects as you wish to (as mentioned in Chapter 4).

We are calling the `onclick` event actions on each of the `<div>`s we have created. We are calling the event actions. Check out what it results in.

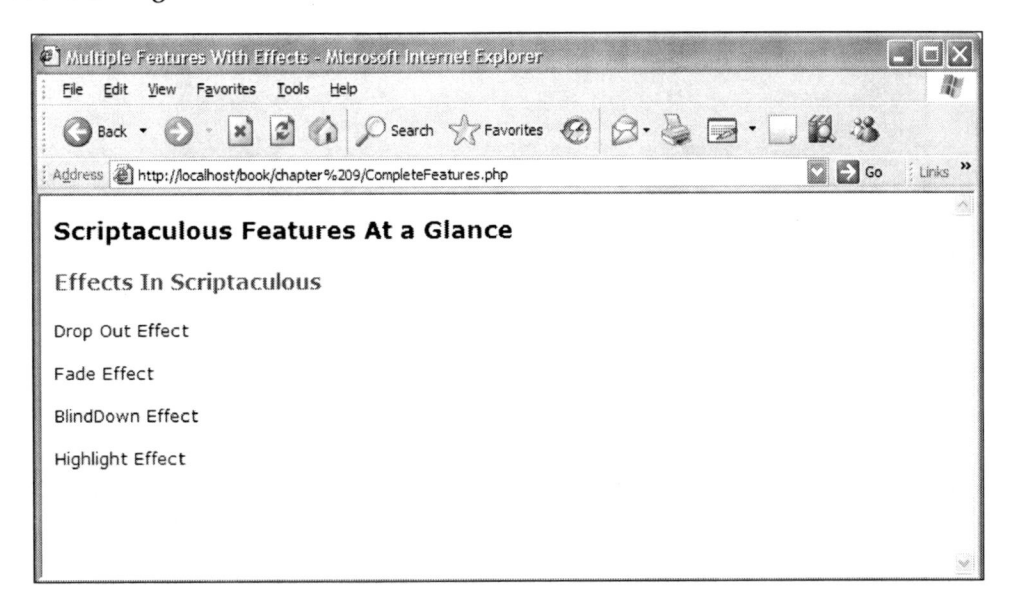

Add CSS to style up the effects in the user interface. Now, try clicking on those links for the effects and you should be able to see the effects on your page. Try adding a few more effects as practice.

Some in-place editing

Moving on, we are going to add the in-place editing element. Let's add the HTML code for the in-place editor.

```
<h4 id="section">In Place Editing With Effects</h4>
<div id="editme">Click To Edit Me</div>
<p>
```

Let's add some JavaScript to the element.

```
new Ajax.InPlaceEditor($('editme'), '/server-side-script.php',
   {highlightcolor:'#BCE6D6'});
```

Check out the following screenshot:

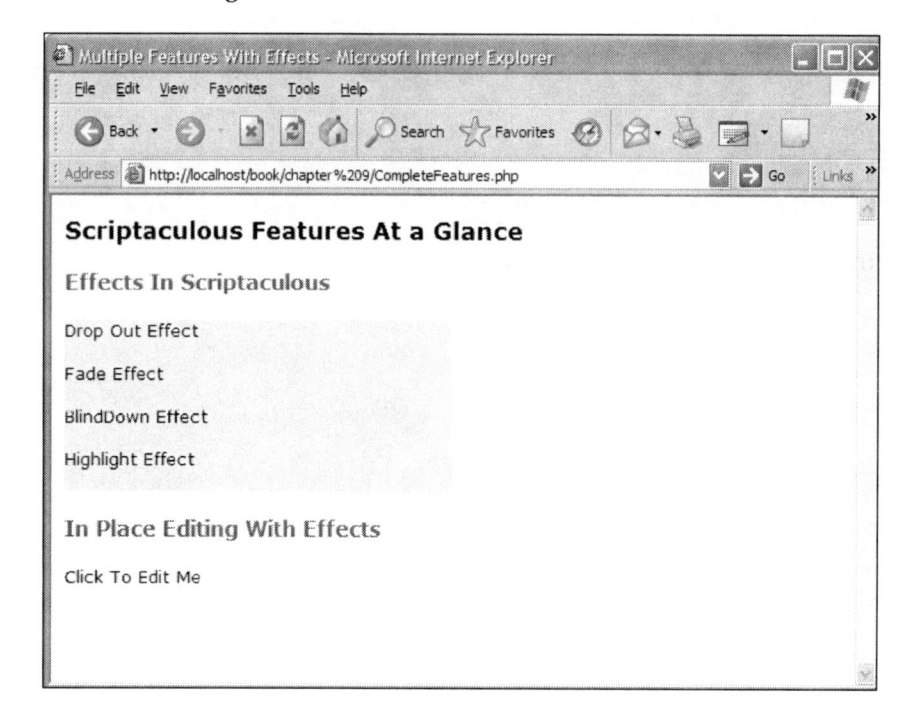

A little bit of drag and drop

Similarly, we will be adding the drag and drop element to the page. The HTML code is given as follows:

```
<h4 id="section">Drag & Drop With Effects</h4>
    <div id="myDrag">iPhone <p>
    </div>
<p>
```

And, the corresponding scripting is shown as follows:

```
new Draggable('myDrag',{revert:true, endeffect: function(element){
                        new Effect.Opacity(element,
                            {from:0, to:1.0, duration:10} )
                    }});
```

The resulting page is shown as follows:

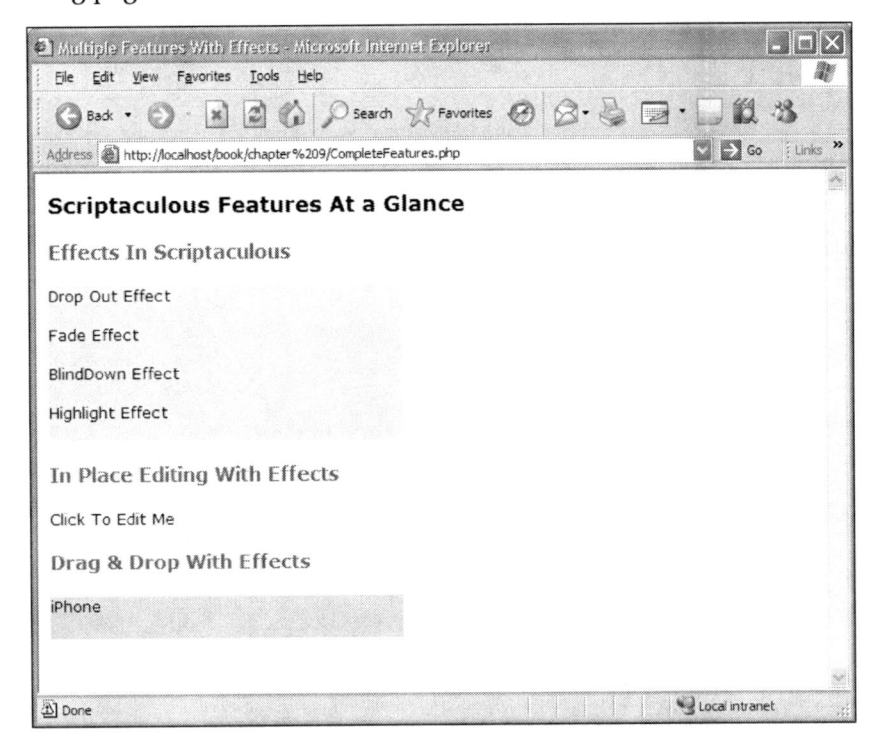

The slider needs to be in picture too

The slider is also a pretty handy feature, so let's add it too. Here's how we go about it:

```
<h4 id="section">Sliders with Scriptaculous</h4>
<div id="track1">
    <div id="handle1"></div>
</div>
```

And the corresponding script for the element is shown as follows:

```
new Control.Slider('handle1', 'track1');
```

We need to dress up the element in a more presentable form. The required CSS code is as follows:

```
#track1 {
    background-color:#BCE6D6;
    height: 1em;
    width: 150px;
}
#handle1 {
    background-color:#30679B;
    height: 0.5em;
    width: 7px;
}
```

And now the new page looks like the following screenshot:

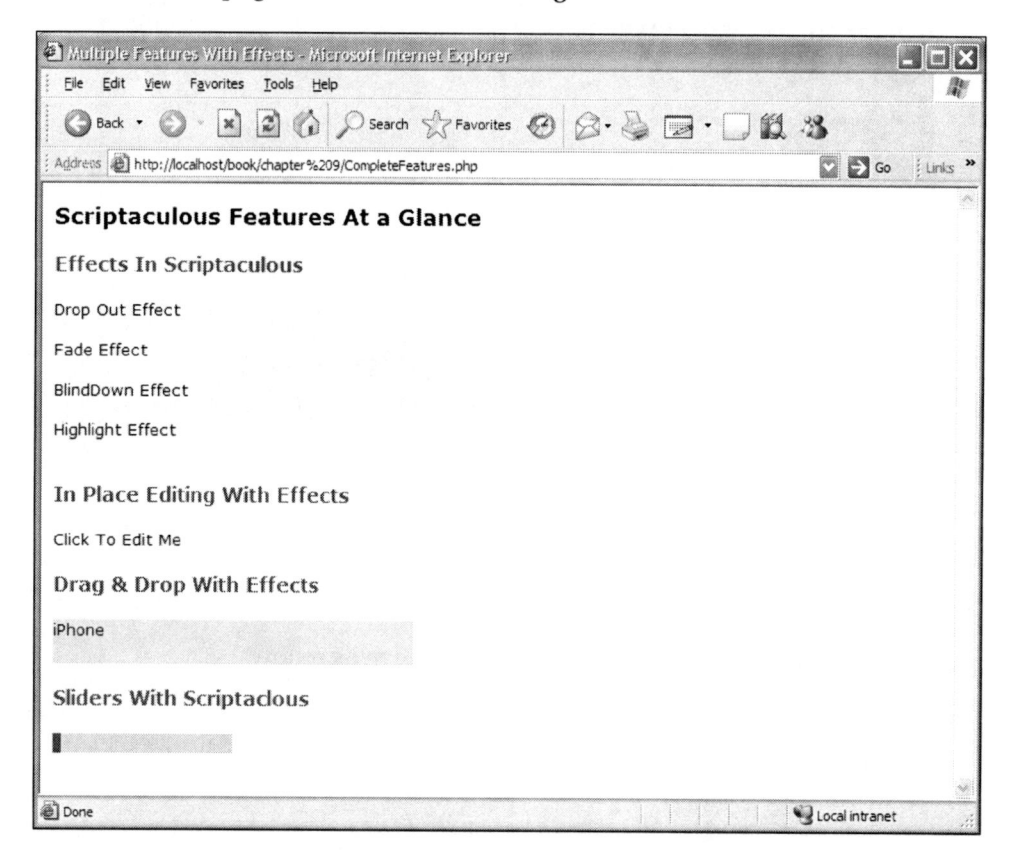

How can we miss music?

Now, assume you need some rest from these features and want to listen to your favorite song. Well, you can do it right here.

Include the required script.aculo.us file to play the song.

```
<script src="includes/scriptaculous/src/sound.js"
        type="text/javascript"></script>
```

Now, play the song right from your browser.

```
<h4 id="section">Multi Media with Scriptaculous</h4>
<a href="#" onclick="Sound.play('Track01.MP3');
    return false">Play Song</a>
```

I am playing *Track01*. Just replace it with the song you want to listen to and hit **Play**.

By the way, which song are you going to play?

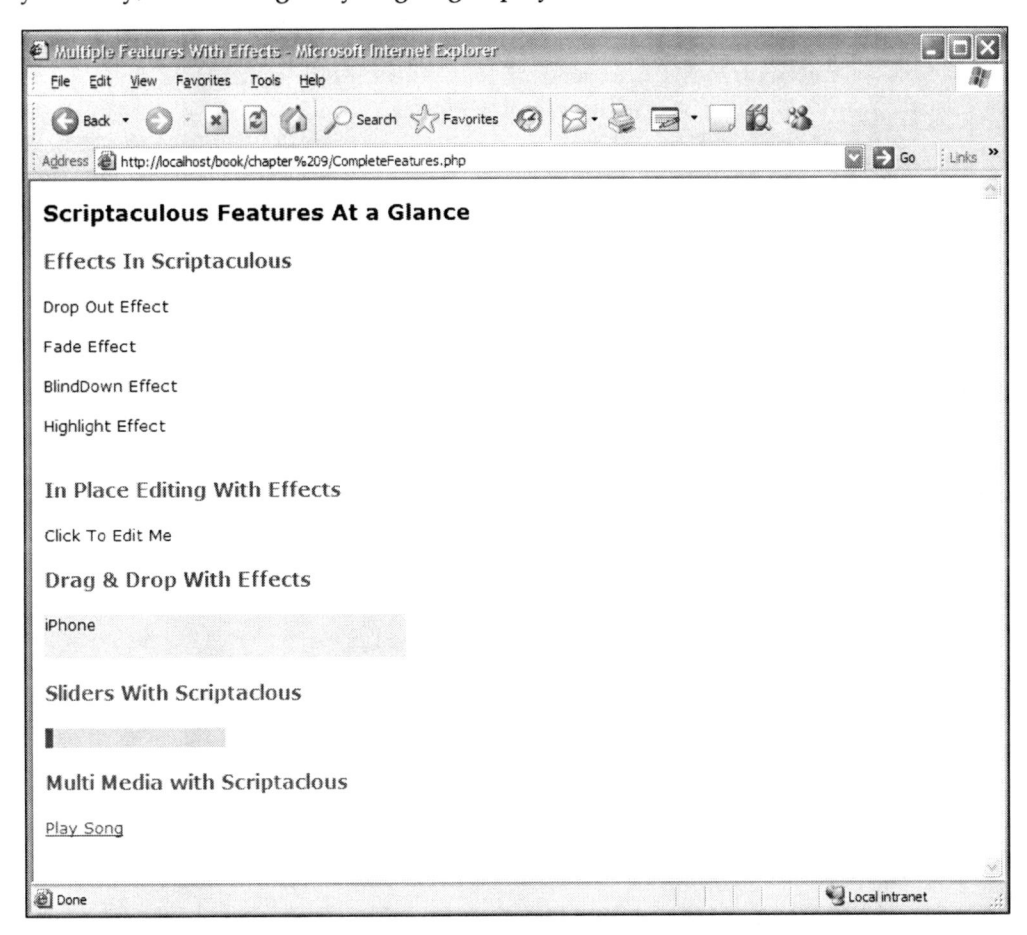

Summary

Exploring the script.aculo.us library was a wonderful journey. We promised you in the beginning that this was going to be a rocking experience.

Learning and working with features such as effects, in-place editing, drag and drop, multimedia, slider, and autocompletion was real fun.

Some of the hands-on examples that we looked at in this chapter are:

- Exploring the features of script.aculo.us as a mash up
- Quick glance of all the script.aculo.us features in one page for reference

We are now skilled and armed with the technical knowledge of the script.aculo.us library. It's time for us to get into building some real-world applications.

To start with, we are going to create a clone of `Tadalist.com` and many more such simple yet *killer* web applications.

And, before we move on to the next section, let's take a moment to thank the wonderful community for supporting script.aculo.us.

10
Todonow: A Tadalist Clone

I have a lot of things on my mind before leaving my house such as visiting the bank, buying vegetables, or office work. But whatever is on my mind is there on my `tadalist.com` application too.

Tadalist is a simple web application for making lists and managing items. It comes in handy all the time. So after learning script.aculo.us, why don't we try to create our own Tadalist clone? Hang on. Before we proceed and create an application, let's give it a Web 2.0-ish name—say **todonow**. Get, set, and code!

Some of the key points we will be covering in this chapter are:

- The BIG picture of the application
- Features and functionalities
- Creating a database for the project
- Implementing all the features of the application

The BIG picture

Let's quickly get a complete picture of what the application is and what it should do. In simple words, we are trying to create a to-do list manager. As a user, we should be able to sign up, log in, and log out as mentioned in Chapter 3 in the *User login management system* module.

- The user should be able to create lists and add items to a list
- The user can mark items as completed, when done
- The user will see completed items as well as incomplete tasks

All these operations will be performed when the user is logged in. And, finally, the user can log out.

Features and functionality

Now that we are clear about what our application will do, let's quickly get an overview of the features and functionality that our application will have.

- User signup
- User login
- View all my lists
- Show a summary of items for lists (in complete status)
- Create new lists
- Add new items
- Mark items as completed
- Mark complete items as incomplete
- Delete lists
- Logout

These features and functionalities are the fundamental requirements for any to-do list manager. You may think there are too many features and functionalities to code. Nope! We have already implemented some of them in our *User login management system*.

Creating a database playground

Having a clear picture of **todonow** gives us clarity about the kind of data we will be dealing with. In our application, users will create lists, add items, update the status of the items, and so on.

We explored and used the phpMyAdmin application to work with the MySQL database in Chapter 3. We will be using phpMyAdmin again for creating our database tables.

We will need three tables for user information, lists, and items, to store the corresponding data in our application. So, let's quickly create the tables for users, lists, and items.

We have already created the schema for the user table in our login management system in Chapter 3.

The fields for the database table `lists` are as follows:

- `listID`: This is the primary key to identify the lists individually. It is defined as `auto_increment`, which means our system will automatically increase the value of this field every time we add entries. In Oracle SQL, we call these fields a *sequence*.
- `ListName`: This is the name of the list provided by the user.
- `ownerID`: This tracks the user of the list.
- `Date`: This is the time when the list was created.

The database schema for storing lists is as follows:

```
CREATE TABLE `lists` (
  `listID` int(11) NOT NULL auto_increment,
  `ListName` varchar(50) NOT NULL,
  `ownerID` int(11) NOT NULL,
  `Date` timestamp NOT NULL default CURRENT_TIMESTAMP on update CURRENT_TIMESTAMP,
  PRIMARY KEY  (`listID`)
) ENGINE=InnoDB DEFAULT CHARSET=latin1 AUTO_INCREMENT=1 ;
```

Similarly, fields for the database table `items` are as follows:

- `ItemID`: It is the primary key to identify the items individually. This is defined as `auto_increment`, which means that the system will automatically increase the value of this field every time we add entries. In Oracle SQL, we call these fields a *sequence*.
- `ListID`: This helps in identifying the parent of items.
- `ItemName`: This is the name of the item provided by the user.
- `Status`: This shows whether the item is complete or incomplete.
- `ownerID`: This tracks the user of the list.
- `Date`: This is the time when the list was created.

The database schema for storing the items is as follows:.

```
CREATE TABLE `items` (
  `ItemID` int(11) NOT NULL auto_increment,
  `ListID` int(11) NOT NULL,
  `ownerID` int(11) NOT NULL,
  `itemName` varchar(40) NOT NULL,
  `status` enum('Incomplete','Completed') NOT NULL,
  `Date` timestamp NOT NULL default CURRENT_TIMESTAMP,
  PRIMARY KEY  (`ItemID`)
) ENGINE=InnoDB DEFAULT CHARSET=latin1 AUTO_INCREMENT=1 ;
```

Todonow: A Tadalist Clone

> We shall loop through the code snippets for each feature to understand it better. The complete code is available to download for free at the URL given in the *Preface* of the book.

Let's log in...

I am sure you must have figured out that I am referring to the login management system that we created in Chapter 3.

Check out the following screenshot from Chapter 3 for a quick reference:

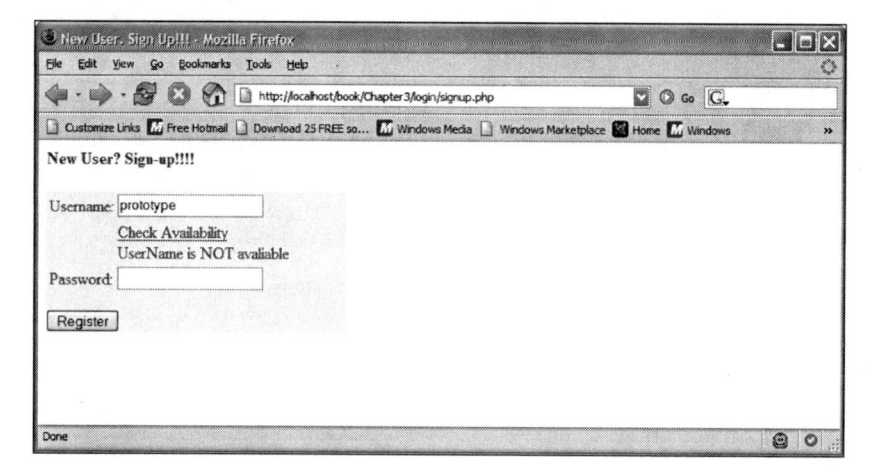

Once we log in to the application, we don't see much happening. What we created in Chapter 3 was just a simple secured page that looked like the following screenshot:

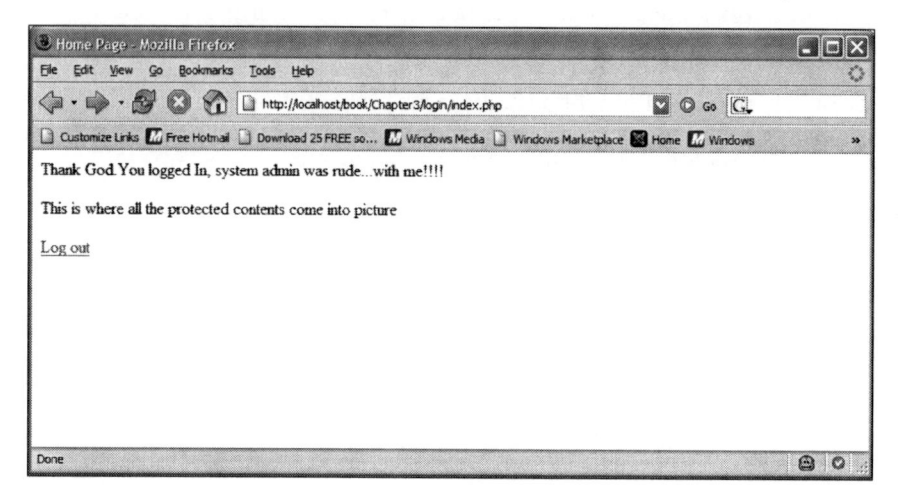

We have created a raw skeleton for the **todonow** application. So let the party begin!

> The login management system is just a simple and basic module for your understanding. In real web applications, you may need to enhance or modify it according to your security and performance needs.

User interface comes first

Coding is a costly affair, and that's why we will start designing the user interface first. We can always change the interface layout, color combinations, and look and feel of the application. This really is a useful feature, since our code functionality will remain the same. Only the user interface changes, and trust me it doesn't hurt!

My friend John thinks that the three-column layout is better than a two-column layout. Different people have different tastes for interface design. And, that's the reason I am suggesting a simple user interface for our **todonow** application. Feel free to modify it on the basis of your comfort.

It's time now for us to create a user interface for our application once the user has successfully logged in. We will try and keep the user interface as simple and beautiful as possible. Below is the simple modification done to our existing index.php file from the login management system. We have added the session variables to our page to read user ID {$_SESSION(uid)} and username {$_SESSION(uid)}.This will help us in further reading the values based on user authorization.

The following code is used to create a simple user interface for our application:

```
<img src="images/logo.png">
<p>
<span class="header-text">
<?php echo 'Welcome, '.$_SESSION['username']; ?>
</span>   |
<span class="MyLists">My Lists</span>
<span class="header-links">  | 
<a class="sideMenu_links" href="AddLists.php">
Create New List </a>  |  
<a class="sideMenu_links" href="logout.php">Logout</a>
</span>  
```

Todonow: A Tadalist Clone

What we have done here is pretty neat and simple. We needed text, **My Lists**, and two hyperlinks each for **Create New Lists** and **Logout**. Check out the result in the following screenshot:

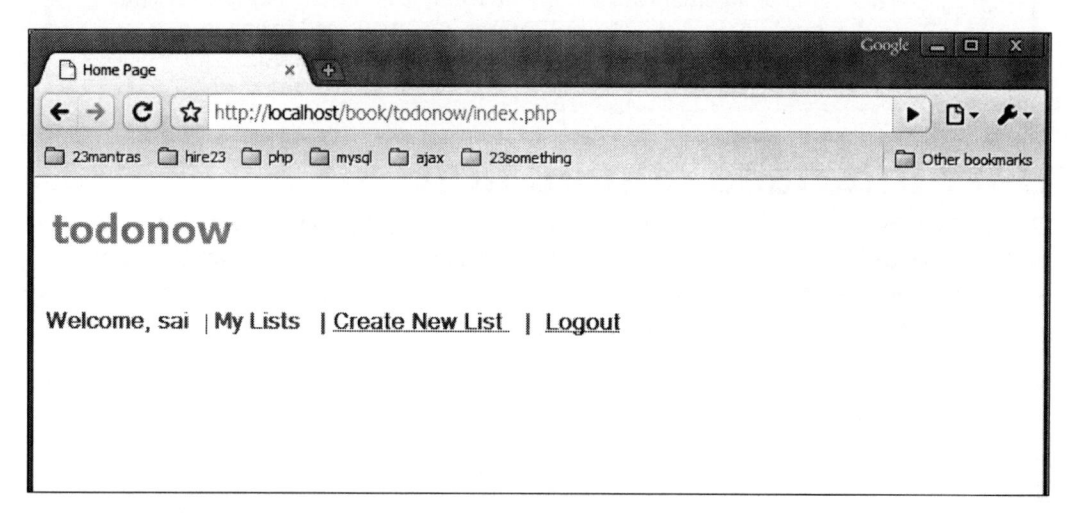

View all my lists

Now that the user is logged in, we need to check if the user has created any lists. If the user has previously created lists, we shall show all those lists on the user home page.

Logic and code

The process to view the lists for a logged-in user is as follows:

- We will read the `userID` from the session variable.
- We will run the query to select the lists, if any, created by the user. We are using `DBClass` defined in our login management system and the related functions by creating an object of the database class.
- We are running the SQL query to read the lists and the lists details such as `ListID`, `ListName`, and `Date` created by the user.

```
require_once 'DBClass.php';
 $db = new DBClass();
 $GetListDetails = "SELECT ListID,ListName,MonthName(Date) as
   Month,Day(Date) as Day  from Lists where
   ownerID=".$_SESSION['uid'];
$ListResult = $db->Query($GetListDetails);
```

- We check whether the user has created any lists before. Using the `Mysql_num_rows` function of MySQL, we get the number of rows returned by our query. If the count is more than zero, we will read the rows individually; else, we will show no lists.

    ```
    $num_rows = mysql_num_rows($ListResult);
    if($num_rows>0)
    ```

- We will loop through the result array. We are calling the `fetchArray` function defined in our `DBClass` to get the array of results and using a `while` loop to read each row.

    ```
    while($row = $db->fetchArray($ListResult))
    ```

- We display each row on the screen. Using the value `ListID`, we will create a link to a `viewList.php` file with `ListID`, so that the user can click on the list to view the details. And yes, make it attractive using the power of CSS.

    ```
    echo '<li>
    <a href="ViewList.php?ListID='.$row[ListID].'">'.$row[ListName].'
    </a>
     </li><p>';
    ```

Check out the resulting output in the following screenshot:

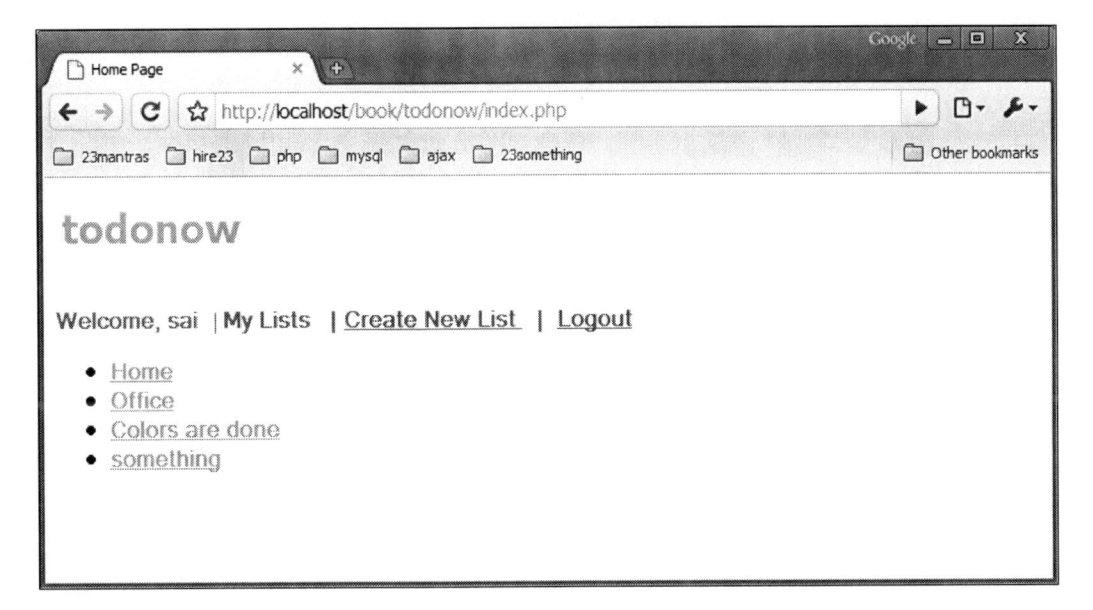

View all my lists along with a summary of incomplete items

A better way of representing the data is by showing a summary. We have displayed the lists created by the user on the home page. It would be of great help to show the user the status of incomplete items from the lists.

Logic and code

Extending the code used for reading the lists, we will create a subquery inside the `while` loop to read the count of the number of items with the status `Incomplete`.

```
while($row = $db->fetchArray($ListResult))
{
    $sql2 = "SELECT COUNT(ItemID) from Items where
    ListID=".$row[ListID]." AND status='Incomplete'";
    $result2 = $db->perform_query($sql2);
    $row2 = $db->fetch_one_row($result2);

}
```

Now, let's also display the timestamp when the list was created. We have read the value in the SQL query used while reading the lists created by the user.

```
$GetListDetails = "SELECT ListID,ListName,MonthName(Date) as
Month,Day(Date) as Day  from Lists where ownerID=".$_SESSION['uid'];
```

Let's display the summary of the incomplete items and the date timestamp to the user along with the lists.

```
echo '<li>
    <a href="ViewList.php?ListID='.$row[ListID].'">
    '.$row[ListName].'</a> 
    <span class="ItemsInfo"> --'.$row2[0].' remaining items </span>
    <br>
    <span class="DateDetails">on'.$row[Day].' 
    '.$row[Month].'</span>
</li>
<p>';
```

Check out the result shown in the following screenshot:

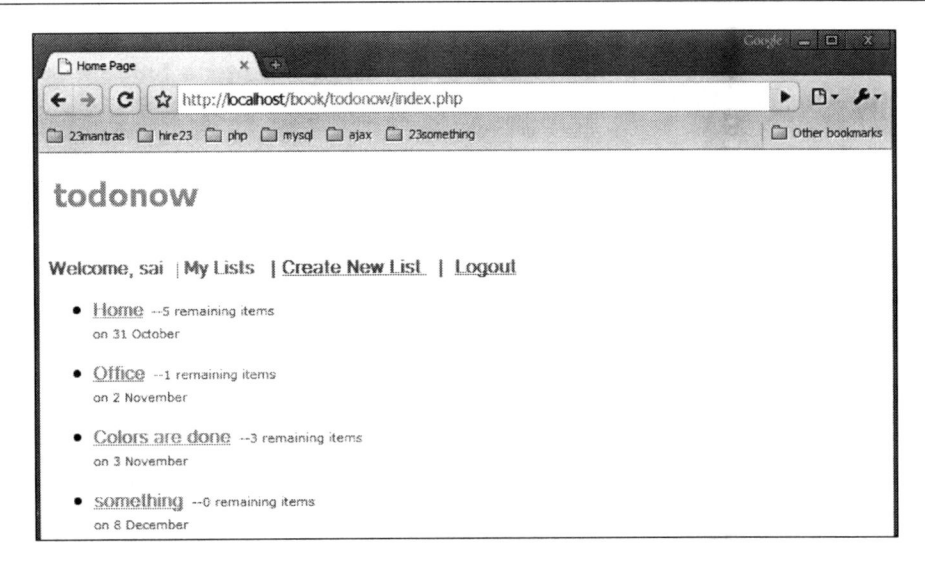

Chapter 10

Creating new lists

I prefer classifying my items into separate lists. It helps me to be what I am actually not—organized! I classify my items as Home, Office, Personal, and so on. This brings us to the core feature of our application: creating new lists to get organized.

Logic and code

The first thing we need to do is show the user a form to create the list. We will be creating a new file `addLists.php`. As we decided earlier, we shall keep the form very neat and pretty simple. Check out the following screenshot to see what our form will look like:

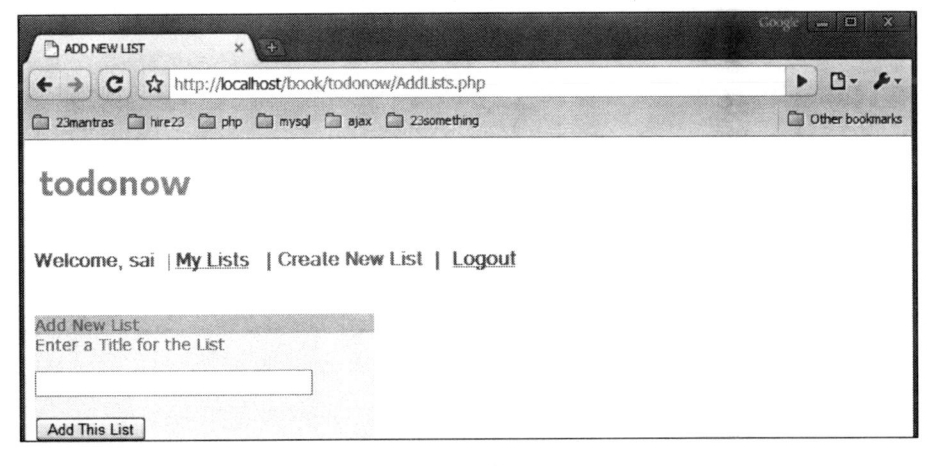

The code to create the user interface in the screenshot is given here. We have to create an input text box and a submit button. The user will **Enter a Title for the List** and hit the **Add This List** button.

```
<div class="AddListForm">
<div class="MyNewList">Add New List</div>
    <form action="AddLists.php" method="POST">
    Enter a Title for the List<p>
    <input type="text" name="ListTitle" size="35"><br><br>
    <input type="submit" name="AddLists" value="Add This List">
    </form>
</div>
```

When the user submits the information, we will check whether or not the user has posted the data (reading POST variables).

We will read userID using the session variable. Using $_POST, we will be reading the value of the list name entered by the user.

For those of you who are **Object Oriented Programming Languages and Systems (OOPS)** lovers, we have created a class called lists. This will have all the constructors and functions related to working with lists, some of which are ad_new_list(), read_list(), and so on. Otherwise, a simpler way is to run the query from the code itself.

```
$db = new DBClass();
$newlist = new lists();
$title = $_POST['ListTitle'];
$ownerid = $_SESSION["uid"];
$query = $newlist->add_new_list($title,$ownerid);
//$AddListQuery = "INSERT INTO Lists (listID,ListName,ownerID,Date)
VALUES (NULL,'$title','$ownerid',CURRENT_TIMESTAMP)";
```

We shall execute the query calling our DBClass function query.

```
$AddListResult = $db->Query($query);
```

We have added the list to our database, and we will now use a Mysql_insert_id() function to read ListID, which is an auto_increment. This function will always return the ID of the last INSERT action performed, and then we will execute the query and check if the query returned a value or not.

```
$sql = 'SELECT ListID, ListName from lists
            where ListID = '.mysql_insert_id();
$result = $db->Query($sql);
if (!$result) {
    echo 'Could not run query: ' . mysql_error();
    exit;
}
```

From the result set, we will read the list details.

```
$row = $db->fetch_one_row($result);
```

Now comes a very tricky part. Once we have read the `ListID` of the newly added list, we shall redirect the user to the list page showing the details. For that, we will write a simple `Redirect` function that will take `time` and page URL as parameters.

- The `time` parameter is used to define after how much and at what interval the user should be redirected
- The page URL will be used to specify to which page the application gets redirected

The code for the `Redirect` function is as follows:

```
function Redirect($time, $topage) {
echo "<meta http-equiv=\"refresh\" content=\"{$time};
      url={$topage}\" /> ";
}
```

Adding items to our lists

OK, now that we have created our lists we need to populate them with items or tasks. Wait, this is where our script.aculo.us magic comes into the picture. We are going to add the items in our AJAX way. We will do this in two steps:

1. Add items to the database.
2. Read the newly added items and place them back on the page.

Adding items to the database

We will add our items using a simple form in the `viewList.php` file. When a user enters the item name and hits submit, the JavaScript function `AddItem()` gets invoked. It uses `Ajax.Request` of Prototype to submit the data to `GetItem.php`.

Values of the item are read, that is the item name entered by the user, using our good old `$F()` function and then passed as parameters using `$_POST`.

The code for the `AddItem()` function is as follows:

```
function AddItem() {
var input = 'myinput='+$F('myinput');
var list = 'ListID='+$F('ListID');
var user = 'userID='+$F('userID');
var pars = input+'&'+user+'&'+list;
```

Todonow: A Tadalist Clone

```
new Ajax.Request(
'addItem.php',
   {
       asynchronous:true,
       parameters:pars,
       onComplete: ShowData
   }
);
$('myform').reset();
$('myinput').activate();
return false;
}
```

These values will be passed to our `GetItem.php` file, which will be working in the background asynchronously.

We will read the value of the `itemName`, `ListID`, and `userID`, and insert these values into the database table `items`.

But before we do that, we have to create an XML file through `GetItem.php` since we are using the AJAX way of returning the results. So let's define the headers for the XML file.

```
header("Content-Type: text/xml");
print'<?xml version="1.0" encoding="UTF-8" standalone="yes"?>';
```

Now, let's read the values of the variables and create a query to insert the values in the database. Using our `DBClass`, we will create an object for the class and invoke the query function to execute the query.

```
$the_name = $_POST['myinput'];
$List_name = $_POST['ListID'];
$user_name = $_POST['userID'];
$sql = "INSERT INTO items (ItemID,ListID,ownerID,itemName,status,Date)
VALUES (NULL,'$List_name','$user_name','$the_name','Incomplete',
        CURRENT_TIMESTAMP)";
require_once 'DBClass.php';
$db= new DBClass();
$result = $db->Query($sql);
```

We have added the item to our database table. Since we need to put the item back on the screen, we will read the ID of the recently inserted item using `mysql_insert_id()` and execute the query to read the details of the item.

```
$rowID = mysql_insert_id();
$sql = "SELECT itemName from items where ItemID=".$rowID;
$result = $db->Query($sql);
$row = $db->fetch_one_row($result);
$itemValue = $row[0];
```

As I said, we are going to return an XML file. Therefore, we need to place our data in the XML format.

```
echo '<response>';
echo '<ItemID>'.$rowID.'</ItemID>';
echo '<ItemValue>'.$itemValue.'</ItemValue>';
echo '</response>';
```

Finally, we are done with our XML file. The system is ready to return the data back to the JavaScript function.

Reading the newly added item and placing it back on the page

If you remember, we mentioned the `showData()` function when the AJAX call was completed. We will read the XML values returned by the `Ajax.Request` call and put them back on the screen in the incomplete `<div>`.

We are reading the values using `getElementsByTagName` of `ItemID` and `ItemValue`, which we mentioned while creating the XML file.

```
function ShowData(originalRequest) {
var xmlDoc = originalRequest.responseXML.documentElement;
var value1 = xmlDoc.getElementsByTagName("ItemID")[0].childNodes[0].nodeValue;
var value = xmlDoc.getElementsByTagName("ItemValue")[0].childNodes[0].nodeValue;
```

Now, let's use this information and create a `<div>` element and a checkbox with the values we have read from the XML file.

```
divID = 'DIV'+value1;
var div = document.createElement('div');
div.className ='ItemRow';
div.id = divID;
var val = '"'+value+'"';
var i = document.createElement('input');
i.type='checkbox';
i.id=value1;
i.value=value;
i["onclick"] = new Function("MarkDone(this.id)");
var t = document.createTextNode(value);
div.appendChild(i);
div.appendChild(t);
$('ItemTree').appendChild(div);
```

Todonow: A Tadalist Clone

If you look closely, we have added a function for the `onclick` event called `MarkDone(this.id)`. We shall get to this function in the next topic. Let's just be happy to see how the application is shaping up. Check out the following screenshot:

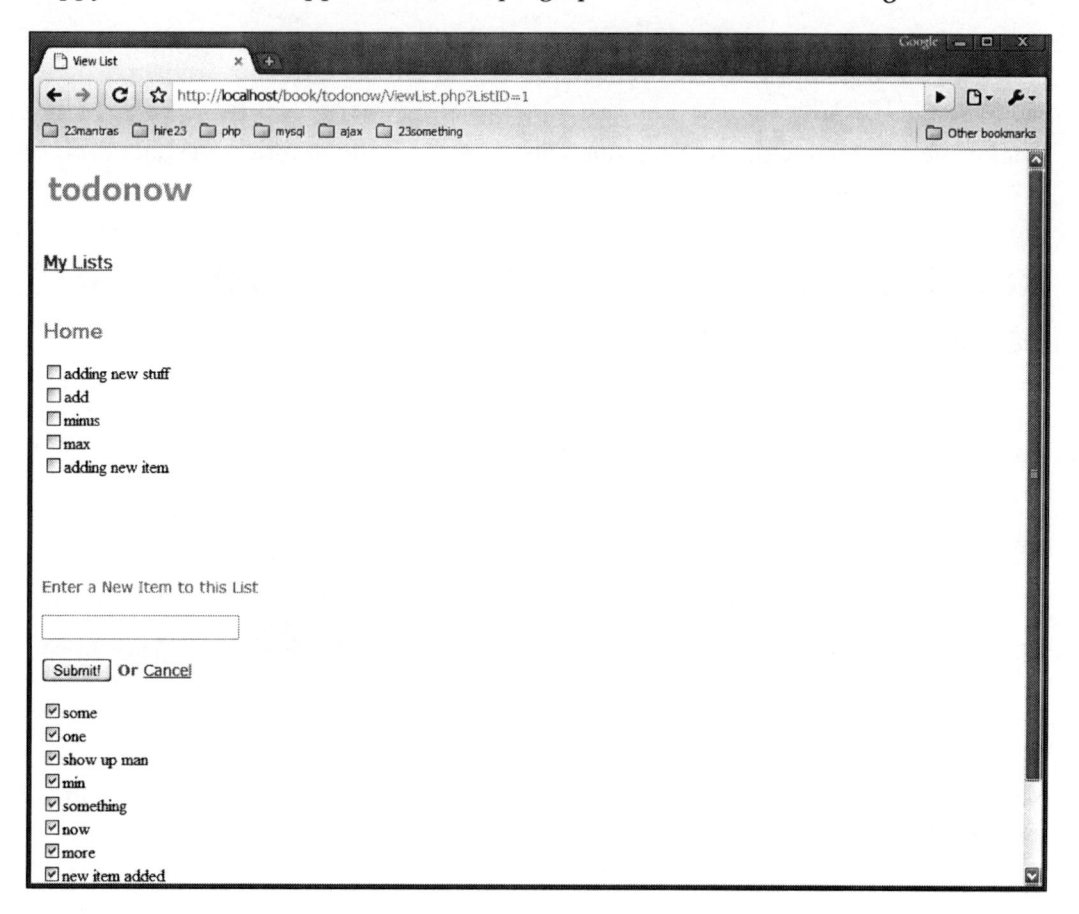

Adding effects to our items

Now that we have added our items in the AJAX way, you must have already started thinking of how to make them more appealing using the effects of the script.aculo.us library. In this section we will add effects to our functionality.

We are now well-versed with the power and beauty of the script.aculo.us library for using effects in our application. Before we do that, let's include the required files.

```
<script type="text/javascript" src="src/prototype.js"></script>
<script type="text/javascript" src="src/scriptaculous.js"></script>
<script type="text/javascript" src="src/effects.js"></script>
```

Chapter 10

Alright, now we are ready to explore the *special* effects in our application.

Just add this one line of code at the end of the above function:

```
new Effect.Highlight($(div));
```

And, you will not believe me. So, go ahead and see the visual treat for yourself!

Check out the following screenshot:

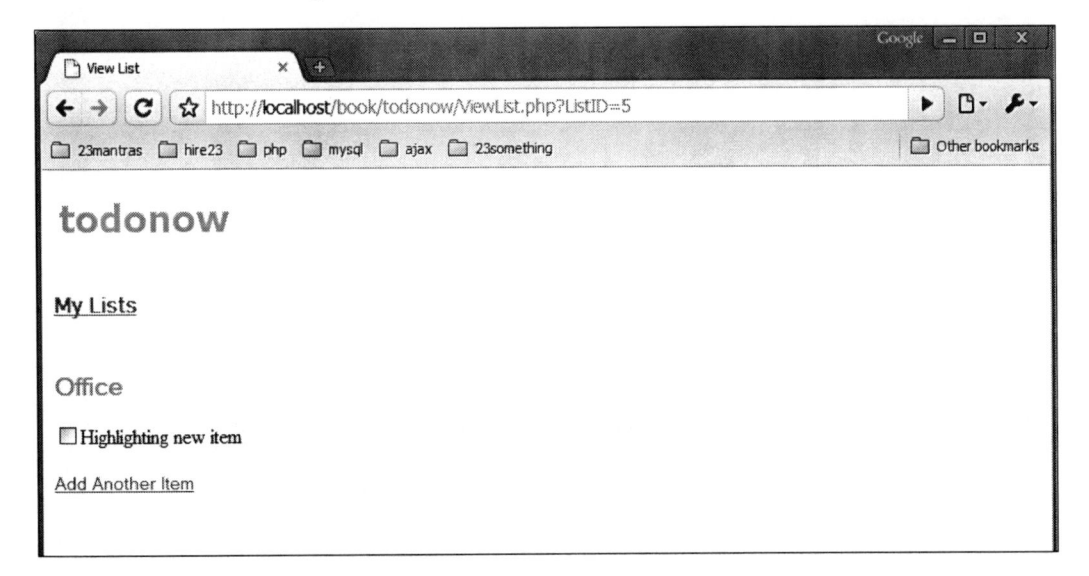

Mark items as completed

OK, this is the story so far. We have created lists, added items to our lists, and highlighted them using effects. Perfect! Now, the user has completed a particular task, so what's the point of showing the same task to the user along with the incomplete items? So the user marks the item as complete. The user will have to just click on the checkbox of the item and the item should get added into the incomplete item `<div>`.

In the previous topic we talked about the `MarkDone(this.id)` function, and we will cover that function in this section.

For that, we have some background work to process.

- Add the item to the completed `<div>`
- Delete the item from the incomplete `<div>`
- Change the status of the item to completed

Before we get into the code, have a look at the following screenshot to see what the application will look like:

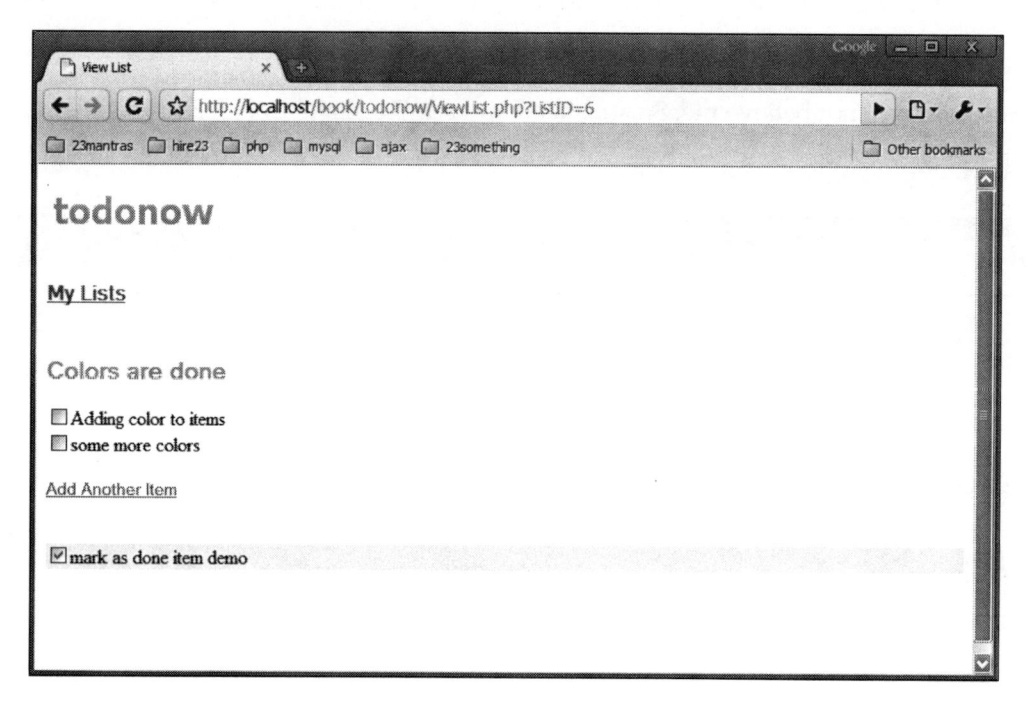

Let's get started. What follows is the snippet for the function `MarkDone(this.id)`. We are just calling the function by passing the ID and the value of the item.

```
function MarkDone(valueID){
   var itemValue = $(valueID).value;
   AddtoCompleted(valueID, itemValue);
}
```

Add the item to the completed <div>

We are calling the `AddtoCompleted` function. The purpose of this function is to create a `<div>` element and append an input checkbox element with the `onclick` event as `MarkUndone(this.id)`. The functions `DeletefromItemTree()` and `ChangeStatus()` will be covered in the next topic.

The `AddtoCompleted` function takes `valueID` and `itemValue` as parameters. We are creating a `<div>` and the checkbox on the fly.

```
Function AddtoCompleted(valueID, itemValue) {
   var str = "DIV"+valueID;
   var divDelete = $(str);
```

```
        DeletefromItemTree(divDelete);
        ChangeStatus(valueID);
        var div1 = document.createElement('div');
        div1.className ='ItemComplete';
        div1.id = str;
        var i = document.createElement('input');
        i.setAttribute("type","checkbox");
        i.id=valueID;
        i.defaultChecked="true";
        i.value=itemValue;
        i.className="ItemList";
        i["onclick"] = new Function("MarkUnDone(this.id)");
        var t = document.createTextNode(itemValue);
        div1.appendChild(i);
        div1.appendChild(t);
        $('Completed').appendChild(div1);
        new Effect.Highlight($(div1));
    }
```

Delete the item from the incomplete <div>

In the above function `AddToCompleted()`, we have called the `DeleteFromItemTree(divDelete)` function. It takes <div> to delete from the completed <div> called `ItemTree`.

```
    function DeletefromItemTree(divDelete)
    {
        $('ItemTree').removeChild(divDelete);
    }
```

Using the code that we just saw, we are removing the child from the completed `ItemTree` <div>.

Change the status of the item to completed

We have also called the function `changeStatus(valueID)` function, which is used to update the status of the item in the database. Again, we will be making `Ajax.Request` and updating the status.

```
    function ChangeStatus(valueID) {
        var list = 'ListID='+$F('ListID');
        var user = 'userID='+$F('userID');
        var itemID = 'itemID='+valueID;
        var pars = itemID+'&'+user+'&'+list;
        new Ajax.Request(
```

```
        'ChangeStatus.php',
          {
          asynchronous:true,
          parameters:pars,
          onComplete: ShowStatus
          }
        );
}
```

We are calling the `changeStatus.php;` script. We will update the status by executing the query, reading back the value, and returning the message.

```
<?php
require_once 'DBClass.php';
$ListID = $_POST['ListID'];
$user_name = $_POST['userID'];
$itemID = $_POST['itemID'];
$sql = "UPDATE items SET `status` = 'Completed'
            WHERE itemID =".$itemID;
$db = new DBclass();
$result = $db->Query($sql);
if (!$result) {
      echo 'Could not run query: ' . mysql_error();
     exit;
}
else {
$sql = "SELECT COUNT(itemID) from Items WHERE `status` = 'Incomplete'
and ListID =".$ListID;
$result = $db->Query($sql);
$row = $db->fetch_one_row($result);
$num = $row[0];
echo 'You Have'.$num.' Of Incomplete Tasks';
     }
?>
```

OK, now we are done completely with marking the item as completed.

Convert completed items to incomplete status

Oh my god! I marked the *place new LCD monitor order* item as completed. But a small problem, I just placed an order and I didn't pay for it. So, it's still an incomplete task. What do I do now? Simple, I will uncheck to make the item incomplete again. So we need to change the status of the item from completed to incomplete.

Before we actually go into making our items incomplete, we will add a function on the onclick event as `MarkUnDone(this.id)`.

The code for the `MarkUnDone` function is as follows:

```
function MarkUnDone(valueID){
   var itemValue = document.getElementById(valueID).value;
   AddtoItemTree(valueID, itemValue);
}
```

The same process applies to converting the completed items back to incomplete status.

- Add the item to the incomplete `<div>`
- Delete the item from the complete `<div>`
- Change the status of the item to incomplete

Add the item to the incomplete <div>

Now you must have guessed it right. We are going to perform the reverse process of the same procedure that we did in the previous topic.

First, we are going to add a `<div>` element and an input checkbox to append with the `MarkDone(this.id)` function on the onclick event.

We are also calling the functions `DeleteFromCompleted()` and `ResetStatus()`. The code for the function `AddtoItemTree()` is as follows:

```
function AddtoItemTree(valueID, itemValue) {
   var str = "DIV"+valueID;
   var divDelete = $(str);
   DeletefromCompleted(divDelete);
   ResetStatus(valueID);
   var div = document.createElement('div');
   div.className ='ItemRow';
   div.id = str;
   var i = document.createElement('input');
   i.type='checkbox';
   i.id=valueID;
     i.value=itemValue;
     i["onclick"] = new Function("MarkDone(this.id)");
   var t = document.createTextNode(itemValue);
   var br = document.createElement('br');
   div.appendChild(i);
```

```
div.appendChild(t);
div.appendChild(br);
$('ItemTree').appendChild(div);
new Effect.Highlight($(div));
}
```

Delete the item from the complete <div>

Now, let's repeat the same logic that we used while deleting the item from the completed `<div>`. We will be removing the item from the completed `<div>` using this function:

```
function DeletefromCompleted(divDelete)
{
    $('Completed').removeChild(divDelete);
}
```

Change the status of the item to incomplete

There is one last thing to do before we place the item back to the incomplete `<div>`. We need to reset the status of the item just as we did in changing the status from incomplete to complete.

We are making `Ajax.Request` to update the status of the item back from complete to incomplete. The `ResetStatus.php` file, which will be used to update the status of the item, is called.

The code for the function `ResetStatus()` is as follows:

```
function ResetStatus(valueID) {
    var list = 'ListID='+$F('ListID');
    var user = 'userID='+$F('userID');
    var itemID = 'itemID='+valueID;
    var pars = itemID+'&'+user+'&'+list;
    new Ajax.Request(
    'ResetStatus.php',
        {
            asynchronous:true,
            parameters:pars,
            onComplete: ShowStatus
        }
    );
}
```

In the `resetStatus.php` script we are updating the status of the item back to incomplete again, and then sending the status update back to the user screen.

The value of the parameters are read and the query to update the status of the items is executed.

```
$ListID = $_POST['ListID'];
$user_name = $_POST['userID'];
$itemID = $_POST['itemID'];
$db = new DBClass();
$sql = "UPDATE items SET `status` = 'Incomplete' WHERE itemID
     =".$itemID;
$result = $db->Query($sql);
```

If the result is true, we will count the total number of items that have an incomplete status. The number will be prompted back to the user.

```
$sql = "SELECT COUNT(itemID) from Items WHERE `status` = 'Incomplete'
and ListID =".$ListID;
$result = $db->Query($sql);
$row = $db->fetch_one_row($result);
$num = $row[0];
echo 'You Have'.$num.' Of Incomplete Tasks';
}
?>
```

After a lot of coding and scripting, I am sure that you are now eager to see the output of the application. Here it is. Check out the following screenshot:

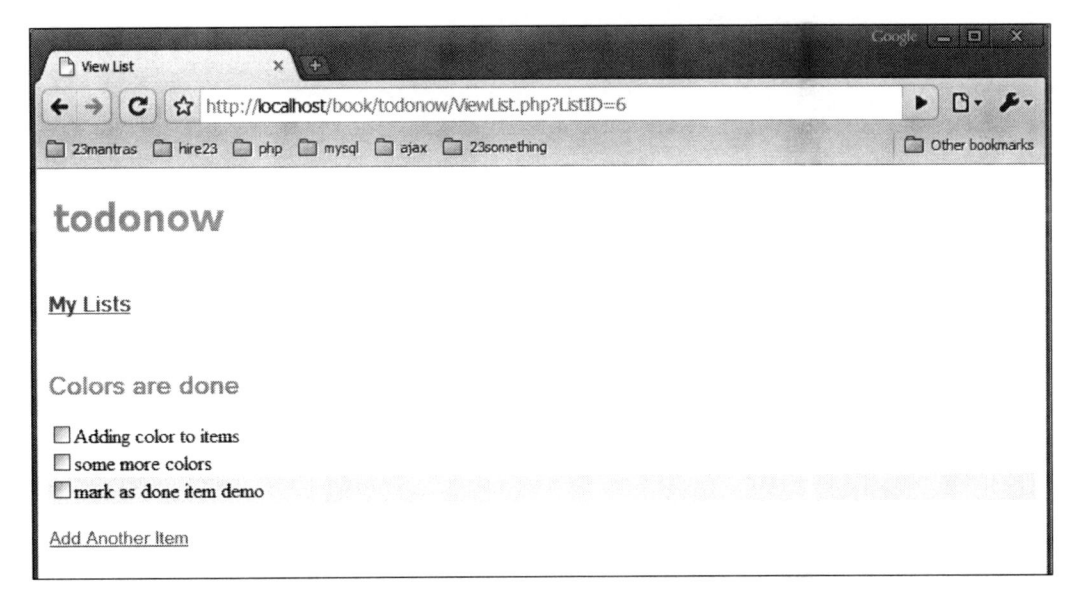

Deleting lists

The other day I was planning for a reunion and it got cancelled. Now that there is no reunion, I want to delete the entire list. We can delete any list on the fly. Be game and let's take this feature as your homework. I shall give the code for this feature in the next chapter. Here is the hint.

> Read the session `userID`, read the `$_POST` value of the list, delete it from the database, and update the user about the status. Try it out.

Let's wrap up and log out

Finally, the user has finished today's tasks and (s)he can join the party downtown. The user can log out. Here, the script is the same as the one we used in our login management system module.

Check out the following screenshot:

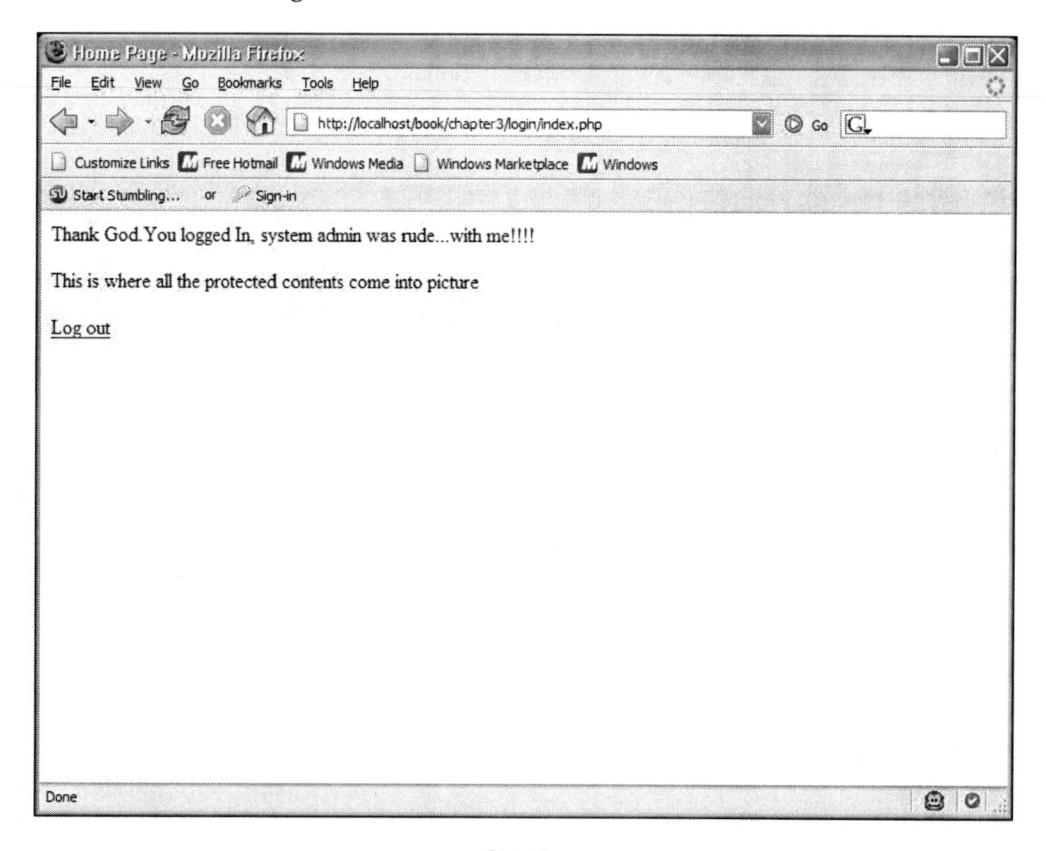

Don't worry about your lists. Now that we have killed the session, no one will be able to see your data. Go ahead and party hard!

Our Todonow is ready to go live

So after a long journey, we reached our first destination. Our **todonow** application is now ready to go live. Here is a glimpse of our application:

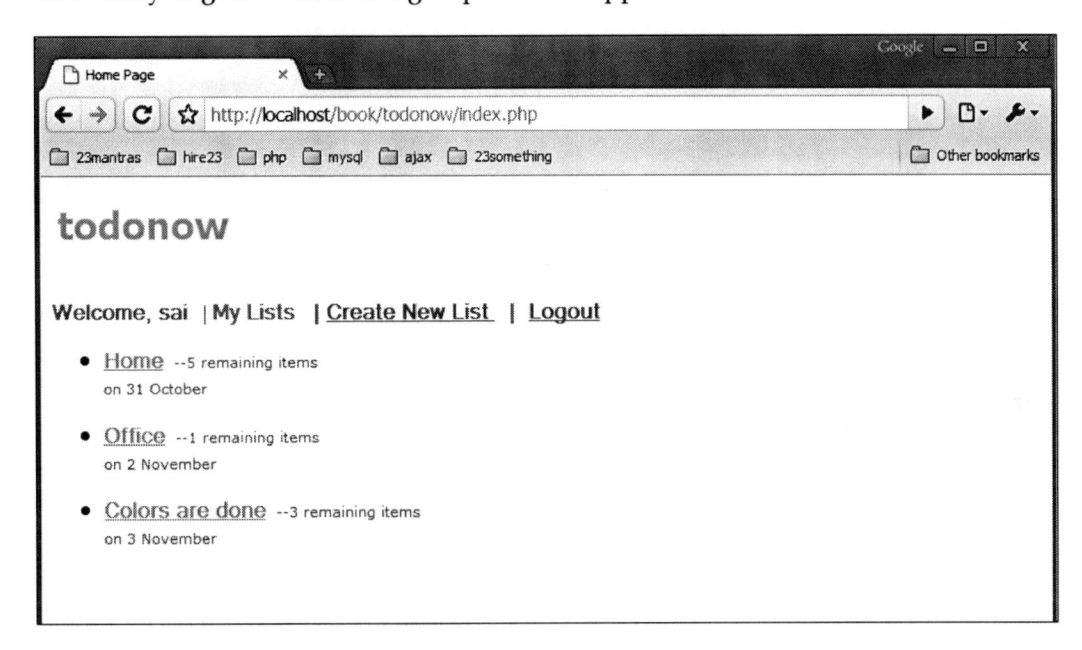

Summary

In the previous chapters we learned about the striking features of script.aculo.us. In this chapter we implemented some of those features and created a ready-to-go-live project (and a to-do list manager), that is, the **Todonow** application.

In this chapter we used features of Prototype and script.aculo.us such as `Ajax.Request` and effects. It's amazing to see that we started our journey with simple features and now we are ready with our own applications.

The sole idea was to show how web developers and user interface designers use the wonderful yet powerful script.aculo.us library to make appealing and useful web applications.

In the next chapter we will create yet another killer web application. Yes, now it's time for you and me to go ahead and plan our lists and tasks for the day.

11
Creating Delicious and Digg Bookmarks Manager

Now that we have planned our to-do list for today (using our **todonow** manager created in the previous chapter), let's quickly get started with the day's work.

Some of the key topics we will be covering are how to:

- Create a database for our application
- Define features and functionality
- Create the user interface for our frontend user
- Implement the features
- View the complete application at a glance

In this chapter we will be creating a mash up of Delicious and Digg applications. Let's admit that we love Delicious and Digg applications. So, why not try and build some of the features in our web application based on these lovely applications?

The whole point of doing this project is to understand how we, as developers, can explore new possibilities and build features in a more agile way.

Application at a glance

Let's quickly get the complete picture of what the application is all about. Let's call this application *bookmarker*.

We are trying to create a mash up of Delicious and Digg applications. As a user, we will be able to submit our URLs and search using real-time search (aka autocompletion). We learned this in Chapter 7.

Creating Delicious and Digg Bookmarks Manager

Users can search for tutorials submitted by other users under different tags (one must not forget the wonderful and powerful tag-based features that have become an integral part of any Web 2.0 applications).

The key features and functionality that we will be implementing for the bookmarker application are listed in the next section. Now is the time to switch to your coding gears!

Features and functionality

Let's quickly get an overview of the features and functionality using our bookmarker application.

- User signup
- User login
- My tutorials
- Submit new tutorial
- Add title, description, and tags to tutorials
- Search all the tutorials based on the title
- Tag cloud search
- Edit my tutorials
- Delete my tutorials
- Logout

Some of the key features covered in this chapter form the basis of Web 2.0 features. For example: Generate the tag cloud and search using the tags—you see the results accordingly. This is a powerful feature and most of the search engines will render it. We will be implementing the real-time search (aka autocompletion) using the title for quick searching.

The database playground for our application

As we did in Chapter 10, before we start building our application user interface and functionality, let's work towards getting our database ready.

Since we will be reusing the login management system from Chapter 3, we will use the same database table for storing the user information.

Chapter 11

For our bookmarker application, we will be adding two new tables:

- tutorials
- tutorial_tags

The tutorials table will store all information regarding the tutorial submitted by the user. Similarly, tutorials_tags will store information about tags.

Have a look at the schema of the tutorials table.

```
CREATE TABLE `tutorials` (
   `tutorialID` int(11) NOT NULL auto_increment,
   `tutorial_url` varchar(200) default NULL,
   `tutorial_title` varchar(200) default NULL,
   `tutorial_desc` varchar(400) default NULL,
   `ownerID` int(11) NOT NULL,
   `date` timestamp NOT NULL default CURRENT_TIMESTAMP,
   PRIMARY KEY  (`tutorialID`),
   UNIQUE(`tutorial_url`)
) ENGINE=InnoDB DEFAULT CHARSET=latin1 AUTO_INCREMENT=0;
```

The attributes of the tutorials table are explained as follows:

- **tutorialID:** This is the primary key attribute to uniquely identify each tutorial. The field is made auto_increment. For every insertion into the table, the value automatically increases. It has an integer value.
- **tutorial_url:** This stores the URL of the tutorial submitted by the user.
- **tutorial_title:** This field stores the title of the tutorial defined as varchar, since it's a text.
- **tutorial_desc:** This is the description of the tutorial added by the user.
- **ownerID:** The owner refers to the user who added the tutorial maps from the users table.
- **date:** This field stores the timestamp of when the tutorial was submitted.

The other table we need is the tutotials_tags table. The following is the schema definition of the table:

```
CREATE TABLE `tutorial_tags` (
  `tutorialID` bigint(20) unsigned NOT NULL,
  `tag` varchar(255) NOT NULL,
  PRIMARY KEY  (`tutorialID`,`tag`)
) ENGINE=InnoDB DEFAULT CHARSET=latin1;
```

[195]

The attributes of the table are as follows:

- `tutorialID`: It is added as a reference to identify which tutorials tags were added.
- `tag`: It is the name of the tag. It can be anything that the user adds or wants to identify the tutorial by.

That's it! Our database tables are ready and we can build our application on them.

User profile home page

Let's quickly design a common header layout that the users will see once they log in. We will try to keep it simple, but feel free to add your own creativity to the user interface.

Have a look at the following screenshot for the user profile home page:

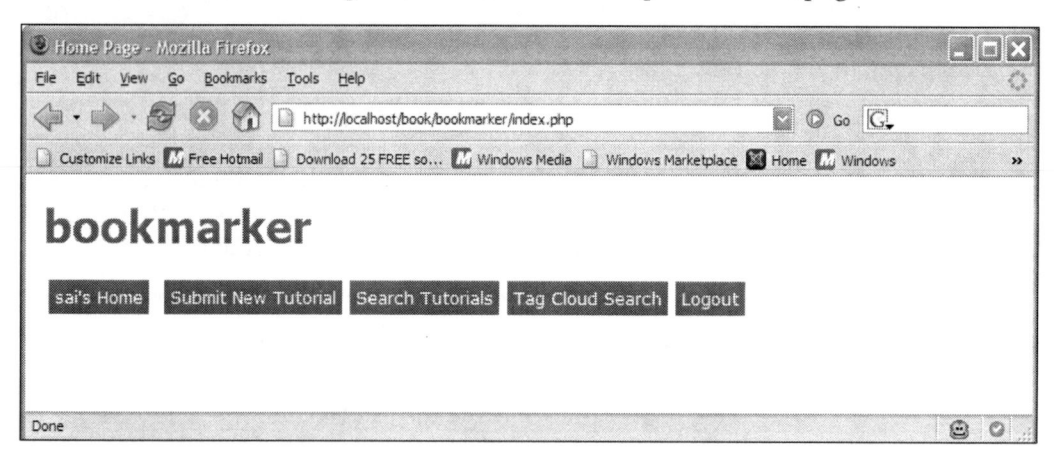

We have created five simple tabs. Each tab represents a feature that we will be working on.

Submit new tutorials

Once the user logs in by providing the necessary credentials, s(he) can submit new tutorials. In this section we will learn how to add tutorials. This will be done in two steps:

1. We will allow the user to submit the tutorial URL.
2. If the URL submitted is unique, the user will be allowed to add a title, description, and tags for the tutorial.

Submitting a tutorial URL

While creating the database schema, we have defined the `tutorial_url` field as `UNIQUE`. This means there can only be one entry for a tutorial. If the tutorial has already been added, no other user can add the same tutorial again.

Let's quickly create a user interface for adding new tutorials. We will need a text box where a user can type the URL and click on the **Submit Now** button to post to the server.

```
<body>
   <img src="images/logo.png">
<p>
   <div class="header-links">
   <a href="index.php">
   <?php echo $_SESSION['username']."'s";?> Home</a>
   <a href="submitTutorial.php">Submit New Tutorial</a>
   <a href="searchTutorials.php">Search Tutorials</a>
   <a href="tagCloud.php">Tag Cloud Search</a>
   <a  href="logout.php">Logout</a></div>
</body>
```

The following screenshot shows the user interface for submitting tutorials:

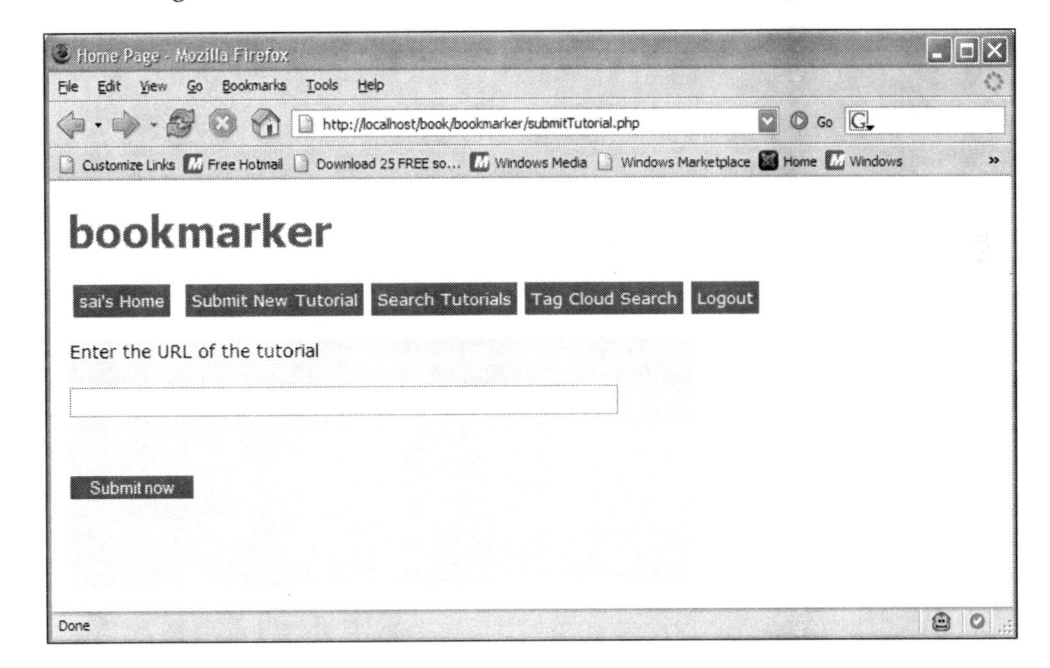

We have our user interface ready, so let's quickly get the server-side code prepared.

We will be checking if the session is valid on every page.

```
<?PHP
session_start();
if (!(isset($_SESSION['login']) && $_SESSION['login'] != '')) {
   header ("Location: login.php");
}
?>
```

Once the session is set, we read the user ID and the tutorial URL that the user has posted.

```
$url = $_POST['titleURL'];
$ownerid = $_SESSION["uid"];
```

OK, so far so good! Let's move on to create a class called `Tutorials`. It will have all the functions related to tutorials such as adding, deleting, and editing tutorials.

The complete `Tutorials` class is given as a part of the code download. For now, we will see a snippet of code to add tutorials to the database.

```
function add_new_tutorial($url, $ownerid){
   $query = "INSERT INTO Tutorials
   (tutorialID,tutorial_url,ownerID,Date) VALUES
   (NULL,'$url','$ownerid',CURRENT_TIMESTAMP)";
   return $query;
}
```

We are adding `tutorial_url`, `ownerID`, and `Date` to our database using the following query:

```
$query = "INSERT INTO Tutorials (tutorialID,tutorial_url,ownerID,Date)
VALUES (NULL,'$url','$ownerid',CURRENT_TIMESTAMP)";
```

On success, the user will be redirected to the submit details page.

```
$query = $newtutorial->add_new_tutorial($url,$ownerid);
$AddURLResult = $db->perform_query($query);
If ($AddURLResult)
   {
      //re-direct the user to submit details page
   }
else
   {
      // alert message to user
   }
```

Now, when the user submits a tutorial, an alert message will be displayed to the user. If the tutorial does not exist, the next page will be shown where the user can add the title, description, and tags.

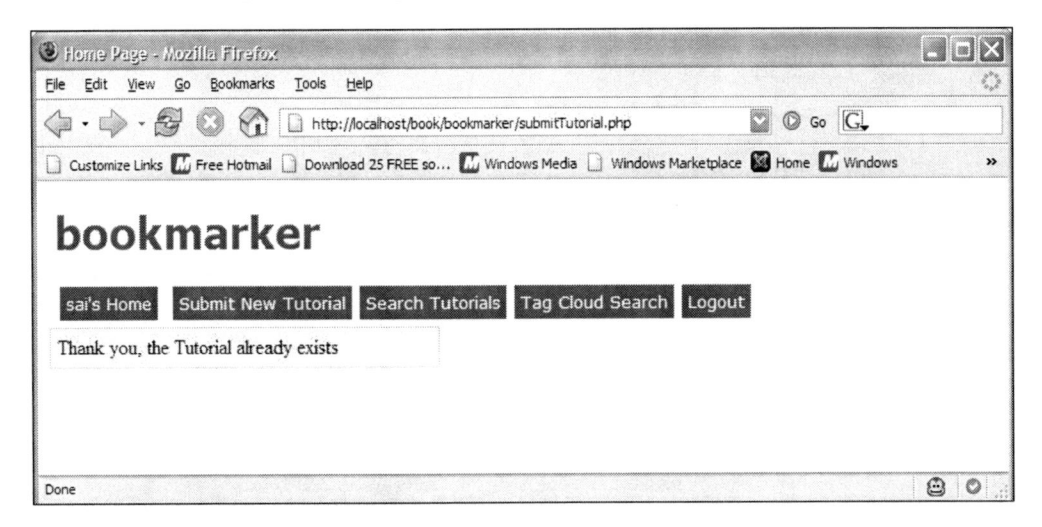

Adding title, description, and tags to the tutorial

Now that the user has submitted the tutorial and we have checked that the tutorial does not exist already, it's time to add the title, description, and tags to the newly added tutorial through `tutorialDetails.php`.

Let's first quickly create a user interface to add the title, description, and tags.

```
<div class="add-details-div">
<form action="tutorialDetails.php" method="POST" >
   <span class="details-text">
      Enter a title for the tutorial
   </span>
   <br>
      <input class="submit-url" type="text" name="title">
   <br>
   <span class="details-text">
      Enter description for the tutorial
   </span>
   <br>
   <span class="submit-url">
      <input type="text" name="desc">
   </span>
```

```
            <p>
            <span class="details-text">
                Enter Tags for the tutorial
            </span>
            <br>
            <span class="submit-url">
                <input type="text" name="tags">
            </span>
                <input type="hidden" name="tutorialID" value="<?php echo
                    $tutorialID; ?>">
            <p>
                <input name="submitDetails" class="submit-button" type="submit"
                    value="Submit now">
        </form>
    </div>
```

The user interface for `tutorialDetails.php` is shown in the following screenshot:

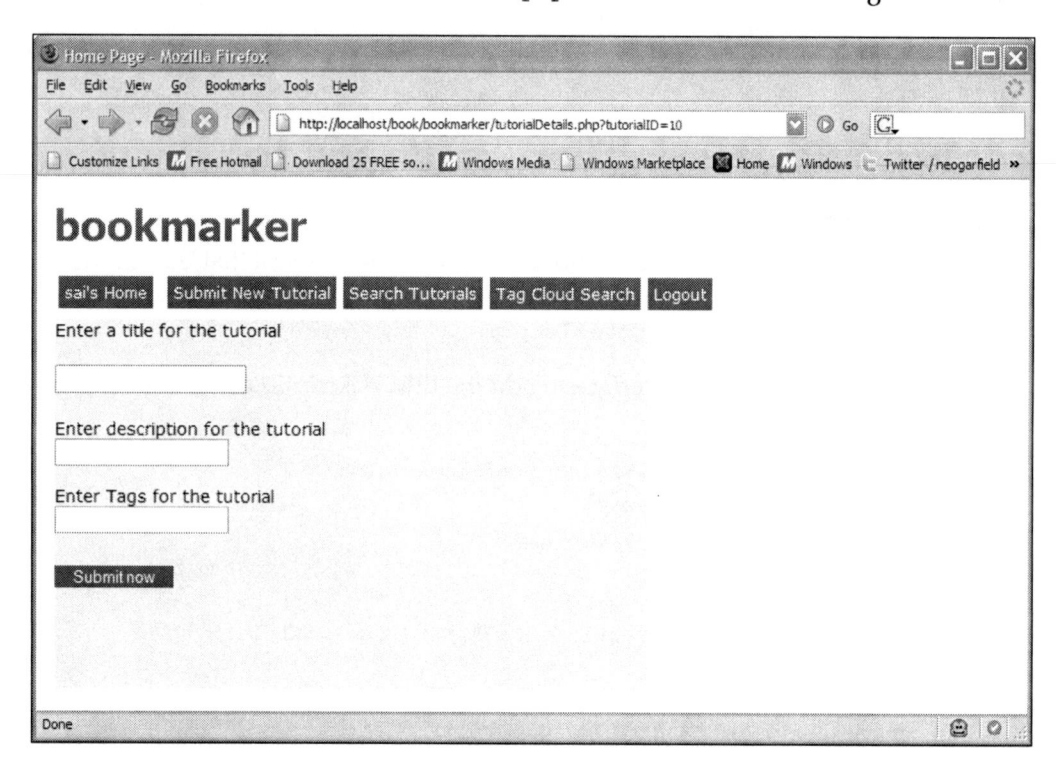

This page will be available to the user only when the session is valid.

We will read the user ID through $_SESSION, and the details of the tutorials posted by the user using $_POST.

```
$ownerid = $_SESSION["uid"];
$tutorialID = $_POST["tutorialID"];
$title = $_POST['title'];
$desc = $_POST['desc'];
$tags = $_POST['tags'];
```

We have all the details of the tutorials. So, let's update the same in the database. In the tutorials class we have a function for adding the tutorials description called add_tutorial_desc($title, $desc, $tutorialID).

```
function add_tutorial_desc($title, $desc,$tutorialID){
    $query = "UPDATE tutorials SET tutorial_title='".$title ."'',
       tutorial_desc ='".$desc."' WHERE tutorialID =".$tutorialID ;
return $query;
}
```

We will insert the details of the tutorials using the query as follows:

```
$query = "UPDATE tutorials SET tutorial_title='".$title ."'',
   tutorial_desc ='".$desc."' WHERE tutorialID =".$tutorialID ;
```

> For now, we are not adding any details about the tags. It needs a separate explanation that is covered in next section.

The resulting user interface after adding the details is as follows:

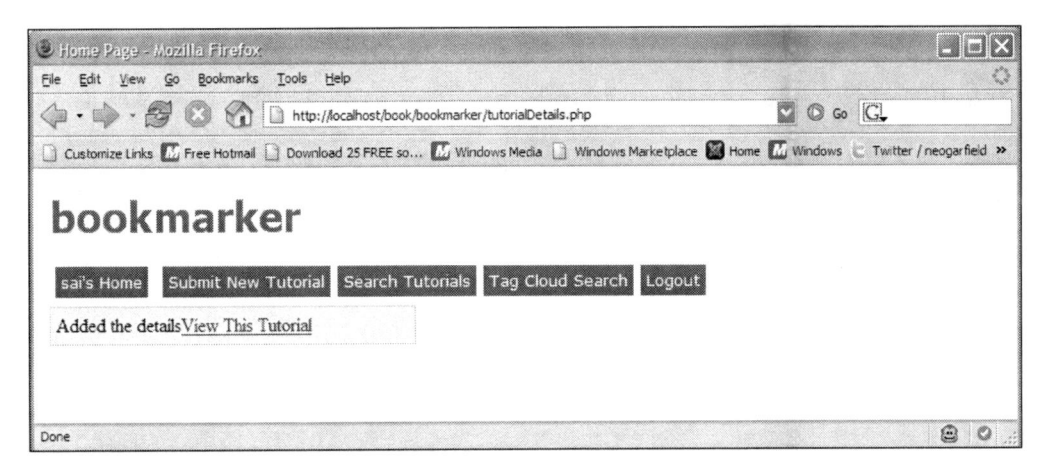

We also give a link to `viewTutorial.php` with the ID so that the user can see the recently added tutorial.

View tutorial

In the previous section we successfully created a tutorial. We were able to read back `tutorialID` of the latest inserted tutorial. Now, let's create a script called `viewTutorial.php` that will take `tutorialID` via `$_GET`.

We need to query the database table `tutorials` for details with `tutorialID` as the last inserted ID.

The following is the query to read the values for the recently inserted tutorial:

```
$query="SELECT * FROM tutorials WHERE tutorialD=".$tutorialID;
```

The query returns an array with all the details of the particular tutorial. Loop the details, decorate it with CSS, and display it to the user.

> We have used the same logic and steps for reading the details of the list in our **todonow** application in Chapter 10. Refer to the `viewList.php` script.

Deleting tutorials

It's not enough to just submit tutorials. Sometimes, we realize that we have made the mistake of submitting a wrong tutorial. So, it's important to have a mechanism to delete the unwanted tutorials.

We refer to these basic set of actions as CRUD, which stands for Create, Read, Update, and Delete. In this section we will be creating our delete function for the tutorials using the AJAX way.

In the user profile page we will see all the tutorials submitted by the user. Along with each tutorial, we will also have the links for editing and deleting the tutorial. The point is to do it in such a way that we use an AJAX call and do not take the user to a new page.

We will prompt the user with a JavaScript confirmation message to verify whether the user really wants to delete the tutorial.

Take a look at the following screenshot to see what happens when a user clicks on the **Delete** link:

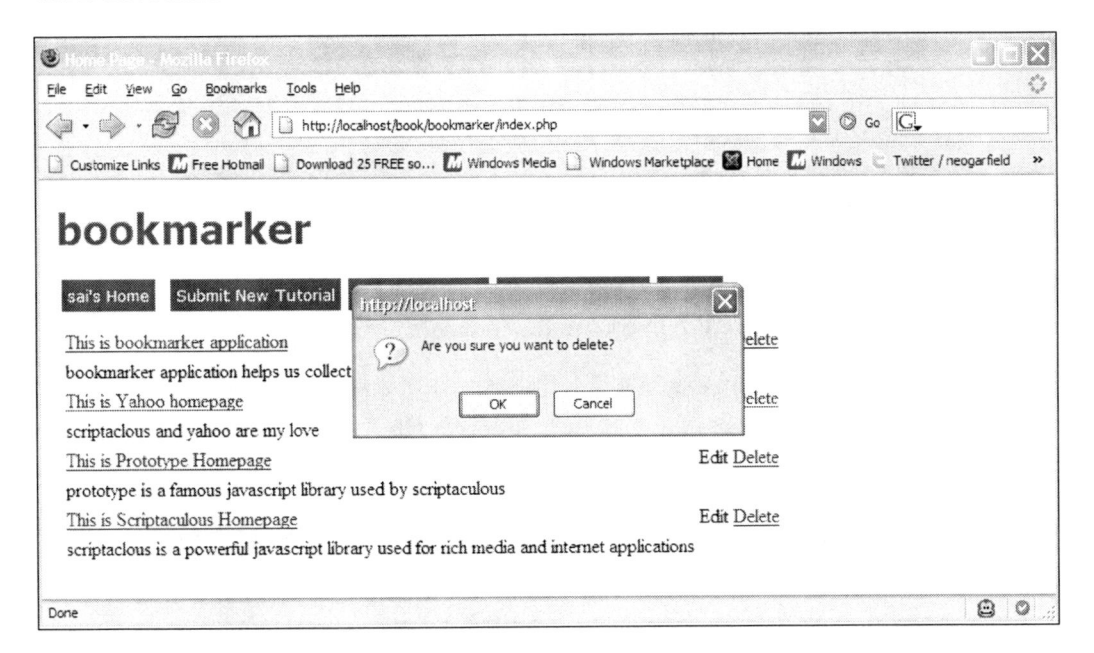

When the user clicks on **Cancel**, nothing happens. If the user clicks on **OK**, the following steps take place in the given sequence:

1. Read the `tutorialID`.
2. Read the `tableID` and `rowID`.
3. Delete the child row from the table.
4. Call the AJAX function to delete the data from the database.
5. Use the effects to highlight the updated row.

While presenting the information about the tutorials submitted by the user, we also read `tutorialID` and place it under the **Delete** link along with the ID.

The **tutorial** ID will be passed by calling a JavaScript function `deleteTutorial(ID)`.

```
function deleteTutorial(id)
{
    var result = confirm("Are you sure you want to delete?");
    if(result==true)
        {
            deletechildrow('mytutorials-table',id);
        }
}
```

This function in return calls another JavaScript function `deletechildrow(tableID, rowID)`, where we actually delete the child row from the table.

```
function deletechildrow(tableID,rowID)
{
   var d = document.getElementById(tableID);
   var olddiv = document.getElementById(rowID);
   d.deleteRow(olddiv);
   alert("Tutorial Deleted");
}
```

Did we miss out anything? Yes, we did! We did not make a remote call to the server to delete the tutorial. I leave it to you to make that call.

Let's add a little spice of effects while deleting the child row from the table.

```
new Effect.Highlight($(id));
```

Search using real-time autocompletion

Does real-time autocompletion sound familiar? It's the same awesome feature of script.aculo.us that we learned about in Chapter 7.

In this section we will build a simple real-time search of tutorials based on titles.

> When we aim at scaling large data in a real-world application, the autocompletion feature might slow down as it has to search through a lot of records. The idea here is to show how we can integrate the autocomplete feature into a web application.

So, let's quickly create a user interface for searching. We will need a text box where the user will start typing the query and our system will search for it in real time.

```
<div class="tutorial-search">
    <label>Enter Your Search Terms</label>
    <input type="text" id="title" name="title"/>
    <div id="myDiv"></div>
<p>
   <div id="result" name="result"></div>
</div>
```

The screenshot corresponding to the above user interface script for searching is as follows:

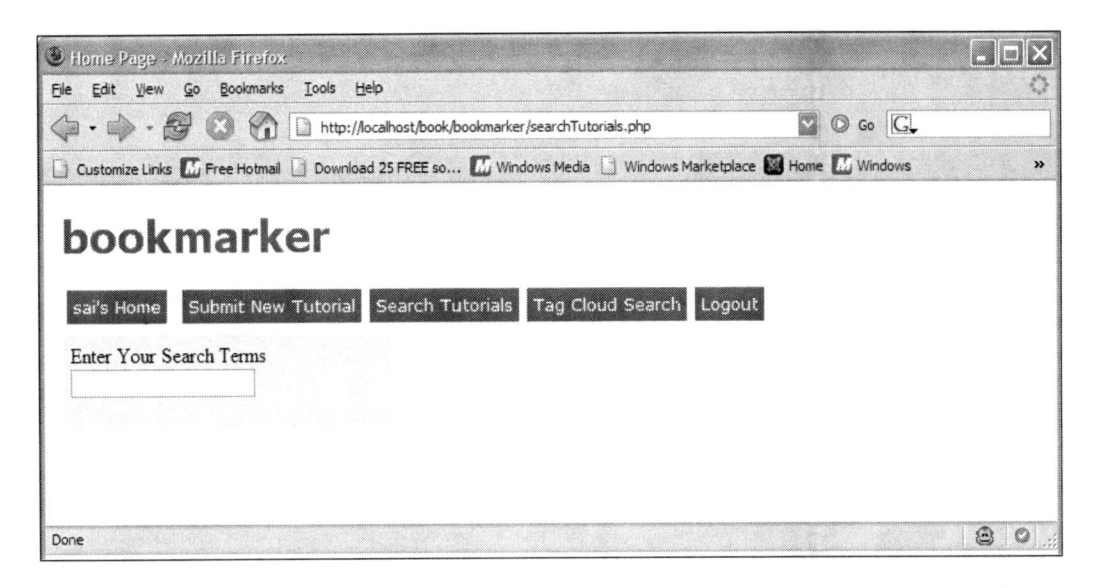

Now it's time to start searching for the tutorials. On loading the page, we will invoke our JavaScript code for autocompletion.

```
<script type="text/javascript">
    window.onload = function() {
        new Ajax.Autocompleter(
            'title',
            'myDiv',
            'fetchChoices.php'
        );
    }
</script>
```

In the code snippet that we have just seen, we are passing the ID of the text box as `title`, a `<div>` to host the result set as `myDiv`, and our script in `fetchChoices.php` that will get us the results.

The code for `fetchChoices.php` remains the same as the one we used in Chapter 7. The only difference is in the query that we pass to get the results.

```
$query="SELECT * FROM tutorials WHERE tutorial_title LIKE
'%".$value."%'";
```

This wildcard search will get all the tutorials using `LIKE`, which gets the matching records. We are restricting the number of tutorials to 20 by using `LIMIT` in our query.

Check out the following screenshot to see the resulting user interface:

On selecting the row from the list, we automatically redirect the user to view the tutorial.

Exploring the tag cloud features of 2.0 applications

Tags in web applications have become a standard for 2.0 applications. To a user and a developer of web applications, it really makes things simpler in terms of organizing or searching content.

For example, the Delicious application really explored the power of using tags. The whole world started appreciating the *art* of quick-searching relevant content based on tags.

In this section we will learn and master the *art* of tags.

> The same concept and approach can be applied to any content in any web application. The logic remains the same.

Some of the key functionalities related to the tags in our bookmarker application include how to:

- Add tags to tutorials
- Read all the tags in the database
- Create a tag cloud
- Search using tags

For implementing the tags, we have to create a separate class called `tags`, which we will be using in our applications. The `tags` class can be used with any web application.

Adding tags to tutorials

While adding the tutorial, we have skipped this part. So, let's first implement the process of adding tags to our tutorials.

A user can add any number of tags to a tutorial. We have to collect all the tags that the user inputs, and then explode the string to get each word separately. The words are then put in an array and each word is inserted as a row in the `tutorials_tags` table.

```
function add_tutorial_tags($tags, $tutorialID){
$temp_tags = explode(',', $tags);
foreach ($temp_tags as $tag)
{
      $tag = strtolower($tag);
      $query = "INSERT INTO tutorial_tags(tutorialID, tag)
               VALUES ('$tutorialID','".$tag."')";
      $result = mysql_query($query);
      if($result)
      {
         continue;
      }
   }
}
```

In the code above, we are reading the values as `$tags`. Using the `explode()` function, we will separate the words and the criteria for separation is ','.

For each tag read, we will loop using the `foreach` loop and insert the data into the database table. It's time for you to go ahead and add lots of tutorials along with tags.

Creating Delicious and Digg Bookmarks Manager

Reading all the tags in the database

Now that we have added our tags to tutorials, it is important to read them back. These tags will be used in the creation of our tag cloud, which we will display to the users.

> We are reading all the tags submitted by the users of the application, which can be a massive number. You may want to restrict the number of tags displayed by applying `LIMIT` to the query. We can also match the tags and display only the most used tags by counting the tags.

The function to read the tags from the database is as follows:

```
function read_all_tags() {
$query = "SELECT tag FROM tutorial_tags LIMIT 0,30 ";
$result = mysql_query($query);
if($result) {
    while($row = mysql_fetch_array($result)) {
        $all_tags[$row['tag']] = $row['tag'];
    }
return $all_tags;
}
```

Creating a tag cloud

The playground has been prepped. We have added tags to the tutorials and read the tags from the database. What are we waiting for? Let's go ahead and create a tag cloud.

> In our applications we need to know how many times a tag was used by the users. Depending upon the weight of the usage of the tag, we will return the tags. Alternatively, we can also use the `LIMIT` clause in our query to restrict the number of tags displayed to users.

If you remember, we have an array of `$all_tags` returned from the above feature that is reading the tags from the database.

```
$all_tags = $tutorials->read_all_tags();
```

Now, let's read these values and create our own tag cloud.

```
foreach ($all_tags as $tag =>$value)
{
    echo '<a style="font-size:'. rand(50,20). 'px'
```

[208]

```
    .'" class="tag_cloud" href="http://localhost/content/searchTag.php?s='
. $value.'" title="\'' . $tag . '">'.$value.'';
}
```

We are looping through each tag and creating a random-sized font (for each tag) on the page.

Take a look at how the tag cloud looks in the following screenshot:

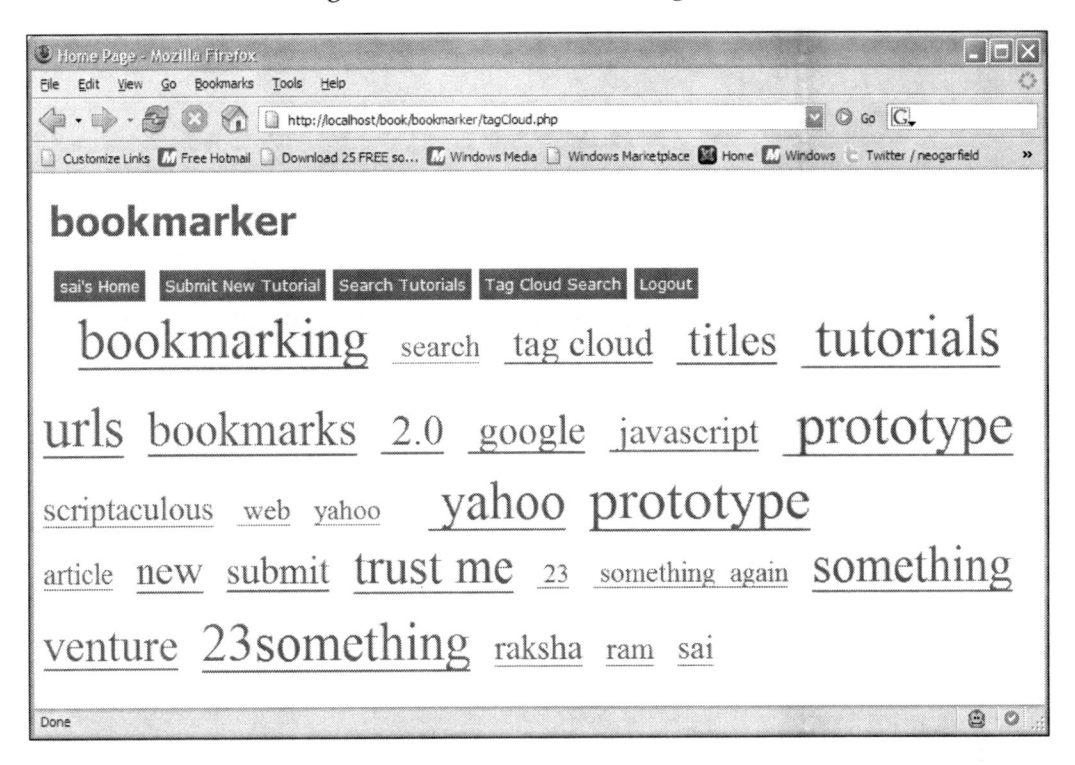

Search using tags

We have covered all the aspects from adding the tags and reading the tags to creating the tag cloud. Let's now take a look at the search function using tags.

> In the following piece of code, we are searching through all the tutorials submitted by the users. In a real-time application, you may need to display limited tutorials based on your application requirements. This module is an example for searching through all tutorials.

Creating Delicious and Digg Bookmarks Manager

If you look at the code that we used while creating a tag cloud, we have given a link for the `searchTag.php` script. This script is used for searching through the tags. I will only give you a hint in the form of a query. Just use this query and see what it results in.

```
$query = "SELECT tutorialID FROM tutorial_tags WHERE tag='".$tag."'";
```

This query will give you the resultant set for all the matching tutorials. Just loop the set and display the results to the user.

Don't forget to log out

This brings us to the most important task, especially if you are using a public system. Users need to log out so that the session is no longer valid and they need to give their credentials to access the system again.

> You can also use a session time-out feature from our login management system that we built in Chapter 3. Set `session.gc.maxlifetime` in the `php.ini` file. Using a variable, you can check the idle state time and the current session start time.

We will use the same log out script that we created in Chapter 3 for the login management system. The following screenshot shows the logout screen:

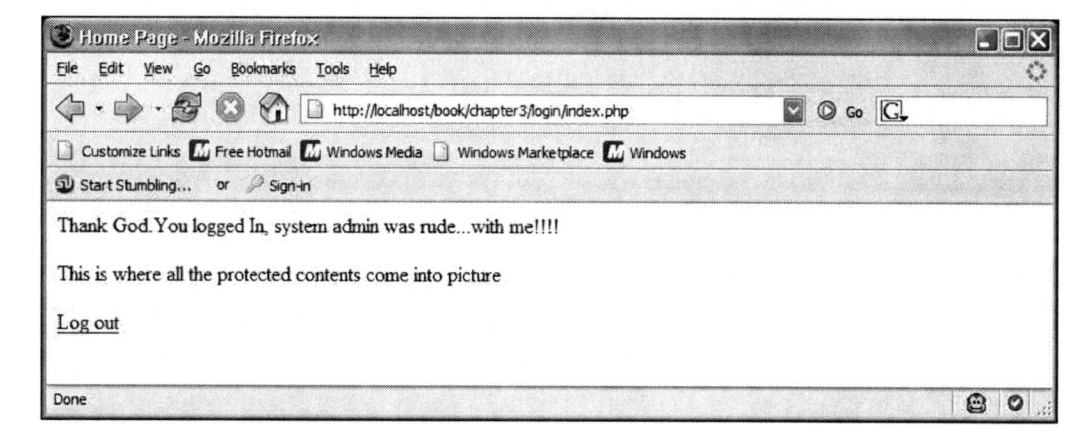

Ideas for life

The Delicious and Digg applications are two huge projects. Here are some of the ideas that can also be added to our bookmarker application:

- Adding the user's picture
- Searching using description
- Adding categories for tutorials
- Editing tutorial information using AJAX
- Visiting a URL

Summary

Did you show off your application to your friends? You should! When everyone seems to be appreciating Digg and Delicious based applications, we can boast of having our own versions of the same.

We have built some cool features such as submitting tutorials, real-time search, tag clouds, and adding tags. We must admit it was fun building them.

In the next chapter we will explore and build a better shopping search experience. Oh, I forgot! I have a lot of tutorials and I am off to bookmark my tutorials using the bookmarker application. Happy hacking!

12
Creating a Shopping Search Engine

Still playing with our bookmarking application? Here is a reason to cheer up. In this chapter, along with the bookmarking tutorials, we will create a new shopping search engine. The shopping application is more about adding a rich user interface experience to the search functionality. We will learn how to integrate the features of the script.aculo.us library to our application. Keep your shopping list ready!

Application at a glance

Before we start coding our shopping application, let's give it a nice 2.0 name. For now, we will name it as **Shop-Me**. You can give it any name that you want.

So let's get started and get a complete picture of our application.

As a user, our friend Jenny signs up with the application. She will be able to see the user profile home page. It has an option to **Buy Products** in which she has to drag products and place them under her selection zone.

She can also search various products using real-time search, and the product details will be displayed in an AJAX way.

We will provide Jenny with a tag cloud. For each tag, search products will be displayed to her.

And finally, Jenny can log off.

To put all the above explained words in a user interface, check out the following screenshot:

Features and functionalities

Now that we are clear about the application, let's quickly walk through the features we are going to build into the **Shop-Me** application. The features we will be working on are listed here:

- The user management system
- Searching products
- Selecting the products to buy
- Adding effects
- Searching products using the tag cloud

So, let's help our friend Jenny with her shopping.

The user management system

We are going to build a user management system for our application. Not really! It is said that *good programmers code, great programmers re-use*. Honestly, we all want to be great programmers. Hence, we will re-use the user management system module created in Chapter 3.

We will use the same database table schema for users, which we created earlier. The schema definition is given as follows:

```
CREATE TABLE `users` (
  `userID` int(11) NOT NULL auto_increment,
  `Username` varchar(40) NOT NULL,
```

```
     `Password` varchar(40) NOT NULL,
     PRIMARY KEY  (`userID`)
   ) ENGINE=InnoDB DEFAULT CHARSET=latin1 AUTO_INCREMENT=1 ;
```

We will also be using the `users` class. The screenshot that follows will help us to quickly get started with the application:

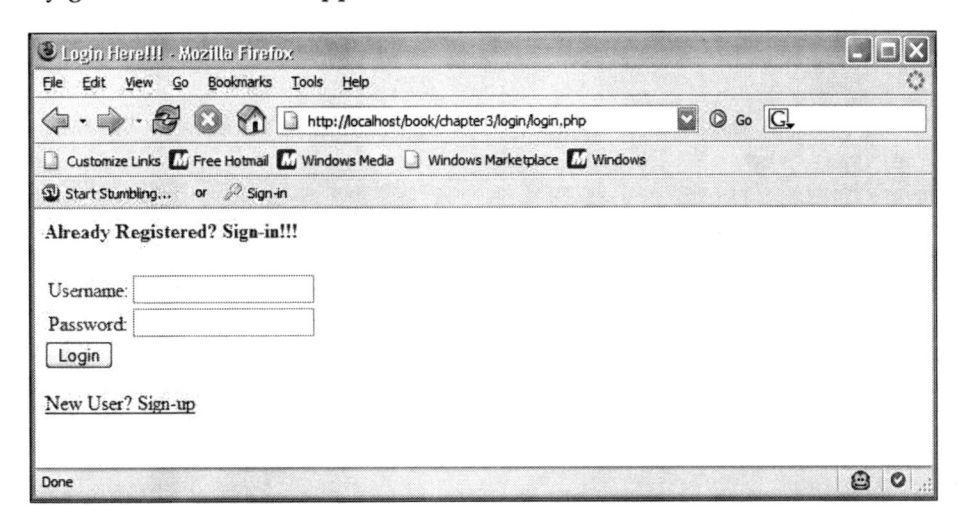

Selecting the products to buy

We have a user management system and our user wants to select the products to buy. We all know Jenny. She just can't wait to buy her new handbag.

Let's do a simple memory test here. Check out the following screenshot and see if you find it familiar:

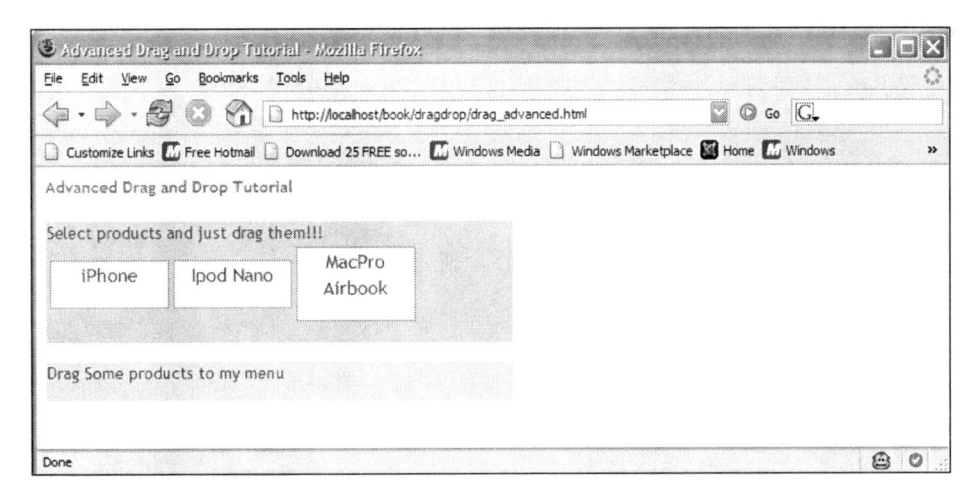

There you go! Yes, we made this module in Chapter 5 while learning the drag and drop feature of script.aculo.us.

Here, we are going to integrate the same module with our application. We will be using the same code and we will add our PHP sessions to make sure that only a registered and logged-in user can access and buy the products.

```
<?PHP
session_start();
if (!(isset($_SESSION['login']) && $_SESSION['login'] != '')) {
   header ("Location: login.php");
}
```

We ensured that this page can be accessed only by the users who are logged in. We have created three products and have made them draggable.

> When dealing with data about products coming from database, you may need to change certain JavaScript code to make things draggable.

The products that we need to buy can be dragged and placed under the droppable area that we have created to hold the products.

We make the created products draggable by using the following code:

```
new Draggable('myProduct2',{revert:true});
```

When we make a product draggable, we can play with the product and drag it anywhere on the page.

The products have been made draggable. Now, we will need a container to hold the products, or an area where we can drop the draggable elements.

We can create a droppable area by defining the `<div>` with the code, as follows:

```
Droppables.add(
 'myDiv',
  {
    onDrop: addItem
  }
);
```

The attributes in the piece of code snippet that we have just seen are:

- `myDiv`: This is the area, `<div>`, or any portion of the page we want to make as the droppable area
- `onDrop`: We call the function `addItem` once we are done with dropping the products in the droppable area

Have a look at the following screenshot and see how the application behaves:

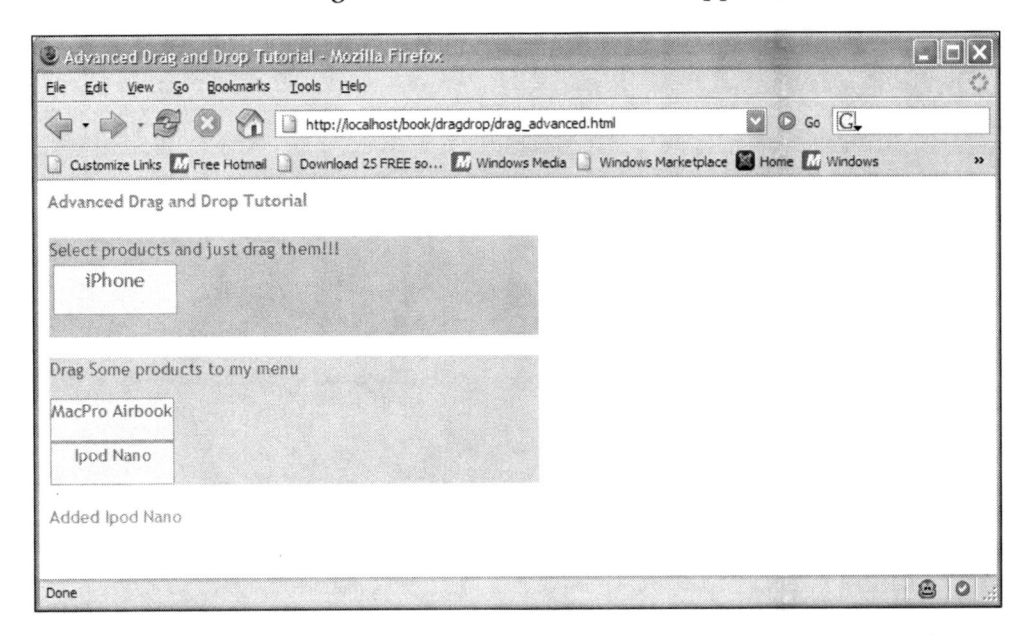

Adding effects

Effects have been one of the most adorable features of script.aculo.us. We surely have done justice to this feature by using it in all the modules and applications that we created.

We have used the effects to inform the user about any update, results, or responses. Users just love them!

Some effects will also be added to our **Shop-Me** application to inform the users—in plain text—about what's happening in the application. As explained before, we can add effects with only one line of code.

In the **Shop-Me application**, in the `buyProducts.php` file, we add this magic line of code to add effects to our results:

```
new Effect.Highlight($('note'));
```

Adding this line of code results in a neat, clean, and attractive text been shown to the user. Check out the following screenshot to see the code in action:

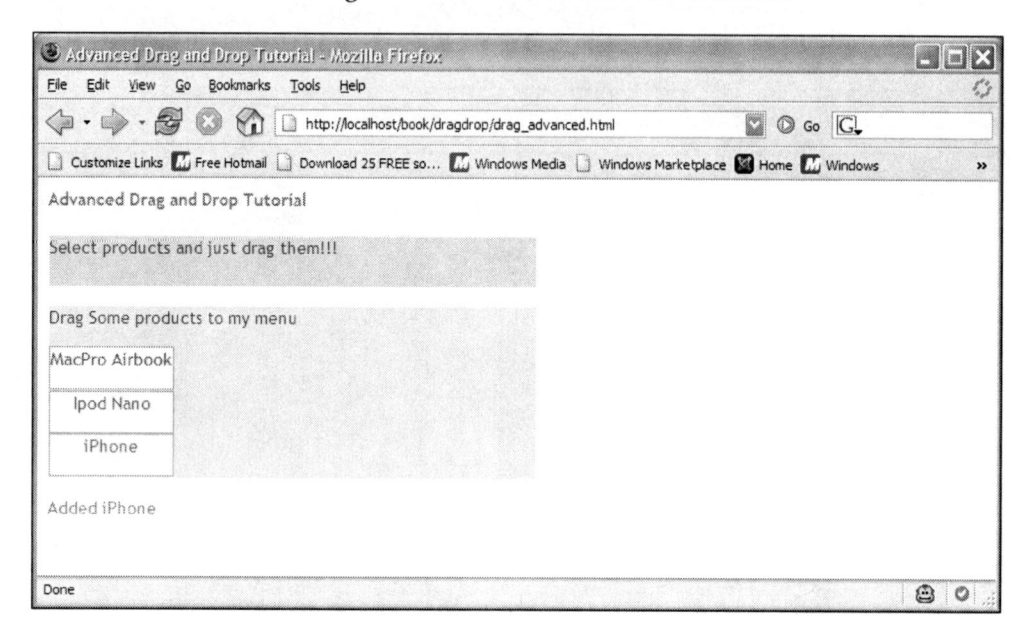

Searching products

We have given Jenny an option to buy the products that we have defined. But that's not really fair. We can do much better! We are now going to create a `products` table in our database. The schema for the `products` table is as follows:

```
CREATE TABLE `products` (
  `product_id` int(11) NOT NULL auto_increment,
  `product_title` varchar(200) NOT NULL,
  PRIMARY KEY ('product_id')
) ENGINE=InnoDB DEFAULT CHARSET=latin1 AUTO_INCREMENT=1;
```

We have used very basic attributes for the products. `product_id` and `product_title` are the only attributes we are considering for our Prototype.

We will power this search feature with the autocompletion feature of script.aculo.us.

After readying the database, it's time to create the user interface for `searchProducts.php`. The code for the interface is as follows:

```
<div class="product-search">
  <label>Enter Your Search Terms</label>
  <input type="text" id="title" name="title"/>
  <div id="myDiv"></div>
<p>
   <div id="result" name="result"></div>
</div>
<div class="show-product" id="show-product"> </div>
```

Check out what the interface looks like in the following screenshot:

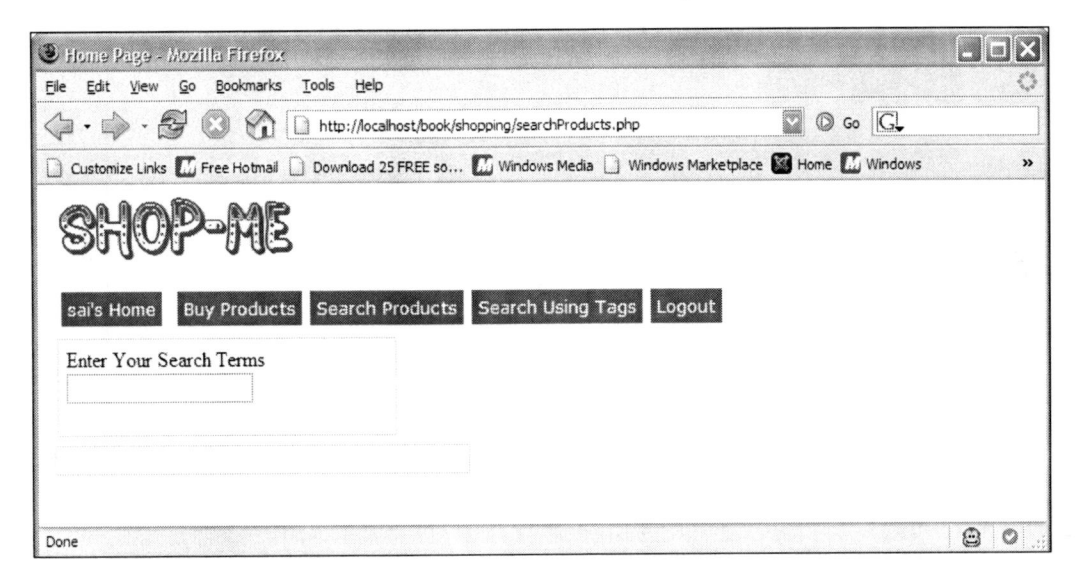

It's show time! We are now going to add the autocompletion feature of script.aculo.us to our search.

The following is the spicy JavaScript code to add the functionality to our application:

```
window.onload = function() {
   new Ajax.Autocompleter(
       'title',
       'myDiv',
       'fetchChoices.php',
       {afterUpdateElement:showProduct}
   );
}
```

[219]

Creating a Shopping Search Engine

The code is pretty much similar to what we did in Chapter 7 and even in our bookmarking application. The only difference is the `afterUpdateElement` event in our definition.

Let's get a clear picture by taking some help from the user interface. When our user, Jenny, starts typing the product name or title using the autocompletion feature, we give her suggestions about the available product names in the database. This is seen in the following screenshot:

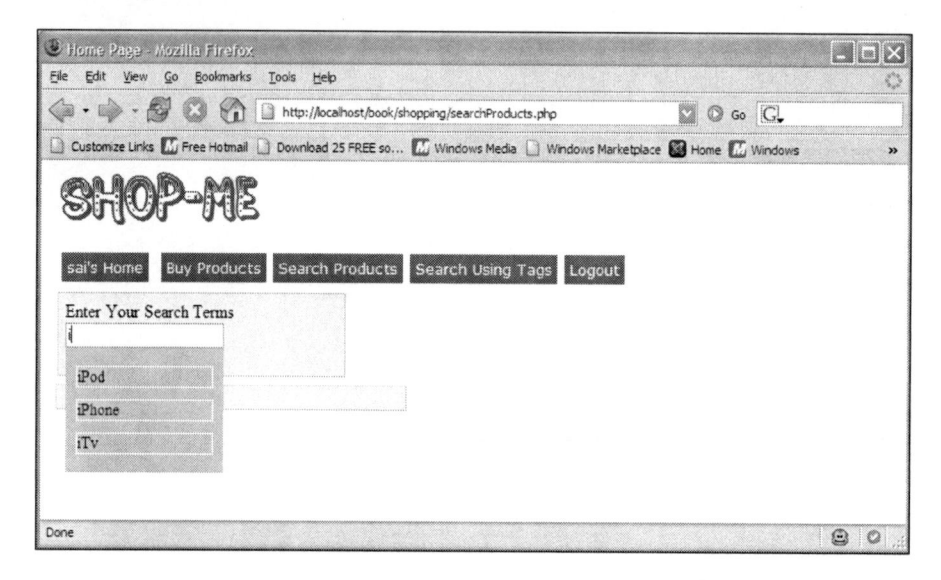

So, now when Jenny selects a particular product using the `Ajax.Request` feature, we fetch the product information and display it in the empty `<div>`. Jenny sees the product information without having to refresh the page.

When the user selects a product from the list of suggestions, the `afterUpdateElement` event gets called and the `showProduct()` function is invoked.

The code for the `showProduct()` function is as follows:

```
function showProduct(text,li)
{
var pars = 'product_id='+li.id;
var url = 'getProduct.php';
new Ajax.Request(url, {
     method: 'POST',
     parameters:pars,
     onSuccess: showResult,
     onFailure:showError
  });
}
```

We are reading the product ID information, and we are passing it to
`getProduct.php` using `POST`.

The `getProduct.php` script at the server side will process the data and send the response back to the JavaScript function.

Let's quickly take a look at the `getProduct.php` script. To read the product information, we are using the following query:

```
$query="SELECT product_id, product_title FROM products
        WHERE product_id=".$value;
```

Executing the query above with `$value` as `product_id`, we read the product information and pass it back to our function `showProduct`. Using `onSuccess`, we will read the response from the server and put it back on the user interface.

The snippet to display the response from the server is as follows:

```
$('show-product').innerHTML = response;
```

Check out the corresponding interface to display the response from the server.

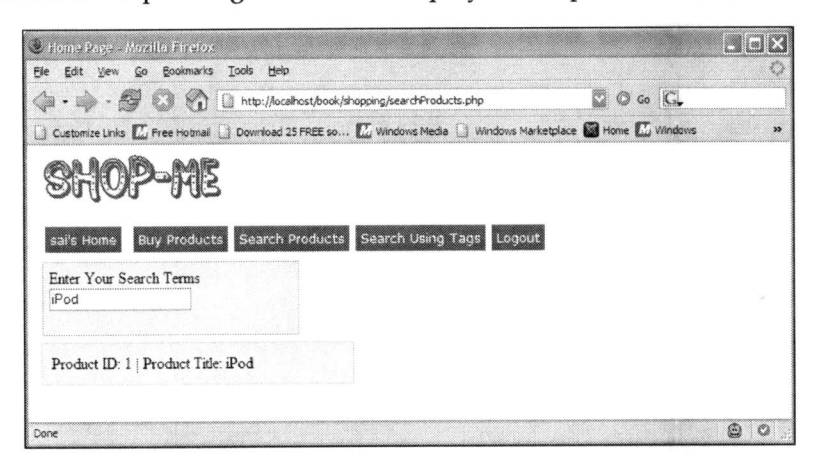

Searching products using the tag cloud

We created the tags class in our application in Chapter 11, and we will make use of the same class in our application here. Of course, we will be making the necessary changes to our database settings, queries, and table names.

We will be searching products in two steps:

1. Generate a tag cloud.
2. View the products for a tag name.

Generating a tag cloud

We have generated the tag cloud in the Chapter 11 tutorials using the `read_all_tags()` function from the `tags` class.

Let's quickly see the code that helped us create a tag cloud. The following query will read all the tags for the products:

```
function read_all_tags() {
$query = "SELECT tag_name FROM product_tags";
$result = mysql_query($query);
   if($result) {
       while($row = mysql_fetch_array($result)) {
       $all_tags[$row['tag_name']] = $row['tag_name'];
       }
       return $all_tags;
    }
}
```

The query we used in the code that we just saw is to read all the tags from the `product_tags` table.

```
$query = "SELECT tag_name FROM product_tags";
```

Now, let's see the necessary changes we need to create our tag cloud.

```
foreach ($all_tags as $tag =>$value)
{
   echo '<a style="font-size:'. rand(50,20). 'px'.'" class="tag_cloud"
   href="http://localhost/book/shopping/searchTags.php?tag='
   .$value.'" title="\'' . $tag . '">'.$value.'';
}
```

In the code that we just saw, we are looping through each tag in the `tagCloud.php` script and making magic with CSS.

[222]

View products for a tag name

So far, we have created our tag cloud and we have all our tags presented to the user. Now, when a user clicks on a tag, we need to display the products associated with the tag.

Let's quickly add the function to our `products` class and then invoke it in our `searchTags.php` script. The code for the function that will fetch us all the products with a particular tag is as follows:

```
function search_by_tags($tag) {
$query = "SELECT product_id FROM product_tags WHERE tag_name = '".$tag."'";
return $query;
}
```

OK, now when we are done with executing our query, we will have a result set with the values of products that are matching our tag.

We will take that result set, loop through it, and display it to the user. The code to loop through the result set is as follows:

```
$result = $db->perform_query($query);
    if($result) {
    while($row=$db->fetch_array($result))
    {
        echo "<div class='show-product-id'>Product
            ID:".$row[0]."<br></div>";
    }
}
```

Take a look at the following screenshot and see how the application looks:

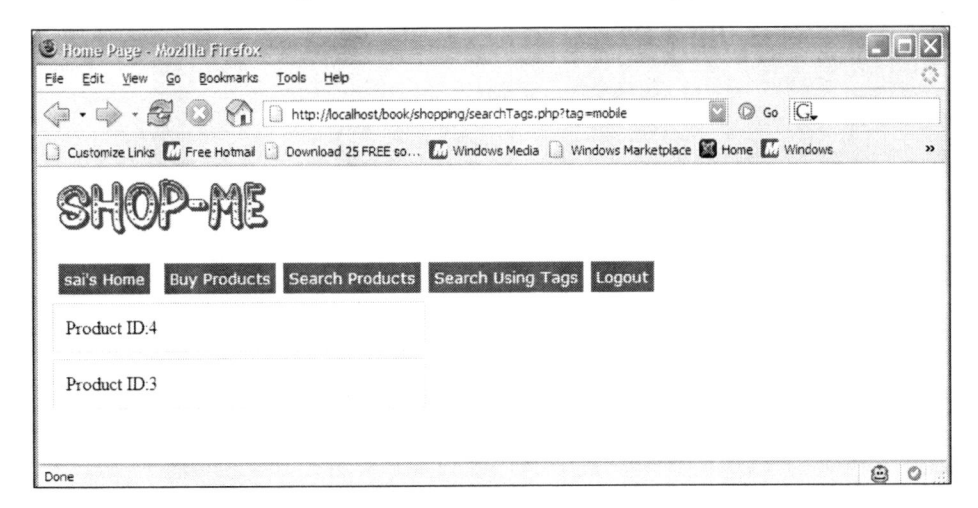

Summary

Shopping has been a thing of interest as well as business. In this chapter we created a new shopping search experience. We have integrated a couple of script.aculo.us features into our application, **Shop-Me**.

From searching products to tag clouds and from drag and drop features to effects, we have added them all in our application.

In the next (and the last) chapter, we will revisit all the modules that we have created so far and see how we can integrate them into any web applications. We will also create a new commenting system for our applications. See you in the next chapter!

13
Common 43: 43 Things, 43 Places, and 43 People Clones

How many tutorials did you bookmark? And how many products did you add to your shopping cart? We had fun developing our applications and the applications stand as a testimony to our claim.

In this chapter we will be building the clones of 43 things, 43 places, and 43 people. These clones are also some of the most famous applications of the Web 2.0 era. We will create a raw structure and see how we can integrate our modules to build clones for these applications.

Some of the key features we will be learning and working with in this chapter are:

- Getting the database ready for the common 43 applications
- The AJAX commenting system
- The modules built so far
- A quick view of the script.aculo.us features
- Clubbing the pieces together

So let the party begin!

Getting the database ready

The first thing we learned in all the chapters till now is to start with designing the database schema. We certainly believe in breaking rules, but not when it comes to making killer web applications. So, let's quickly create the database tables for places, people, things, and also for tagging.

Database for places

We will be creating a basic schema for storing information about places. The schema is defined as follows:

```
CREATE TABLE `places` (
   `place_id` INT NOT NULL AUTO_INCREMENT PRIMARY KEY ,
   `place_name` VARCHAR( 200 ) NOT NULL ,
   `place_desc` VARCHAR( 300 ) NOT NULL
) ENGINE = innodb;
```

The attributes of the `places` table are as follows:

- `place_id`: This is the unique `id` for each place. The field is defined as the `PRIMARY KEY` and will be auto incremented every time places are added in the database.
- `place_name`: This field contains the name of the place.
- `place_desc`: This field contains some description about the place.

Database for people

Now, let's quickly create a schema definition for the `people`'s table. This will be on the same lines as our `places` table.

```
CREATE TABLE `people` (
   `people_id` INT NOT NULL AUTO_INCREMENT PRIMARY KEY ,
   `people_title` VARCHAR( 200 ) NOT NULL ,
   `people_desc` VARCHAR( 300 ) NOT NULL
) ENGINE = innodb;
```

The attributes of the `people`'s table are as follows:

- `people_id`: This a unique `id` using which the application can identify each user as separate
- `people_name`: This is the name of the user
- `people_desc`: This contains some description about the place

Database for things

OK, so now we have created a schema definition for people and places. On the same lines, you can try and create the schema for things. The database code is given as a part of code download at the URL mentioned in the Preface to test your skills.

Advanced commenting system

We have covered and created a lot of modules for our web applications. Ask your friend, and he will tell you that we have missed out one important feature—comments.

Comments have become an integral part of all web applications. They allow the users to discuss and share their view points.

In this section we will learn how to create an AJAX-based comments module. This module is a Prototype. Please feel free to add your creative ideas to make it as powerful as your applications.

So, let's get started and add the comments module to our bookmarker application. In `viewtutorial.php` from Chapter 11, we have seen the details of the tutorial and now let's add the comments section to it.

Creating a comments form

Let's quickly put some code together and make the user interface for our comments module. We need to have a link called **Add Comments** and on clicking it, the user will be shown the add comments form.

Another link that we need is the **Hide Comments** link, which will be hidden from the user and will only be shown to the user when the add comments form is displayed.

```
echo '<div>
    <table id="show-comments" class="show-comments">
    </table>
</div>';
echo '<div id="add-comments">
    <a href="Javascript:showCommentsForm()">Add Comments</a>
</div>';
echo '<div id="hide-comments" style="display:none">
    <a href="Javascript:hideCommentsForm()">Hide Comments</a>
</div>';
```

Common 43: 43 Things, 43 Places, and 43 People Clones

Check out the following screenshot with the **Add Comments** link:

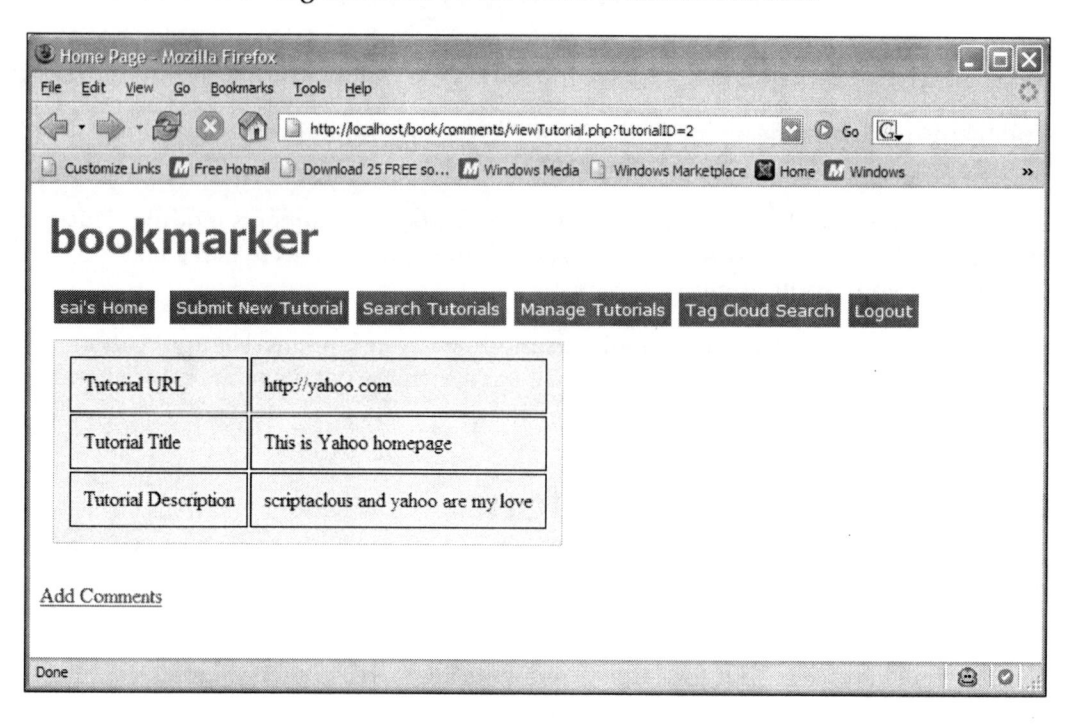

[Screenshot of bookmarker Home Page in Mozilla Firefox showing URL http://localhost/book/comments/viewTutorial.php?tutorialID=2. Navigation buttons: sai's Home, Submit New Tutorial, Search Tutorials, Manage Tutorials, Tag Cloud Search, Logout. A table shows Tutorial URL: http://yahoo.com, Tutorial Title: This is Yahoo homepage, Tutorial Description: scriptaclous and yahoo are my love. Below the table is an "Add Comments" link.]

An empty table named `show-comments` will be used to hold all the comments posted by the user.

```
echo '<div class="comments-form" id="comments-form"
         style="display:none">
   <form id="myform" method="POST" onsubmit="return false;">';
      echo '<input type="hidden" size="45" name="tutorialID"
            id="tutorialID" value="'.$tutorialID.'">
   <input type="hidden" size="45" name="ownerID" id="ownerID"
            value="'.$ownerid.'">Add Your Comments<br>
   <input type="text" size="45" name="your_comments"
            id="your_comments"><br>
   <input type="button" onclick="addComments()"
            value="Add Comments">
   </form>
</div>';
```

In the code that we just saw, we have created a simple text box and a submit button to post the data. The following screenshot shows us the output:

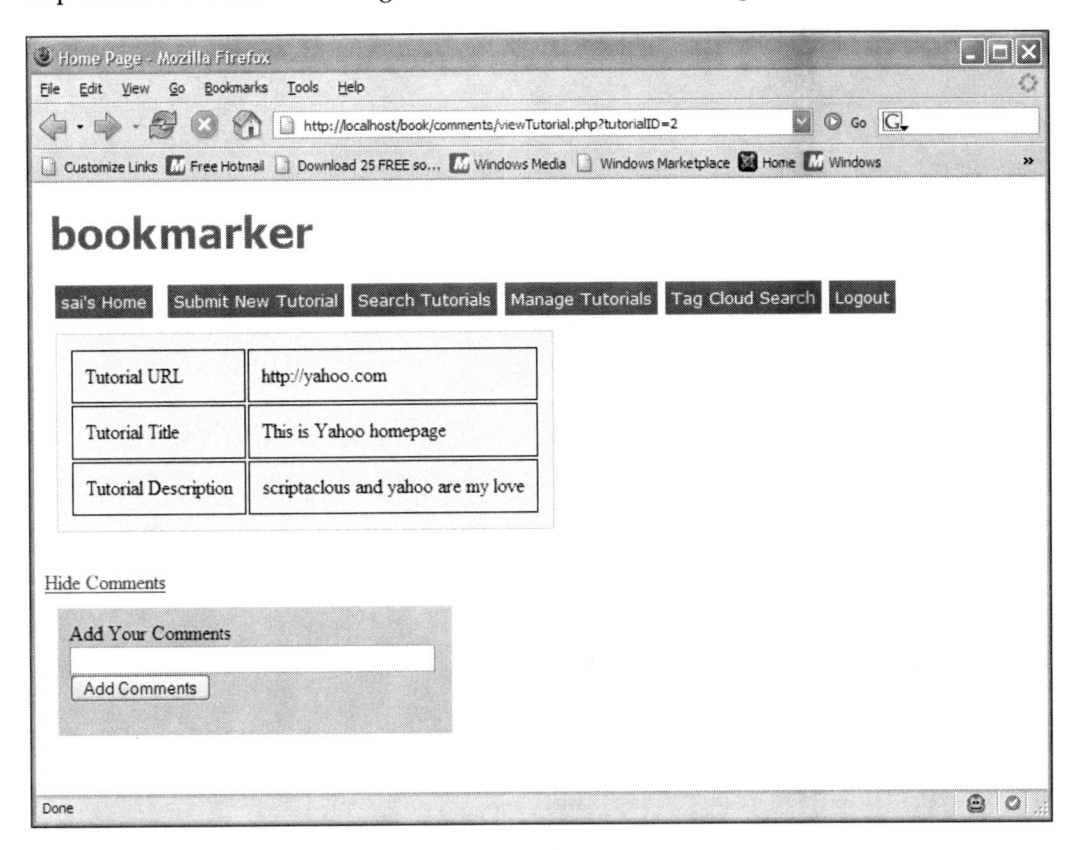

Now let's wrap things up and hide the user interface components that we do not intend to show to the user at this point in time.

```
function showCommentsForm(){
    $('comments-form').style.display="";
    $('add-comments').style.display="none";
    $('hide-comments').style.display="";
}
```

Posting comments

OK, so now that we have our comments interface ready, we will post the data to server the AJAX way. When the user clicks on the submit button, the data is posted using the `Ajax.Request` feature that we learned in Chapter 2.

We will add the following piece of JavaScript code to add the comments functionality:

```javascript
function addComments() {
    var your_comments = 'your_comments='+$F('your_comments');
    var tutorialID = 'tutorialID='+$F('tutorialID');
    var ownerID = 'ownerID='+$F('ownerID');
    var pars = your_comments+'&'+tutorialID+'&'+ownerID;
    new Ajax.Request(
        'GetItem.php',
        {
            asynchronous:true,
            parameters:pars,
            onComplete: ShowData
        }
    );
    $('myform').reset();
    return false;
}
```

In the above piece of code, we are creating a function called `addComments()` and it will read `userID`, `tutorialID`, and the comments posted by the user.

We will pass these values to the server file, `getItem.php`, using `Ajax.Request`. When the request is completed, we will call another JavaScript function, `ShowData()`, which will handle the response sent by the server.

We mentioned that we are passing the values to the `GetItem.php` script. So, let's explore what we will be doing in `GetItem.php`.

A couple of things that we will have to do in sequence at the server side are as follows:

1. Create an XML file.
2. Insert the data.
3. Read back the recently added comment.
4. Create an XML tree with the data read.

Let's start by creating the XML file. The lines of code that we need to add to create an XML file are as follows:

```php
header("Content-Type: text/xml");
print'<?xml version="1.0" encoding="UTF-8" standalone="yes"?>';
```

In this way, we are passing our header information to the PHP compiler and informing it that the file has XML content.

We need to read the values of `tutorialID`, `ownerID`, and the comments posted by the user. The code for reading the values is as follows:

```
$your_comments = $_POST['your_comments'];
$tutorialID = $_POST['tutorialID'];
$ownerID = $_POST['ownerID'];
```

The next step is to insert the comment information to our database tables. The query to insert the data is as follows:

```
$sql = "INSERT INTO comments (commentID,tutorialID,ownerID,
comment_desc,Date) VALUES (NULL,'$tutorialID','$ownerID',
'$your_comments',CURRENT_TIMESTAMP)";
```

After inserting the data in the table, we will have to read back the recently added `commentID`.

```
$rowID = $db->get_last_insert_id();
```

We have `commentID` for the latest inserted comment. We will read the values for this `commentID` and put them in the XML tree format.

```
echo '<response>';
echo '<commentID>'.$rowID.'</commentID>';
echo '<comment_desc>'.$comment_desc.'</comment_desc>';
echo '</response>';
```

That makes the `getItem.php` file complete. This will return the response in the XML format. We need to handle and read the response in the JavaScript file.

A function called `showData()` in our `Ajax.Request` will be called once the server sends the response.

The code for the `showData()` function is as follows:

```
function ShowData(originalRequest) {
   var xmlDoc = originalRequest.responseXML.documentElement;
   var value =
      xmlDoc.getElementsByTagName("comment_desc")[0].childNodes[0].
         nodeValue;
   var value1 =
      xmlDoc.getElementsByTagName("commentID")[0].childNodes[0].
         nodeValue;
}
```

In the function that we just saw, we are reading the response sent by the server. The response sent is in the XML format. Hence, we will loop through the `childNodes` and read the values.

But wait! We are missing something.

We have read the comments inserted in the database and received the response. Now, we need to put it in our user interface and display it to the user.

The table rows will be added dynamically using DOM with the data that we received from the server.

The code for creating dynamic table rows and data is as follows:

```
var newTR=document.createElement('tr');
newTR.class='show-comments';
var newTD=document.createElement('td');
newTD.appendChild(document.createTextNode(value));
```

But that's not all! We need to present the user with the **Edit** and **Delete** options along with the data.

Here is the complete code for the function `showData()`:

```
function ShowData(originalRequest) {
   var xmlDoc = originalRequest.responseXML.documentElement;
   var value =
      xmlDoc.getElementsByTagName("comment_desc")[0].childNodes[0].
         nodeValue;
   var value1 =
      xmlDoc.getElementsByTagName("commentID")[0].childNodes[0].
         nodeValue;
   var newTR=document.createElement('tr');
   newTR.class='show-comments';
   var newTD=document.createElement('td');
   newTD.appendChild(document.createTextNode(value));
   var newTD2=document.createElement('td');
   var textNode2=document.createTextNode('Edit')
   var editLink=document.createElement("a")
   editLink.setAttribute("title",'Delete')
   editLink.setAttribute("href",'#')
   editLink.appendChild(textNode2);
   newTD2.appendChild(editLink);
   var newTD3=document.createElement('td');
   var textNode=document.createTextNode('Delete')
   var delLink=document.createElement("a")
   delLink.setAttribute("title",'Delete')
```

```
        delLink.setAttribute("href",'#')
        delLink.appendChild(textNode);
        newTD3.appendChild(delLink);
        newTR.appendChild(newTD);
        newTR.appendChild(newTD2);
        newTR.appendChild(newTD3);
        $('show-comments').appendChild(newTR);
}
```

The above code might have confused you. But if you look at the code carefully, you will find that we are just doing the simplest thing with DOM.

Now, after all this coding, it's time to see what our hard work results in. Check out the following screenshot:

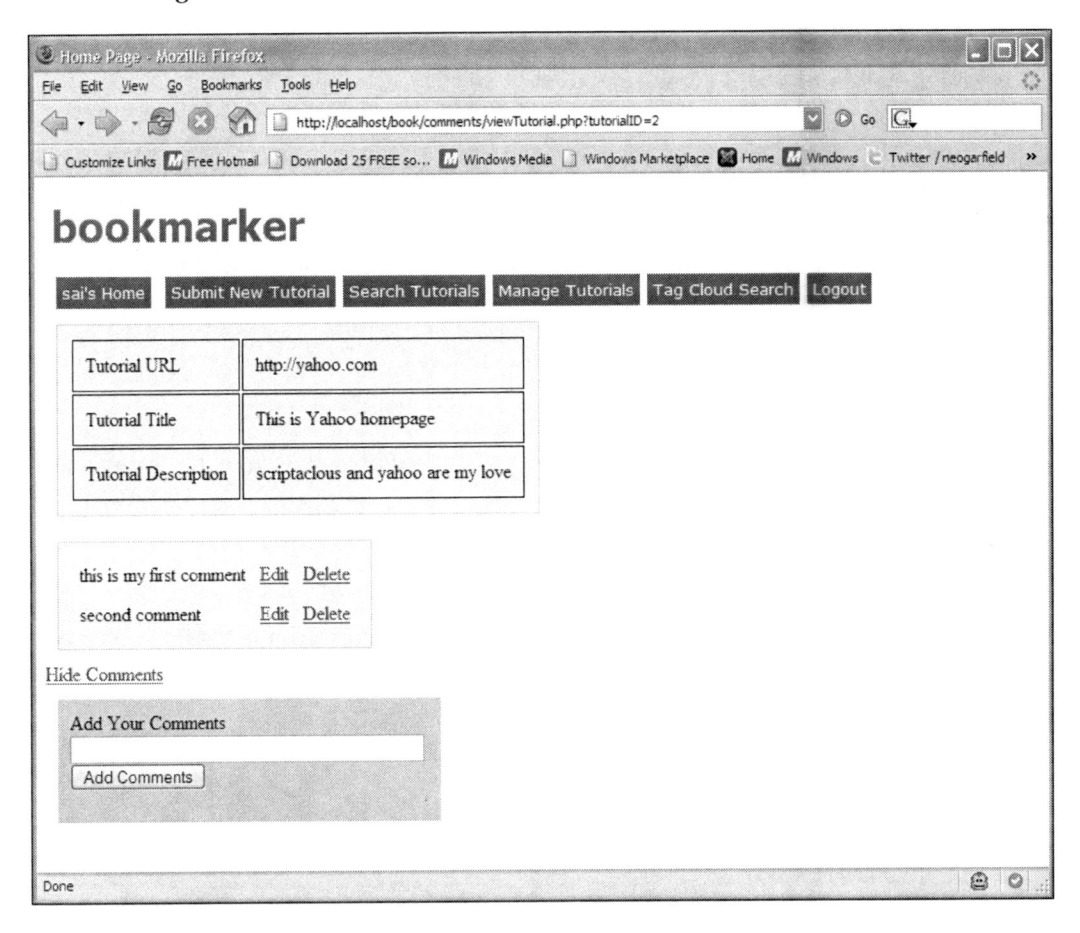

Edit or Delete comments

OK, so we have added **Edit** and **Delete** options as links with `href="#"`. Here, we need the two functions `editComment()` and `deleteComment()` that will be linked to the **Edit** and **Delete** options.

That's your homework. OK, let me give you a few hints. Just follow these steps in the sequence mentioned and you should be able to see the resulting output.

- Read the comment ID
- Using `Ajax.Request`, pass the value of `commentID` and `userID`
- Check if the user can delete or edit the comment
- Edit or Delete and get the response from the server
- Display the result to the user

Those are all the hints I will give you.

Modules ready to go live

Throughout this book we have learned and built different modules, most of which can be easily integrated into any web application. In this section we will look at some of these modules that can be used at the server side.

- User management system
- Tag cloud features

Let's quickly walk through each of the modules and see how we can extend them to any web application.

User management system

We created a user management system in Chapter 3, which we have also re-used in our real-world applications.

Some of the key features we created are:

- User signup
- Log in
- Register new user
- Log out

These are the most basic features for any web application. In a real scenario, you may have to work and tweak the code to add necessary security and other important features as per the requirement of the projects.

We have created separate classes for `Users` and `Database` that can be extended further and can easily be used in invoking the objects for the classes.

Tag cloud features

I am sure that by now you are a fan of tags and want to use them effectively in your web applications. We have created the tag class in Chapter 11.

Using the tags class, we have been able to do the following functionalities:

- Add tags
- Search using tags
- Create a tag cloud
- Delete tags
- Edit tags

With a simple change in database schema definition, we can extend the tags to any web application.

Adding 2.0 flavour to applications

We covered the basic modules at the server side in the previous section. Now, let's also quickly recollect and add the 2.0 aspects to our web applications. All these features have been covered extensively in the previous chapters.

AJAX modules

We are in the Web 2.0 era and AJAX has become a part of applications and also of developers like us.

AJAX helps us in making our applications fast and efficient. Prototype and script.aculo.us provide us with a very powerful combination to add beauty to powerful features. We have explored in detail some of the following features in Chapter 2:

- `Ajax.Request`
- `Ajax.updater`

Effects

One of the most amazing features of script.aculo.us, and my personal favourite, is effects. Effects can be used to inform users, highlight some key aspect of features, or just to add beauty to applications. Just about anything and everything can be done using effects.

We have seen how to use various types of effects. Some of the key effects are as follows:

- `Effect.Opacity`
- `Effect.Scale`
- `Effect.Morph`
- `Effect.Move`
- `Effect.Highlight`
- `Effect.Parellel`

There are some more effects that can also be used along with applications. We have explored them in detail in Chapter 4. The application we created in Chapter 4 is shown in the following screenshot:

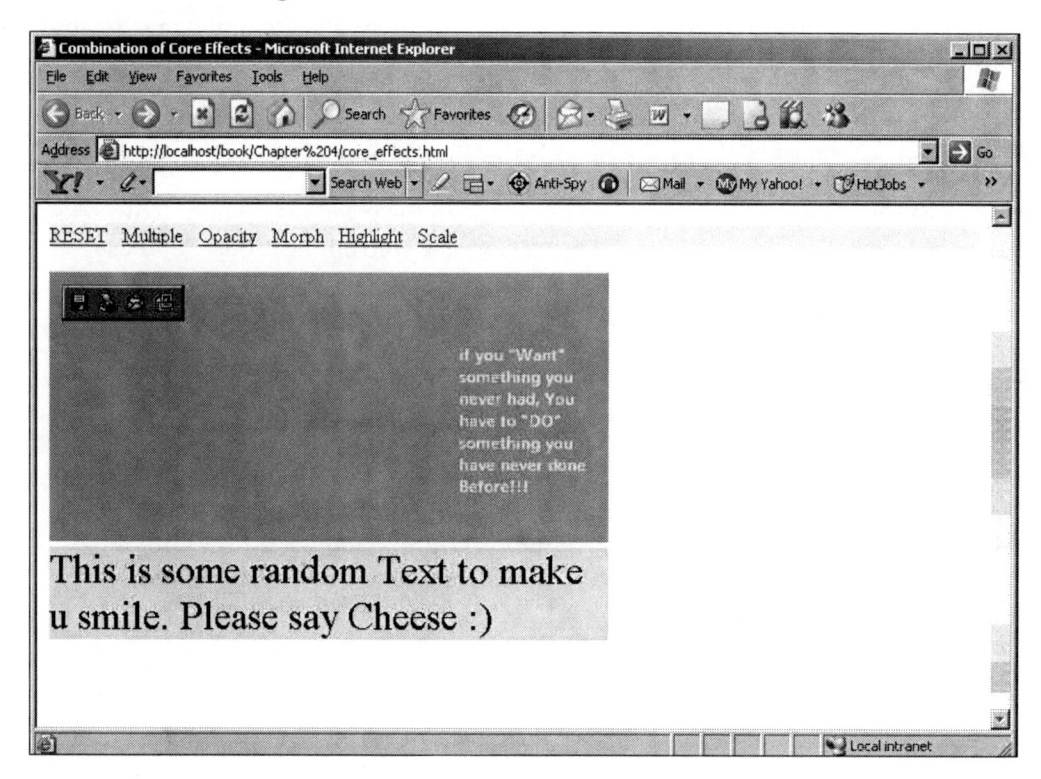

Real-time search

We have created real-time search using the autocompletion feature of script.aculo.us that we covered in detail in Chapter 7.

We implemented the same in our projects. In the bookmarker application, we used it to search tutorials. In our **Shop-Me** application, we used it to search the products as well.

The logic behind the feature remains the same. For reference, look at the following screenshot from the bookmarker application. So, go ahead and plug this feature into your applications.

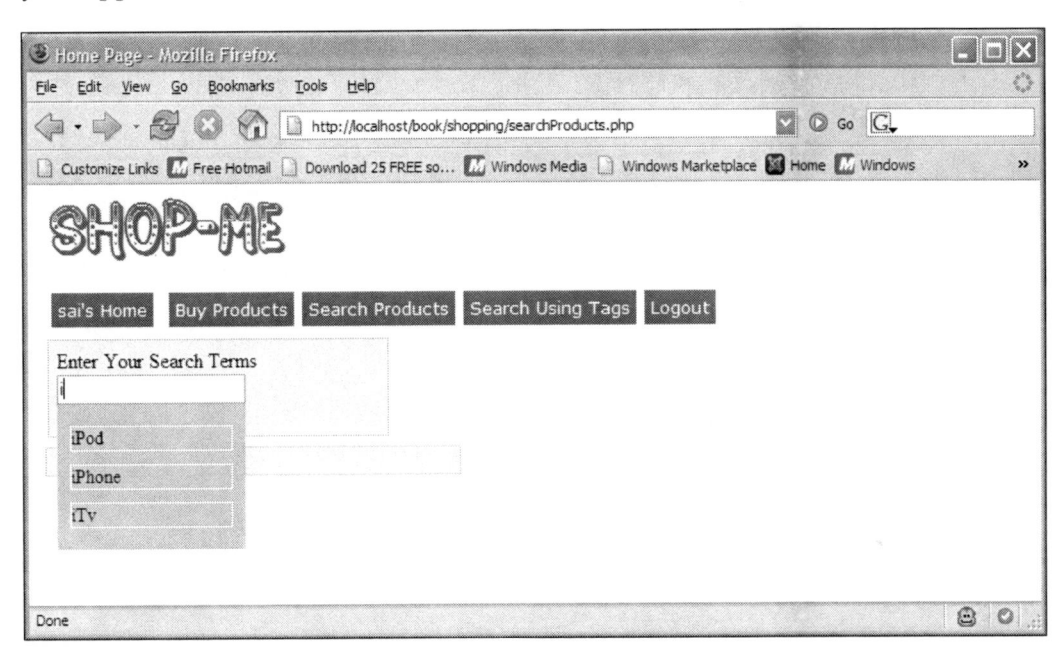

In-place editing

This feature makes things dead simple for basic editing, and especially for any text field. We covered this feature in detail in Chapter 6.

> Any portion of application user interface can be customized for in-place editing. But be choosy about where you apply it!

Drag and drop

How simple would it be if we could just drag and drop things in real life? A great thought by the way! We learned in detail about the drag and drop feature in Chapter 5. Remember how we dragged and dropped our products in the **Shop-Me** application?

> The drag and drop feature is mainly used for a limited set of items. If this set of items is huge, think twice!

For a quick revision, check out the following screenshot:

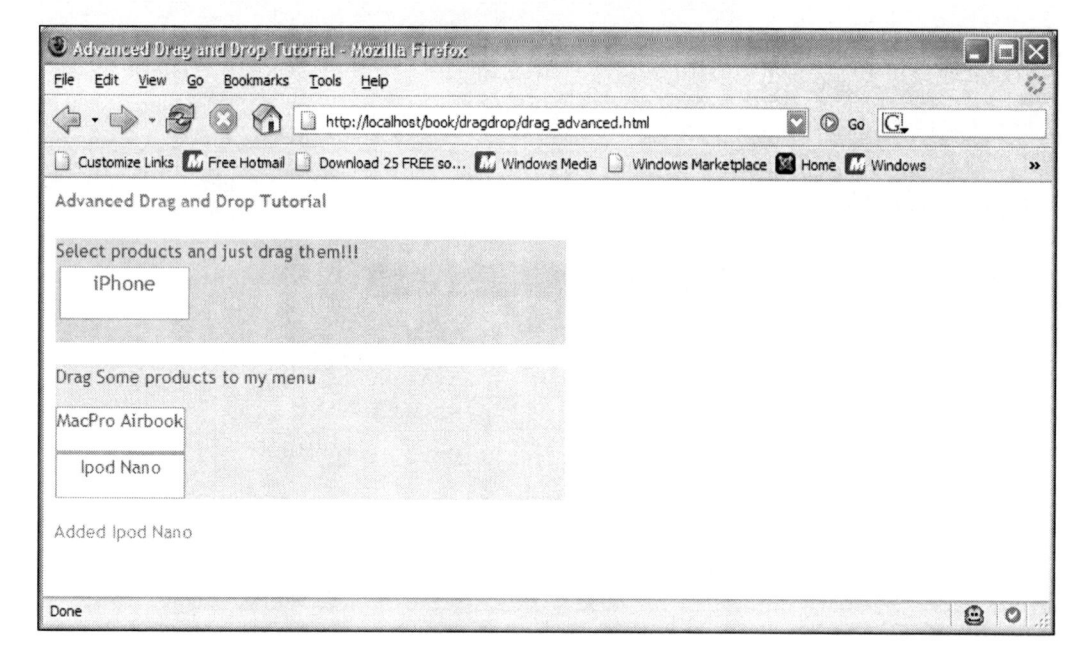

Putting the building blocks together

OK, so now we have covered all the modules at both the server side and the client side. Let's club them together and make new applications.

Features and functionalities

These are some of the key features and functionalities that we will create just by integrating all the modules and code we have created so far.

- User signup
- Login
- Forgot password
- Logout
- User profile
- Tag cloud search for people/places/things
- Add new people/places/things
- Edit people/places/things
- Delete people/places/things
- Effects to notify the user
- `Ajax.Request` to add the 2.0 way of handling data
- In-place editing for title/description
- Real-time search for people/places/things

We have covered and created all the above features in various modules and also in our projects.

So, just play around with the code, tweak it, and plug it into any web application.

Summary

OK, so that brings us to the end of the chapter and the journey of script.aculo.us. We learned many exciting and useful features throughout the book.

Some of the key features that we learned are:

- Effects
- In-place editing
- Autocompletion
- Slider
- Drag and drop

The key modules that we used at the server side are:

- User management system
- Tag cloud features

And, as I have said throughout the book, script.aculo.us has a lot of promise. The only thing that will completely explore its potential is your creativity and imagination. Here's wishing you good luck. May your friends and users be impressed!

Index

Symbols

$() prototype 13
$_POST 178
$A() prototype 13
$F() prototype 13
$H() prototype 13
$R() prototype 13

A

ad_new_list() 178
add() method 88
Add Comments link, comments 227
AddItem() function, code 179, 180
add method, droppables namespace 88
Add This List button 178
AddtoCompleted function
  itemValue parameter 184
  valueID parameter 184
AddtoItemTree() function, code 187
afterUpdateElement option,
      remote sources 120
AJAX 8, 9
Ajax.PeriodicalUpdater class, prototype 18
Ajax.Request object, prototype 17, 18
Ajax.Responders class, prototype 19, 20
Ajax.Updater class, prototype 18
AJAX components 16
AJAX modules 235
AJAX objects
  Ajax.PeriodicalUpdater class 18
  Ajax.Request object 17, 18
  Ajax.Responders class 19, 20
  Ajax.Updater class 18

display username availability script, Ajax.
      Updater used 23, 24
examples 20
username availability script, Ajax.Request
      used 20-22
Asynchronous JavaScript and XML. *See*
      AJAX
auto completion feature
  about 115-117
  auto completion sources 118
  auto completion sources, options 119
  auto completion sources, types 118
  code usage, local sources used 123
  code usage, remote sources used 121, 122
  container parameter 117
  element parameter 117
  example, local sources used 132, 133
  example, remote sources for multiple fields
        used 128-132
  example, remote sources used 124-127
  explanation 117
  local sources 119
  local sources, auto completion sources 118
  local sources:about 118
  options parameter 118
  parameters 117
  remote sources 118
  remote sources, auto completion
        sources 118
  source parameter 118
  sources, types 118
auto completion feature, local sources used
  code usage 123
  example 132, 133
  options, adding to constructor 123

auto completion feature, remote sources for multiple fields used
  example 128-132
auto completion feature, remote sources used 123
  code usage 121
  example 124-128
  options, adding to constructor 122, 123
auto completion sources
  options 119
  options, for local sources 120, 121
  options, for remote sources 119, 120
axis, slider options 137

B

Backpackit application 8
bookmarker application
  2.0 application, tag cloud features 206, 207
  database playground 194
  description, adding to tutorial 199-201
  features 194
  functionality 194
  logging out 210
  new tutorials, submitting 196
  real-time auto completion search 204-206
  search function, tags used 209
  tag cloud, creating 208
  tags, adding to tutorial 199-201
  tags, adding to tutorials 207, 208
  tags in database, reading 208
  tips and tricks 211
  title, adding to tutorial 199-201
  tutorials, deleting 202-204
  tutorials, viewing 202
  tutorial URL, submitting 197, 198
  user interface 199-201
  user profile home page 196
bookmarker application, tips and tricks 211

C

callback option, in-place editing feature 102
callback option, remote sources 120
callsomeFunction 20
cancelLink option, in-place editing feature 101

cancelText option, in-place editing feature 101, 103
change option, drag and drop feature 87
ChangeStatus() function 185
changeStatus(valueID) function 185, 186
choices option, local sources 120
clickToEditText option, in-place editing feature 101, 105
cols option, in-place editing feature 102, 105
commentID 231
comments
  about 227
  Add Comments link 227
  deleting 234
  editing 234
  form, creating 227-229
  Hide Comments link 227
  posting 229-233
common parameters
  delay parameter 69
  duration parameter 69
  from parameter 69
  to parameter 69
common scripts 49
constraint option, drag and drop feature 87
container parameter, auto completion feature 117

D

database
  for people 226
  for places 226
  for things 226
database playground, bookmarker application
  tutorials_tags table 195
  tutorials_tags table, attributes 196
  tutorials_tags table, schema 195
  tutorials table 195
  tutorials table, attributes 195
  tutorials table, schema 195
database playground, todonow
  database table items, fields 171
  database table lists, fields 171
  Date, items field 171
  Date, lists field 171

[242]

ItemID, items field 171
ItemName, items field 171
ListID, lists field 171
ListName, lists field 171
ownerID, items field 171
ownerID, lists field 171
Status, items field 171
DBClass.php 47, 49
DBConfig.php 47
DeletefromItemTree() function 185
DeleteFromItemTree(divDelete)
 function 185
Delicious application 206
disable method 30
Digg application 193
disabled, slider options 138
drag and drop feature 7, 238
 about 86
 advanced tutorial 93-97
 callback options 87
 code usage 88
 draggable element, initializing 87
 exercise 157-159
 options 87
 sample, in one line code 91, 92
drag and drop feature, callback option
 change option 87
 droppables, namespace 88
 onDrag option 87
 onEnd option 87
 onStart option 87
drag and drop feature, options
 constraint option 87
 endEffect option 87
 ghosting option 87
 handle option 87
 revertEffect option 87
 revert option 87
 snap option 87
 startEffect option 87
draggable element, initializing 87
droppables, namespace 88
 add method 88, 90
 onDrop callback 88, 90
 onHover callback 88
 remove method 88, 90

E

Effect.Highlight, effect 68
Effect.Morph, effect 68
Effect.Move, effect 68
Effect.Multiple, effect 68
Effect.Opacity, effect 68
Effect.Scale, effect 68
effect engine feature 6, 7, 236
effects
 about 67, 68
 code usage 69-73
 common parameters 69
 core effects 73, 74
 Effect.Highlight 68
 Effect.Morph 68
 Effect.Move 68
 Effect.Multiple 68
 Effect.Opacity 68
 Effect.Scale 68
 example 73
 exercise 157
 types 68
 various effects 76, 78
effects, example
 combining 78
 core effects 73-75
 various effects 76, 78
effects, shopping application
 adding 217
Element.extend() 13
element parameter, auto completion
 feature 117
element parameter, in-place editing
 feature 101
enable method 30
endEffect option, drag and drop
 feature 87-89
enterEnterMode() function, in-place editing
 feature 107
event handling, prototype
 about 25
 general events, handling 25
 keyboard events, handling 26, 27
 keyboard events handling, example 28
 mouse events, handling 26
 mouse events handling, example 29

example
  drag and drop, advanced 93-97
  drag and drop, in one line code 91, 92

F

fetchArray function 175
forms, prototype
  about 30
  disable method 30
  enable method 30
  examples 32-35
  findFirstElement method 30
  focusFirstElement method 30
  getElements method 30
  getInputs method 30
  methods 30
  request method 31
  reset method 31
  serializeElements method 31
  serialize method 31
  usage 31
frequency option, remote sources 119
fullSearch option, local sources 120
findFirstElement method 30
focusFirstElement method 30

G

general events, handling methods
  element method 25
  extend method 25
  findElement method 25
  observe method 25
  stop method 25
  StopObserving method 25
  unloadedCache method 26
  syntax 26
getElements method 30
getInputs method 30
ghosting option, drag and drop
    feature 87, 89

H

handle, slider parameter 137
handle option, drag and drop feature 87, 89
Hide Comments link, comments 227

highlightColor option, in-place editing
    feature 102, 105
highlightendColor option, in-place editing
    feature 102
horizontal slider
  about 139
  code usage 142, 143
  example 149-153

I

ignoreCase option, local sources 120
in-place editing feature 237
  about 99-101
  at server-side handling, example 108-111
  code usage 102-105
  constructor, parameters 101
  constructor initiating, syntax 101
  element parameter 101
  exercise 156
  getting started 101
  InPlaceCollectionEditor
    constructor 112, 113
  InPlaceEditor constructor, initiating 109
  onEnterEditMode, callbacks for 108
  onLeaveEditMode, callbacks for 108
  options 101
  options parameter 101
  url parameter 101
in-place editing feature, callback option
  Callback option 102
  onComplete option 102
  onFailure option 102
in-place editing feature, options
  cancelLink option 101
  cancelText option 101
  clickToEditText option 101
  cols option 102
  highlightColor option 102
  highlightendColor option 102
  loadingText option 102
  loadTextURL option 102
  okButton option 101
  okText option 101
  rows option 101
  savingText option 101
in-place editing feature, tips and tricks
  data submitting, on Blur 107, 108

edit mode, entering into 106
element, displaying 106
enterEnterMode() function 107
submitOnBlur option 107
increment, slider options 137
Index.php, user login management system 57
indicator option, remote sources 120
InPlaceCollectionEditor feature 112, 113
InPlaceEditor constructor
initiating, syntax 101
options, adding 109, 110
items, todonow application
added item, reading 181, 182
adding 179
adding, to database 179
adding, to incomplete <div> 187
AddItem() function 179-181
AddtoCompleted function 184
AddtoItemTree() function, code 187
ChangeStatus() function 185
changeStatus(valueID) function 185, 186
completed items, converting to incomplete status 186
database table, fields 171
Date field 171
DeletefromItemTree() function 185
DeleteFromItemTree(divDelete) function 185
deleting, from complete <div> 188
deleting, from incomplete <div> 185
effects, adding 182, 183
item, adding to completed <div> 184
ItemID field 171
ItemName field 171
items to completed, status changing 185, 186
ListID field 171
MarkDone(this.id)function 184
marking, as completed 183, 184
MarkUnDone function, code 187
ownerID field 171
ResetStatus() function, code 188, 189
status, changing to incomplete 188, 189
Status field 171
storing, database schema 171

K

keyboard events, handling 26, 27

L

lists, todonow application
$_POST 178
ad_new_list() 178
Add This List button 178
creating 177
creating, logic and code 177-179
database table, fields 171
Date field 171
deleting 190
fetchArray function 175
ListID field 171
ListName field 171
Mysql_num_rows function 175
ownerID field 171
read_list() 178
Redirect function, code 179
storing, database schema 171
viewing 174-176
viewing, logic and code 174, 175
viewing, with summary of incomplete items 176
viewing with summary of incomplete items, logic and code 176
loadingText option, in-place editing feature 102
loadTextURL option, in-place editing feature 102
local sources, auto completion sources
about 119
options 120
local sources options, auto completion sources
choices 120
fullSearch 120
ignoreCase 120
partialChars 120
partialSearch 120
location parameter, Ajax.Updater 18
Login.php, user login management system 53-56
Logout.php, user login management system 58, 59

M

MarkDone(this.id)function 184
MarkUnDone function, code 187
maximum, slider options 137
minChars option, remote sources 119
minimum, slider options 138
modules, at server side
   tag cloud features 235
   user management system 234
mouse events, handling methods
   isLeftClick method 26
   PointerX method 26
   PointerY method 26
multiple Script.aculo.us feature
   drag-and-drop feature, adding 157-159
   effects, adding to page 157
   in-place editing in page, adding 156
   multiple features, adding to element 159-161
Mysql_num_rows function 175
MySQL 5.0 42
MySQL installation
   checking, WAMP server used 45

N

new tutorials, submitting 126

O

okButton, in-place editing feature 101
okText option, in-place editing feature 101, 103
onChange, slider callback 138
onComplete callback option, in-place editing feature 102
onDrag option, drag and drop feature 87
onEnd option, drag and drop feature 87
onEnterEditMode callback option, in-place editing feature 108
onFailure callback option, in-place editing feature 102
onFailure, option parameter 17
onLeaveEditMode callback option, in-place editing feature 108
onLoading, option parameter 17
onSlide, slider callback 138
onStart option, drag and drop feature 87
option parameters, Ajax.Request
   method 17
   onFailure 17
   onLoading 17
   parameters 17
options, slider parameter 137
option parameter, auto completion feature 118
option parameter, in-place editing feature 101

P

parameters option, remote sources 120
paramName option, remote sources 119
partialChars option, local sources 120
partialSearch option, local sources 120
people_desc attribute, people table 226
people_id attribute, people table 226
people_name attribute, people table 226
people tables, database
   attributes 226
   people_desc attribute 226
   people_id attribute 226
   people_name attribute 226
   schema 226
PHP 5.0 42
PHP installation
   checking, WAMP server used 44
phpMyAdmin 43
place_desc attribute, places table 226
place_id attribute, places table 226
place_name attribute, places table 226
place table, database
   attributes 226
   place_desc attribute 226
   place_id attribute 226
   place_name attribute 226
   schema 226
products, shopping application
   creating draggable 216
   searching 218-221
   searching, tag cloud used 221
   selecting, to buy 216
   tag cloud, generating 222
   viewing, for tag name 223

prototype
  $() 13
  $A() 13
  $F() 13
  $H() 13
  $R() 13
  about 11
  Ajax.PeriodicalUpdater class 18
  Ajax.Request object 17, 18
  Ajax.Responders class 19, 20
  Ajax.Updater class 18
  compatibility 12
  element, accessing by ID 12
  event handling 25
  features 12
  helper functions 12-16
  version 1.6 12
prototype library
  adding, to code 46

R

range, slider options 138
real-time auto search, bookmarker application 204-206
read_list() 178
real-time search 237
Redirect function, code 179
remote sources, auto completion sources
  about 118
  options 119, 120
remote sources options, auto completion sources
  afterUpdateElement 120
  callback 120
  frequency 119
  indicator 120
  minChars 119
  parameters 120
  paramName 119
  tokens 120
  updateElement 120
RemoveFunction 20
remove method, droppables namespace 88
reset method 31
request method 31
ResetStatus() function, code 188, 189

revertEffect option, drag and drop feature 87, 90
revert option, drag and drop feature 87, 88
Rich Internet Applications (RIA) 5
rows option, in-place editing feature 101, 105

S

savingText option, in-place editing feature 101
Script.aculo.us
  about 5
  auto completion feature 115-117
  bookmarker application 193, 194
  drag and drop feature 86
  Effect.Highlight, effect 68
  Effect.Morph, effect 68
  Effect.Move, effect 68
  Effect.Multiple, effect 68
  Effect.Opacity, effect 68
  Effect.Scale, effect 68
  effects 67, 68
  effects, types 68
  features, revising 162
  in-place editing feature 99-101
  latest version, downloading link 6
  MP3 sounds 80
  multiple Script.aculo.us feature 155
  shopping application 213
  slider 135
  slider, types 138
  sounds 79
  sounds, types 79
Script.aculo.us, features
  AJAX 8
  drag and drop feature 7
  effects engine feature 7
Script.aculo.us, features in one page
  drag and drop 164
  effects, adding 162, 163
  in-place editing 163
  multimedia 167
  slider 165
Script.aculo.us library
  adding, to code 46
Serialize method 31

serializeElements method 31
Secure.php 49
server-side scripting
  PHP used 41
setDisabled, slider functions 138
setEnabled, slider functions 138
setValue, slider functions 138
Shop-Me application. *See* shopping application
shopping application
  effects, adding 217
  features 214
  functionalities 214
  products, searching 218-221
  products, selecting to buy 215, 216
  products, viewing for tag name 223
  products searching, tag cloud used 221
  tag cloud, generating 222
  user management system 214
show comments 228
showData() function 231, 232
Signup.php, user login management system 50-53
simple tag cloud, creating 63-66
slider
  callbacks 138
  code usage 139, 140
  current value, reading 147
  disabling 148
  enabling 149
  functions 138
  horizontal slider, code usage 142
  multiple handles 147, 148
  options 137
  parameters 137
  steps 136
  tips and tricks 146
  types 138
  vertical slider, code usage 140-142
  with options, code usage 143-146
slider, callbacks
  onChange callback 138
  onSlide callback 138
slider, functions
  setDisabled function 138
  setEnabled function 138
  setValue function 138

slider, options
  axis option 137
  disabled option 138
  increment option 137
  maximum option 137
  minimum option 138
  range option 138
  SliderValue option 138
  values option 138
slider, parameters
  handle parameter 137
  options parameter 137
  track parameter 137
slider, tips and tricks
  current value, reading 147
  disabling 148
  enabling 149
  multiple handles 147, 148
slider, types
  horizontal slider 139
  vertical slider 138
SliderValue, slider options 138
snap option, drag and drop feature 87, 88
sounds
  code usage 80
  example 80-82
  MP3 sounds 80
  types 79, 80
source parameter, auto completion feature 118
startEffect option, drag and drop feature 87, 89
submitOnBlur option, in-place editing feature 107, 108

T

Tadalist. *See* todonow application
tag cloud features, Web 2.0 applications
  search, tags used 210
  search function, tags used 209
  tag cloud, creating 208-222
  tags, adding to tutorials 207, 208
  tags in database, reading 208
tags, bookmarker application
  adding, to tutorials 207, 208
  in database, reading 208

search function, tags used 209
tag cloud, creating 208, 209
things, database 226
to-do list manager. *See* **todonow application**
todonow application
 about 169
 completed items, converting to incomplete status 186
 database playground, creating 170, 171
 effects, adding to item 182, 183
 features 170
 functionality 170
 item, adding to completed <div> 184
 item, deleting from incomplete <div> 185
 item, marking as completed 183, 184
 items, adding to database 179, 181
 items, adding to incomplete <div> 187, 188
 items, adding to lists 179
 items, deleting from complete <div> 188
 items status, changing to incomplete 188, 189
 item status, changing 185, 186
 lists, viewing 174, 175
 lists, viewing with summary of incomplete items 176
 logging in 172, 173
 new lists, creating 177-179
 newly added item, reading 181, 182
 to-do list manager 169
 user interface 173
tokens option, remote sources 120
track, slider parameter 137
tutorial_tags table, bookmarker application
 attributes 196
 schema 195
 tag attribute 196
 tutorialID attribute 196
tutorials, bookmarker application
 deleting 202-204
 description, adding to tutorial 199-201
 submitting 196
 tags, adding to tutorial 199-201
 title, adding to tutorial 199-201
 URL, submitting 197, 198
 viewing 202

tutorials table, bookmarker application
 attributes 195
 date attribute 195
 ownerID attribute 195
 schema 195
 tutorial_desc attribute 195
 tutorial_title attribute 195
 tutorial_url attribute 195
 tutorialID attribute 195

U

Universal Description and Discovery Information. *See* **UDDI**
updateElement option, remote sources 120
url parameter , Ajax.Updater 18
url parameter, in-place editing feature 101
user interface, todonow application 173
user login management system
 Index.php 57
 Login.php 53-56
 Logout.php 58, 59
 Signup.php 50-53
user management system, shopping application 214, 215
username availability script
 adding, to login management system 59-62
user profile home page, bookmarker application 196

V

values, slider options 138
versions, downloading link 6
vertical slider
 about 138
 code usage 140-142
 example 149-153

W

WAMP server
 about 42
 MySQL installation, checking 45, 46
Web 2.0 applications
 tag cloud features 206, 207

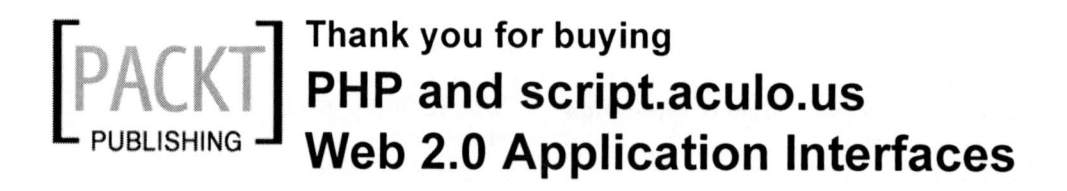

[PACKT PUBLISHING] Thank you for buying PHP and script.aculo.us Web 2.0 Application Interfaces

Packt Open Source Project Royalties

When we sell a book written on an Open Source project, we pay a royalty directly to that project. Therefore by purchasing PHP and script.aculo.us Web 2.0 Application Interfaces, Packt will have given some of the money received to the script.aculo.us project.

In the long term, we see ourselves and you—customers and readers of our books—as part of the Open Source ecosystem, providing sustainable revenue for the projects we publish on. Our aim at Packt is to establish publishing royalties as an essential part of the service and support a business model that sustains Open Source.

If you're working with an Open Source project that you would like us to publish on, and subsequently pay royalties to, please get in touch with us.

Writing for Packt

We welcome all inquiries from people who are interested in authoring. Book proposals should be sent to author@packtpub.com. If your book idea is still at an early stage and you would like to discuss it first before writing a formal book proposal, contact us; one of our commissioning editors will get in touch with you.

We're not just looking for published authors; if you have strong technical skills but no writing experience, our experienced editors can help you develop a writing career, or simply get some additional reward for your expertise.

About Packt Publishing

Packt, pronounced 'packed', published its first book "Mastering phpMyAdmin for Effective MySQL Management" in April 2004 and subsequently continued to specialize in publishing highly focused books on specific technologies and solutions.

Our books and publications share the experiences of your fellow IT professionals in adapting and customizing today's systems, applications, and frameworks. Our solution-based books give you the knowledge and power to customize the software and technologies you're using to get the job done. Packt books are more specific and less general than the IT books you have seen in the past. Our unique business model allows us to bring you more focused information, giving you more of what you need to know, and less of what you don't.

Packt is a modern, yet unique publishing company, which focuses on producing quality, cutting-edge books for communities of developers, administrators, and newbies alike. For more information, please visit our web site: www.PacktPub.com.

Learning jQuery 1.3

ISBN: 978-1-847196-70-5   Paperback: 444 pages

Better Interaction Design and Web Development with Simple JavaScript Techniques

1. An introduction to jQuery that requires minimal programming experience
2. Detailed solutions to specific client-side problems
3. For web designers to create interactive elements for their designs
4. For developers to create the best user interface for their web applications
5. Packed with great examples, code, and clear explanations

AJAX and PHP

ISBN: 978-1-904811-82-4   Paperback: 284 pages

Enhance the user experience of your PHP web site using AJAX with this practical tutorial featuring detailed case studies

1. Build a solid foundation for your next generation of web applications
2. Use better JavaScript code to enable powerful web features
3. Leverage the power of PHP and MySQL to create powerful back-end functionality and make it work in harmony with the smart AJAX client

Please check www.PacktPub.com for information on our titles

Lightning Source UK Ltd.
Milton Keynes UK
19 November 2009

146395UK00001BA/64/P